RACIAL RECONCILIATION AND THE
HEALING OF A NATION

THE CHARLES HAMILTON HOUSTON INSTITUTE SERIES ON RACE AND JUSTICE

The Charles Hamilton Houston Institute for Race and Justice at Harvard Law School seeks to further the vision of racial justice and equality through research, policy analysis, litigation, and scholarship and will place a special emphasis on the issues of voting rights, the future of affirmative action, the criminal justice system, and related areas.

From Lynch Mobs to the Killing State: Race and the Death Penalty in America
Edited by Charles J. Ogletree, Jr., and Austin Sarat

When Law Fails: Making Sense of Miscarriages of Justice
Edited by Charles J. Ogletree, Jr., and Austin Sarat

The Road to Abolition?: The Future of Capital Punishment in the United States
Edited by Charles J. Ogletree, Jr., and Austin Sarat

Life without Parole: America's New Death Penalty?
Edited by Charles J. Ogletree, Jr., and Austin Sarat

Punishment in Popular Culture
Edited by Charles J. Ogletree, Jr., and Austin Sarat

Racial Reconciliation and the Healing of a Nation: Beyond Law and Rights
Edited by Charles J. Ogletree, Jr., and Austin Sarat

Racial Reconciliation and the Healing of a Nation

Beyond Law and Rights

Edited by

Charles J. Ogletree, Jr., *and* Austin Sarat

NEW YORK UNIVERSITY PRESS

New York

NEW YORK UNIVERSITY PRESS
New York
www.nyupress.org

© 2017 by New York University
All rights reserved

References to Internet websites (URLs) were accurate at the time of writing. Neither the author nor New York University Press is responsible for URLs that may have expired or changed since the manuscript was prepared.

ISBN: 978-1-4798-4463-0 (hardback)
ISBN: 978-1-4798-4353-4 (paperback)

For Library of Congress Cataloging-in-Publication data, please contact the Library of Congress.

New York University Press books are printed on acid-free paper, and their binding materials are chosen for strength and durability. We strive to use environmentally responsible suppliers and materials to the greatest extent possible in publishing our books.

Manufactured in the United States of America

10 9 8 7 6 5 4 3 2 1

Also available as an ebook

To Ben with pride and joy (A. S.)

CONTENTS

Acknowledgments   ix

Introduction: Bridging the Black-White Divide   1
  Charles J. Ogletree, Jr., and Austin Sarat

1. Racial Fakery and the Next Postracial: Reconciliation in the
   Age of Dolezal   25
   Matthew Pratt Guterl

2. Race and Science: Preconciliation as Reconciliation   49
   Osagie K. Obasogie

3. From Perceiving Injustice to Achieving Racial Justice:
   Interrogating the Impact of Racial Brokers on Racial
   Antagonism and Racial Reconciliation   62
   Carla Shedd

4. Weaponized Empathy: Emotion and the Limits of Racial
   Reconciliation in Policing   89
   Naomi Murakawa

5. Black Deaths Matter, Too: Doing Racial Reconciliation after
   the Massacre at Emanuel AME Church in Charleston,
   South Carolina   113
   Valerie C. Cooper

6. The "Post-national" Racial State, Domestication, and
   Multiscalar Organizing in the New Millennium   150
   Kirstie A. Dorr

About the Editors   183

About the Contributors   185

Index   187

ACKNOWLEDGMENTS

The contributors to this book first came together at a workshop sponsored by Amherst College's Charles Hamilton Houston Forum on Law and Social Justice and Charles Hamilton Houston Institute for Race and Justice on April 29–30, 2016.

For their skilled research assistance we thank John Malague, Lakeisha Arias De Los Santos, and Lorenzo Villegas.

This is the sixth book on which we have collaborated. Our collaboration has been more stimulating, more fun, and more rewarding than we could have imagined when we began.

Introduction

Bridging the Black-White Divide

CHARLES J. OGLETREE, JR., AND AUSTIN SARAT

Race continues to play an important role in America's society, recent race based events throughout the country have left us gasping for a solution for America's social cancer. These events have only reinforced that race continues to define who we are as Americans and perpetuate the fact that we are not living in a post racial society in the age of Obama.
—Stephen Balkaran, "Post Racial America in the Age of Obama"[1]

During the last few years, from Trayvon Martin to Eric Garner's painful words of "I can't breathe", to Ferguson, to voting rights and more, we as a nation continue to deal with issues of race—and more specifically racial inequality—in the areas of criminal justice, voting, housing, education, health care and just about every area of life.
—Rev. Al Sharpton, "What Ever Happened to Post-racism?"[2]

From Baltimore, Maryland, and Ferguson, Missouri, to the University of Missouri at Columbia and Flint, Michigan, from Charlestown, South Carolina, and Dallas, Texas, to Baton Rouge, Louisiana, and Minneapolis, Minnesota, the dream of a post-racial era in America has run up against the continuing reality of racial antagonism.[3] More than sixty years after *Brown v. Board of Education* put an end to de jure racial segregation in public education, the fact of racial difference in life chances remains very much a part of the American condition.[4] De facto segregation is so widespread in public schools[5] that, as one commentator put it, "Segregation is again being accepted as normal."[6] Thus, in New York, only 13 percent of black students are educated in majority white schools.[7] In California that number is 8 percent.[8] Taking the country as a whole, in 2011, only 23 percent of black students attended a majority white school.[9] The result is that "we live in a complex multiracial society with woefully inadequate knowledge and little support for constructive policies geared toward equalizing opportunity, raising achievement and high school completion rates for all groups, and helping students learn how to live and work successfully in a society composed of multiple minorities (including whites)."[10]

And today, nonwhite families earn about 65 percent of the income earned by white families.[11] While the overall national poverty rate is 15 percent, the black poverty rate is nearly double that at 27 percent.[12] Moreover, on college campuses and in workplaces throughout the country, even where barriers to entry have been lowered, African Americans confront conditions in which implicit bias remains unchallenged and micro aggressions are a fact of daily life.[13] The college graduation rate for black students is still barely half that of whites.[14] Current debates about affirmative action, multiculturalism, and racial hate speech reveal persistent uncertainty and ambivalence about the place and meaning of race and especially the black-white divide in American culture.[15]

Racial polarization is a continuing fact of our political life. As a report of the Joint Center for Politics and Economic Studies noted, recent federal election cycles show that "voting choices by race trumped all other demographic indicators, such as income, education age, and sexual orientation."[16] As that report suggests, "When a core dividing line in a nation becomes so closely aligned with race and ethnicity, larger concerns about inequality, conflict, and discrimination emerge."[17]

In noting these persistent racial divides we do not mean to suggest that no progress in race relations has occurred since *Brown*. Surely that is not the case. Law has banned racial segregation not only in schools but also in workplaces and public accommodations.[18] The black middle class has grown.[19] And, until very recently, a majority of Americans of all races thought that this country had made "real progress" in getting rid of racial discrimination.[20]

Yet there can be little doubt that the aspiration for post-racialism, or simply for benign acceptance of racial difference, is a long way from being realized. All told, the story of racial progress and reconciliation in the America is far from a happy one.[21] The legacy of that story is today seen in what Hazel Carby calls "political apartheid"[22] and in Carol Greenhouse's description of the "criminalization" of racial minorities.[23] And, as the continuing controversy and confusion surrounding race all too dramatically reveals, the civil rights movement unsettled as much as it resolved; it opened up new avenues for contestation, new ideas about how Americans should think about race, new challenges that law could not and cannot resolve.[24]

American uncertainties and ambivalence about race go at least as far back as Tocqueville's pained observations about the three races in America and their sad inability to live together as equals.[25] In the intervening two centuries those uncertainties have not been resolved by civil war, legal prescription, mass protest, or inspiring leadership. Today conflict between blacks and whites, and conflict about black-white relations, are as vexing as they have ever been.[26] Race remains, to use Gunnar Myrdal's famous phrase, the "American Dilemma."[27]

When Americans have thought about the project of promoting racial reconciliation they have thought about it in many different ways, but two of the most important are what we call "racial tolerance" and "racial respect." The former calls on racial groups to "put up" with differences that already exist in the world.[28] Reconciliation in this version is a kind of cold peace in which antagonism is replaced by acceptance.[29] Racial respect is a more demanding version of racial reconciliation. Building respect involves producing the conditions for an embrace and appreciation of difference, for a desire that it exist in the world not just grudging acceptance.[30]

Whether tolerance or respect, building racial reconciliation is often seen as most importantly a project of legal change and of expanding legal rights.[31] *Brown v. Board of Education* is, of course, the key moment in that project, and it has become one of America's sacred texts, a decision to which almost everyone pays homage even when they act in ways incompatible with its central premises.[32] Moreover, it is to the spirit of *Brown* that groups seeking recognition continuously appeal, a spirit that played a key role in recent debates over gay marriage.[33]

As is now widely recognized, until 1954 the project of establishing the American Constitution was radically incomplete. It was incomplete because, in both chattel slavery and then Jim Crow, the law systematically excluded people from participating fully, freely and with dignity in America's major social and political institutions on the basis of their race. But *Brown* changed everything. "*Brown*," J. Harvie Wilkinson contends, "may be the most important political, social, and legal event in America's twentieth-century history. Its greatness lay in the enormity of the injustice it condemned, in the entrenched sentiment it challenged, in the immensity of law it both created and overthrew."[34] It stood for the proposition that "race is an impermissible basis for governmental decisions."[35]

While it did not end the indignities that the law itself had heaped on African Americans, *Brown* was at once a turning point and a source of resistance, a point of pride and an object of vilification. It was seen by many to have laid the basis for racial reconciliation between blacks and whites and to have offered a model for other racial groups.

Its legacy, like the legacy of all great historical events, is, even today, contested and uncertain. While almost everyone recognizes that *Brown* has not resulted in the elimination of racism in American society, some suggest that the civil rights movement in general and *Brown* in particular have been given too much credit for sparking progress toward racial reconciliation. "From a long-range perspective," Michael Klarman argues, "racial change in America was inevitable owing to a variety of deep-seated social, political and economic forces. These impulses for racial change . . . would have undermined Jim Crow regardless of Supreme Court intervention."[36]

For scholars like Klarman, the victories of the civil rights movement stand, not as a monument to the law's ability to bring about social change and to foster tolerance or respect, but instead as a monument to its failure to do so. In their view, whatever racial progress America has achieved cannot be traced back to *Brown*. "Courts," Gerald Rosenberg contends,

> had virtually no effect on ending discrimination in the key fields of education, voting, transportation, accommodation and public places, and housing. Courageous and praiseworthy decisions were rendered, and

nothing changed. . . . In terms of judicial effects, then, *Brown* and its progeny stand for the proposition that courts are impotent to produce significant social reform.[37]

And some now say that the integrationist vision, most closely associated with *Brown*, is inadequate to deal with the continuing subordination of African Americans in contemporary American society.[38]

Integration, of the kind promised by *Brown*, offers a model of racial reconciliation built on the assumption that if blacks and white could just get to know each other they would get over mutual distaste.[39] The father of the idea that integration can lead to reconciliation is Gordon Allport, who developed "Contact Theory" in his 1954 book *The Nature of Prejudice*. Contact between different groups, Allport argued, is both the cause and cure of prejudice. Casual contact with other groups, seeing them on the streets or in the subway, often magnifies negative stereotypes, exacerbating prejudicial attitudes. More intimate contact, however, can contest stereotypes, diminish bigotry, and build respect. After examining studies of integrated military units, Allport noted that "prejudice may be reduced by equal status contact between minority groups in pursuit of common goals. The effect is greatly enhanced if this contact is sanctioned by institutional supports, and if it is of a sort that leads to the perception of common interests and common humanity between the two groups."[40]

Others, following the promise of *Brown*, look to desegregated schools to provide opportunities for the kinds of interactions that Allport argued would lead to racial reconciliation. In this view, educators then have a unique responsibility to promote what David Johnson and Roger Johnson call the "three Cs:" establishing a cooperative community, creating constructive conflict (such as debates in which participants must argue both sides), and fostering cooperative, rather than individualistic, values.[41] Not everyone, however, shares their optimism about the opportunities presented in schools. Status differences, prior biases, and school practices recreate a segregated environment in schools and have neutered the effects of school integration.[42]

Integration might also facilitate reconciliation by leading to the formation of common "superordinate" identities, such as those created by going to the same school or living in the same neighborhood, that can supplant racially based subgroup identities. However, Marilynn Brewer notes that such dual identification often leads racial subgroups to generalize their own values, making members of outgroups who do not share those values seem disloyal to the larger group. In the end, loyalties to subgroups win the day, effectively undermining the superordinate identity.[43]

Some critics of integration say that reconciliation requires a dissolution of diverse cultures. They aim to make race irrelevant, making it no more socially significant than eye color.[44] Richard Alba, looking at the trajectories of the Irish, Italians, and Jews, identifies three conditions necessary for reconciliation by assimilation: the ability of the minority group to attain high-paying jobs, converting higher socioeconomic status into social proximity to white people, and a cultural shift in how the whites view the moral status of other racial groups.[45]

Of course, making these conditions applicable to black-white relations faces numerous barriers, perhaps none more important than the continuing reality of implicit racial bias. The Harvard Implicit Associations Test, made famous by Malcolm Gladwell in *Blink*,[46] revealed that a large percentage of the population, white and black, is to some degree affected by implicit bias.[47] However, people with high internal motivation to avoid prejudice can be taught to avoid their implicit bias once they are introduced to the cognitive dissonance between their ideals of equality and their bias-driven actions.[48] The effect, of course, disappears in those without such internal motivation.

Beyond integration or assimilation, some suggest that there can be no racial reconciliation without an explicit acknowledgment of America's long history of racial wrongdoing and injustice. Sometimes drawing on Christian theology, they argue that reconciliation requires a confession of wrong, a pledge to cease wrongdoing, and penance.[49] Without apology, atonement, and reparations blacks will not, and should not, they claim, forgive the country's history of brutal oppression.[50] Some claim that reparations are the only way to show meaningful regret, while others claim that it is a cheap way to trade on the honor and suffering of black ancestors. Some call for an apology by the government as an important first step,[51] while others see it as a superficial and insulting attempt to close the book on historical injustice.[52]

J. Angelo Corlett claims that those who are wronged deserve compensation. He notes that the United Nations's Universal Declaration of Human Rights includes the right to "an effective remedy . . . for acts violating the fundamental rights granted [the wronged person] by the constitution or by law."[53] America's continued inaction on the matter of reparations, in Corlett's view, betrays a lack of concern and respect for black people. Reparations, therefore, are a matter of moral necessity and not social utility.[54] There can be no reconciliation without restitution.[55]

Roy Brooks outlines a plan of apology, coherence, and reparations that he believes the United States should adopt.[56] In his view, the government should establish a reparations trust fund that would fund young blacks for twenty-five years, long enough to take a person through college and some types of graduate or professional school.[57] Once this is done, Brooks believes that black Americans have a civic responsibility to participate in a meaningful reconciliation process.[58]

Litigation has been proposed, and occasionally attempted, as a way to bypass political obstacles to reparation. No suit has yet been successful. Charles Ogletree, a leader in this movement, describes the challenges faced by plaintiffs in these suits.[59] The first is identifying the parties and finding a definitive nexus between plaintiff and defendant. Another problem arises, however, in the form of a statute of limitations. Ogletree believes that the statute of limitations should be tolled in these circumstances. Statues of limitations are designed to protect defendants from being tried on stale evidence and fading memories, but in cases like this, when evidence is suppressed owing to the defendant's own misdeeds, that justification is irrelevant.[60]

Reparations itself is not an entirely unproblematic proposal. It seems to some foolish for American taxpayers, very few of whom are descendants of slaveholders and many more of whom are descendants of immigrants, northerners, or Union soldiers, to pay reparations to the descendants of the victims of a practice that ended a century and a half ago. Critics of reparations also point to the current existence of affirmative action and welfare, claiming that they are adequate reparation for past injury.[61]

Others worry about the way that reparations will frame the black experience in America. Armstrong Williams notes that the rhetoric surrounding reparations leads black people to believe that they are lost souls without hope of advancement.[62] Blacks, he says, do not wish to be defined by a narrative or stereotype of failure.[63] Moreover, Williams worries that reparations will reinforce the idea that maintaining blackness requires a rejection of the worldly and sophisticated.

Reparations are but one vehicle for trying to redress material inequities in the lives of blacks and whites and of "righting" history. The creation of truth and reconciliation commissions, such as was done in South Africa, is one potential option. The W. K. Kellogg Foundation launched a truth, reconciliation, healing, and transformation process that seeks to change community narratives and broaden American understanding of diverse experiences. Surveys show that this process has led previously "colorblind" whites to acknowledge the racial divides plaguing modern America and to open the way for racial tolerance, if not racial respect.[64]

Randall Robinson, in *The Debt: What America Owes to Blacks*, argues that lack of candor surrounding pernicious race issues is the largest obstacle to reconciliation. "Smoke kills," he says. The more that white people tell themselves that they are racially unbiased, the more easily they can justify acts of discrimination. The more that black people see themselves as only victims, the harder it will be to build new forms of racial tolerance and respect.[65]

In our time the questions of whether Americans can clear away the smoke, and of how we live with racial differences, are very much alive. Moreover, the work of racial reconciliation remains incomplete. This book seeks to assess where we are in that work and to examine sources of continuing racial antagonism among blacks and whites. It also highlights strategies that hold promise of promoting racial reconciliation in the future. Rather than revisit arguments about the importance of integration, assimilation, and reparations to the project of racial reconciliation, it explores perspectives on reconciliation between blacks and whites that have not had pride of place in the existing literature. It connects identity politics, the rhetoric of race and difference, the work of institutions and actors in those institutions, and structural inequities in the lives of blacks and whites to our thinking about tolerance and respect among blacks and whites.

This book does not offer a systematic assessment of the capacity of law to facilitate racial reconciliation. Instead, it invites readers to think beyond law and rights and to examine social, political, cultural, and psychological factors that fuel racial antagonism as well as others that might facilitate racial reconciliation. The work collected here offers varying ideas about the meaning of racial reconciliation and differing visions of what it would look like were it to be achieved. In those ideas and visions it calls attention to questions of power and the limits of the nation-state. It highlights both individual factors and large-scale social forces that mark our current racial condition.

The first chapter in this book acknowledges that structures matter.[66] A different future—one in which bodies marked by race aren't shot dead in the street, in which communities of color have access to excellent schools, clean and safe living conditions, jobs that pay more than a living wage, to real hope and real change—will require significant structural change. But this chapter focuses as much on the self as on structure.

Matthew Pratt Guterl discusses the practice of racial passing in the supposed post-racial age for what it can tell us about the conditions and possibilities of racial reconciliation. Reconciliation, of course, has many meanings. It doesn't just mean peace with equality or even a fair and just world. It refers, as well, to what might be called "abridgment of the ideal and the real." Guterl contends that racial passing is often presented as a reconciliation of the inner truth "we know" with structures all around us.

Guterl's chapter takes up the story of Rachel Dolezal and her "transracial" subject position. Dolezal was born to two Caucasian parents. She has four adopted black siblings. She attended Belhaven University and received a scholarship to attend the historically black Howard University. She taught at Eastern Washington University and was president of the Spokane Chapter of the National Association for the Advancement of Colored People. She attempted to sue Howard University for reverse discrimination and failed. She claimed to be the victim of at least nine racist hate crimes, although police had difficulty verifying her claims. For much of her life Dolezal had been "black passing." She tans her skin and styles her hair, clothing, and speech in such a way that causes most people to perceive her as black.

Guterl reads Dolezal, as she did, through the experiences of Caitlyn Jenner, the trans-gender sports figure. He asks what it means to celebrate racial self-fashioning as if it were akin to gender transitioning and thinks about the broader cultural responses to Dolezal's story of passing and subterfuge.

Just a day after Dolezal appeared on the Melissa Harris-Perry Show to discuss this "fakery," Dylann Roof shot and killed nine black people at Emanuel African Methodist Episcopal (AME) Church in Charleston, South Carolina. Shortly after, Bree Newsome removed the confederate flag from the South Carolina State House in Columbia and was taken away in handcuffs. Both occurrences highlight the costs of being and appearing black. In comparison to such a serious tragedy and such a radical political act, Dolezal's actions seem trivial. However, her fakery offers more than just a contrast to "serious" racial issues. Rather, it offers another angle from which those issues can be viewed.

Dolezal's racial fakery reveals, Guterl claims, that race is fictional and performative. Race is based in culture and appearance rather than bi-ology. The permeability of the race line and its lack of foundation in concrete identifiers seriously challenge the soundness of a political or social system structured around race. Dolezal's transgression of the race line complicates the traditional conception of racial passing and fakery.

Guterl offers a number of historical examples of people crossing color and class lines. Light-skinned black people who can pass as white can adopt new family histories, new jobs, and new customs, leaving their old racial identity behind. In such instances, passing confers monetary, social, and psychological benefits.

Guterl draws a parallel between the way that we see and sense class and the way that we see and sense race. He then suggests that perhaps "faking" class is no less real than having class, with the implication that perhaps race should be considered in the same way. Regardless, he ar-gues, neither the state nor the public should be verifying the authenticity of peoples' race or class. Rather, we should be concerned with the fact that we consider claims on race or class to be verifiable in the first place.

Guterl's chapter moves back and forth between this story about the remaking of the racial self and one woman's quixotic quest to become black and the everyday, violent truths of modern America: "In a mo-ment when whiteness is afforded great structural advantage, when dark skin color can make you a literal target, is there an odd, offbeat lesson here in the story of a woman born to privilege who chooses to 'become black'?" Does "meaningful" or "progressive" racial reconciliation require a reification of race? Or does it allow for an abridgment of the gap between categories?

The next chapter continues the work of thinking from the level of individuals to the conditions of racial reconciliation and of trying to move beyond a biological conception of race. Osagie K. Obasogie argues that many of the racial antagonisms that have existed in the United States from slavery up through the end of World War II have been based largely upon a singular idea: that of biological race, or the notion that social categories of race reflect inherent group differences. From scientific racism to phrenology to the eugenics movement and more, science and medicine have played central roles in creating and sustaining the idea that racial differences and disparities are natural phenomena instead of being produced by human choices.

The Holocaust provided a horrifying example of how dangerous and harmful the concept of biological race could be. Obasogie identifies three efforts at reconciliation that resulted from the Holocaust: the Nuremberg Codes of 1947, a series of statements by UNESCO in 1950, and the mapping of the human genome in 2000 (which demonstrated that all human beings, regardless of race, are more than 99.9 percent the same).

In these moments of reconciliation, science appears to openly refute the idea of biological race. Nonetheless, this notion, Obasogie argues, persisted in medical literature and thought. Multiple theories of race, including biological race, motivated research projects. The biological conception of race was used to identify "pure" groupings of humans. Race categories also were used to understand disease and disease patterns.

Obasogie argues for what he calls "preconciliation" as a way to address and mitigate the consequences of the continued prevalence of a biological explanation of race. He draws on Section 5 of the Fourteenth Amendment and argues that it gives Congress the power to remedy a problem of equal protection before an individual's rights are violated. Congress can proactively legislate to root out future harms that recollect old problems. Legislation, Obasogie notes, is necessary because "race is such a dynamic and structural detriment of everyday life that it is woefully insufficient to rely upon individual or isolated moments of reconciliation."

Obasogie argues for what he labels "race impact assessments" that might be used to mitigate the adverse outcomes of racist ideologies. Race impact assessments could be used within administrative agencies in the scientific and medical fields to root out faulty notions of racial biology. Hospitals and medical schools are other "sites" that have the unfulfilled potential to promote racial reconciliation. The continued skepticism toward and resistance to social constructionist understandings of race in scientific and medical research serves as a primary barrier to racial reconciliation. Until science and medicine move away from the idea that human difference, disease patterns, and disparate social and health outcomes lie in molecular or other physiological distinctions and take seriously the ideological origins and import of race, in Obasogie's view, no meaningful racial healing can take place.

In chapter 3, Carla Shedd focuses on individuals who act as brokers in urban institutions. She notes that there is a symbiotic relationship between urban neighborhoods, public education, and criminal justice. In the name of justice, and often in the name of protecting America's most vulnerable residents, the nurturing arm of the state, she says, now looks more like the punishing arm of the state. Formative urban institutions, such as schools and neighborhoods, now resemble more penalizing, reformatory institutions like juvenile detention centers and prisons. Simply put, our public institutions are failing. Thus we must examine the fundamental relationship that citizens of every racial and ethnic designation have with the state.

This chapter uses ethnographic and interview data to explore how racial brokers—notably parents, teachers, police officers, and judges—foment racial antagonism via the perceptions and experiences of urban youth. Shedd sees race and the spaces that people occupy as closely related, a theory also espoused by David Sibley, Robert Sampson, and Dawn Bartusch. Physical spaces, in particular the neighborhoods and communities in which people live, reinforce racial and socioeconomic segregation. In other words, it is difficult for people of color to leave the physical boundaries of their neighborhood and escape the fetters of racial antagonism.

Shedd focuses on Chicago to study this intersection of race and space. Neighborhoods are incredibly segregated, with most whites living on the North Side and most blacks and Hispanics living on the South and West Sides. Students either attend their neighborhood high school or test into magnet schools. Thus some students remain in their racially homogenous neighborhoods to attend school, while others travel to racially diverse magnet schools located in racially distinct neighborhoods.

To study the impact of this movement, or lack thereof, Shedd interviewed students from four Chicago schools: Tilden High School, Harper High School, Lincoln Park High School, and Walter Payton College Prep.

Tilden and Harper are both neighborhood schools located on the South Side of the city. The neighborhoods they serve, and consequently the majority of the student they enroll, are predominantly black, Hispanic, and poor. Both schools have severe problems with gang violence and crime. Even when given the opportunity to leave their neighborhood and attend a school with better funding, greater diversity, and more opportunity for personal advancement, many students choose to remain in the familiar environment of their neighborhood schools. Shedd notes that the transgressions of geographical and social boundaries required to attend a magnet school have physical and emotional consequences that deter students from leaving their neighborhoods.

Walter Payton College Prep and Lincoln Park High School are located in significantly wealthier neighborhoods on the North Side. Walter Payton College Prep is a selective enrollment school with a racially diverse student body. Lincoln Park High School is a neighborhood school that serves the affluent Lincoln Park neighborhood and once served the Cabrini-Green Public Housing Projects. It has an international baccalaureate program that draws students from all across the city. Both schools provide the opportunity for interaction across racial boundaries, though student accounts suggest that self-segregation within both schools prevents racial reconciliation from occurring.

Shedd found that students who do traverse geographic and social boundaries are more likely to be aware of the discrimination that they face as persons of color and perceive civil and criminal institutions as unjust. Segregation by place isolates and deprives young persons of color of educational opportunities, job opportunities, and housing choices.

For neither group of students do public schools promote racial reconciliation. Although schools have the potential to act as a site of racial justice and social equality, they currently reinforce racial segregation.

Chapter 4, by Naomi Murakawa, focuses on one of the institutions discussed by Shedd, namely the police. The current language used to describe racialized over-policing and over-punishment suggests that they are both problems of mistrust and misunderstanding between police and communities of color. Such language suggests that the solution to police violence is increased dialogue, increased interaction, and increased police training. These reforms, Murakawa argues, increase the power of the police and fail to address the underlying causes of conflict.

This chapter traces the history of calls for "racial reconciliation" in policing and, in so doing, identifies the potential pitfalls of current reform efforts. New proposals for "racial reconciliation" fit within an old architecture of policing reform, extending from the pursuit of stable police "race relations" in the 1950s, to healthy "police-community relations" in the late 1960s, and to proactive "community-oriented policing" of the 1990s. Tracing this post–civil rights history of racial reconciliation in policing, Murakawa identifies potential dangers that lurk within well-intentioned efforts to reconcile police and black communities through truth-telling forums and procedural justice.

As Murakawa sees it, the central problem with current law enforcement policy is the scale and scope of policing. Eleven million to thirteen million police arrests are made each year, the majority of which are petty misdemeanor offenses. The damage that many of these arrests do is almost imperceptible owing to their quotidian character. A citation, fine, or summons might not seem violent, but they can diminish life chances and economic stability. Many misdemeanor offenders are not entitled to a lawyer even though they can face up to six months of prison time and years of probation for alleged infractions. Fines can compound over time, leading to massive debt. Nonwhite communities and neighborhoods experience higher levels of surveillance and stricter policing. Nearly a third of arrestees are black. Although this high-frequency, low-profile policing is less striking than other forms of violence, it is indeed racist and a serious barrier to racial reconciliation.

Historically, Murakawa says, racial reconciliation efforts mystify racial power in ways that ultimately consolidate carceral power. By conceiving of black discontent with policing as a matter of misunderstanding, miscommunication, atavistic suspicion, or misplaced grudge, racial reconciliation efforts end up justifying reforms that fortify police power. In effect, the framework justifies more funding to hire more police officers (of color), more training, and more procedural particularities that ultimately bolster the professional status of police. In short, the language of "racial reconciliation" demands reform but resists normative commitments, effectively translating the potentially transformative work of the Black Lives Matter organization into a set of technocratic, proceduralist fixes with an air of emotional sensitivity.

In an effort to solve problems of mistrust and miscommunication, many police departments have augmented the training of their officers with lessons in "tactical empathy" or similar communication skills. Although empathy has positive connotations, police use it, Murakawa argues, to capture, fool, and seduce. "Tactical empathy" is advantageous to the police as an insurance measure against allegations of unconstitutional policing and because it reduces resistance to police power. It can be used to defuse dangerous situations and elicit compliance.

Murakawa describes "Verbal Judo," a model of tactical communication, to highlight the dangers of tactical empathy. Verbal Judo is teachable as a set of gestures and phrases that give the practitioner the appearance of empathy. Murakawa compares this to theories on counterinsurgency that teach gestural commands to earn the people's trust. In order to teach "humane" policing, one must dehumanize policed subjects. There must be an implicit distancing between police and citizen before they can be united again as equals. Verbal Judo relies on the orientalist notion of the self-mastered military man. This lends both a masculine and a combative character to police-citizen encounters.

Murakawa urges us to identify terror where it is least discernable and recognize the various forces that contribute to the delegitimization of structural critiques of racism. Body cams, police training, and cops of color are "aesthetic" solutions to state violence. Racism may be less visible or discernable, but it is still present. Meaningful racial progress and racial reconciliation in policing requires the deconstruction of police power. Murakawa calls for massive decriminalization and for consistent enforcement of the law as prerequisites to racial reconciliation. A spike in arrests of "respectable" people for minor crimes could produce a public demand for decriminalization.

Like Shedd and Obasogie, Murakawa identifies an institution (the police) that is failing to advance racial reconciliation. Murakawa believes that there can be no meaningful racial reconciliation until we strip the police force of much of its power and transfer it to other institutions. We must frontally challenge the racial scale and concentration of policing; meaningful reconciliation should therefore focus less on police professionalization and more on police power.

The next chapter, by Valerie C. Cooper, focuses on another of the institutions that Shedd contends is critical to the possibilities of racial reconciliation, the church. It calls attention both to the significance of religious institutions as well the significance of individual patterns of belief.

Cooper begins with a remark often attributed to Martin Luther King, Jr., decrying the fact that "11 A.M. Sunday morning" is the "most segregated hour of the week in America." In the more than fifty years since King proclaimed his dream that "one day . . . the sons of former slaves and the sons of former slave owners will be able to sit down together at the table of brotherhood," little has changed. Churches remain overwhelmingly segregated, and very little progress has been made in transforming communion tables around the country into tables of real, interracial brother- and sisterhood.

In June 2015, Dylann Roof—a white male—killed nine black people at Emanuel AME Church in Charleston, South Carolina, with a concealed firearm. The shooting was intended to derail efforts at racial reconciliation in the church and ignite a race war. The shooting, Cooper argues, highlights the continued racial tensions within the Christian faith in America and the failure of the church to act as a site to end racial segregation.

A study by Rice University found that, if a diverse congregation is defined as one in which 20 percent of its members provide racial or ethnic diversity, only 8 percent of congregations in the United States are racially diverse. Christian congregations are hyper-segregated, with a diversity level of approximately zero. Unlike segregation enforced by law, congregational segregation is self-enforced. People choose to return to the same congregation year after year.

The origins of segregation in Christian churches, Cooper argues, can be traced to the impetus for the creation of the first independent black denomination, the African Methodist Episcopal (AME) Church. Whites denied blacks entrance to many of their congregations, thus limiting the number and character of organizations available to black Christians. Even when blacks were allowed to attend white churches, they were segregated and dehumanized. The historical role that Christianity has played in the justification of the American slave system meant that black worshipers needed to separate from white co-religionists and construct a church that acknowledged their full humanity. Consequently there are many areas that have theologically similar but racially distinct congregations that originated from the same organization.

Recent efforts to foster racial tolerance and/or respect among Christian churches have been confounded by a number of factors. Churches are voluntary associations. The government cannot mandate congregational diversity. Members who feel uncomfortable or unhappy with increasing diversification of their congregation can simply leave and join a less diverse congregation. Even if blacks gain entrance into an integrated church, there is no way to ensure that they will be treated like Christians or that the church will become a desirable place for blacks to worship.

Whites may consider integration an assault on a safe and comfortable place of worship. The music may become "too black," or race may be a topic too frequently discussed in sermons. Whites are often less aware of and less committed to efforts to racially desegregate than their black counterparts. Yet for blacks, the integration of whites into their congregations can feel like Anglo-conformation and the loss of the last black dominant social spaces.

Cooper concludes that religious institutions have been some of the most important sites and organizations in the construction of modern racial identities and relations. As such, they have the ability to either valorize or challenge the status quo. The shootings at Emanuel AME demonstrate that multiracial congregations can leave dominant white racial frameworks unchallenged and that challenging the status quo presents significant emotional and physical dangers to participants. Churches may advocate racial reconciliation as a social goal while at the same moment resisting it in their own practices.

Our book concludes with an exploration of national politics, structural antagonisms, and racial justice via transnational, indigenous, and women-of-color perspectives. It also puts the black-white racial binary that has animated the rest of the book into a broader racial perspective.

Kirstie A. Dorr argues that the way that social justice movements operate—both historically and currently—reinforces the systems that they are attempting to dismantle, making it difficult to create substantive change in the long term. She questions whether racial reconciliation is a realistic possibility in twenty-first-century America and discusses how American society would have to change in order to achieve racial justice.

Dorr discusses how globalization has changed the networks of production and consumption from contained systems within a nation-state to a complex, decentralized, transnational system. This in turn has changed the nature of race, gender, and capital. Struggles for inclusion and redress often fail to recognize these changes and, as a result, "recapitulate or fortify the geo-political structures of dominance that they seek to reform or destabilize." We must be careful to foster anti-racial thought and action, she contends, that is conscious of this new and changing landscape.

Efforts at racial reconciliation are all too often domesticated. This takes several forms. Social justice movements use nationalist rhetoric that reinforces social differentiations such as that between the foreign and the domestic or the citizen and the migrant. Rhetoric about progress, reform, and inclusion relies on heteropatriarchal notions of the homeland and the traditional family unit that are used, Dorr notes, to support racial capitalism. Domestication also impedes our ability to form cross-community coalitions and transnational alliances.

Dorr points to the situation of ethnic studies programs at institutions of higher learning and the backlash they have received. In the decades following their inception, ethnic studies programs have become increasingly domestic—focusing mainly on the study of communities of color within the United States. The assimilation of ethnic studies programs into American studies programs is indicative of how the radical efforts at racial reconciliation are being tamed and assimilated to fit and even support the extant racist system.

Another example of domestication and the ways in which anti-racism movements reinforce systemic racism is the division of ethnic studies programs into black studies, Asian American studies, and Chicano studies programs. This sterilizes, pigeonholes, and separates different racial identities, interests, and relations. Additionally this domestication (wrongly) superimposes racial norms from the United States onto other countries and cultures.

In Dorr's view, racial formation is a dynamic and relational process. Dorr argues that the pursuit of racial justice in the new millennium will require thinking through the discursive logics and material conditions that organize "the state-sanctioned or extralegal production and exploitation of group-differentiated vulnerability to premature death"[67] beyond the scale of the nation-state and across axes of difference. She concludes that, in our current political moment, analyses of racial discourse and practice must contend with the ways in which racial formation processes are at once *geo-historically specific*—that is, as temporally emplaced in particular, local, regional, and national contexts—and *geo-historically relational*—that is, as situated within and articulated with other geographies of racial capitalist formation and networks of cultural circulation. Racial reconciliation, if it is to occur, must work across and beyond the accepted boundaries of the nation-state to imagine new, intersecting, and relational models of racial, social, and economic justice.

Taken together, the work presented in this book reminds us that, as we celebrate and struggle over the meaning and reach of civil rights post-*Brown*, when it comes to race and racial issues these are strange times, confused and confusing times. This is especially true when the issue of race involves relations between African Americans and caucasians. As Wilkinson argues, "America stands at a critical juncture with respect to its race relations—a juncture every bit as important as that which confronted the Supreme Court in 1954."[68] This book takes stock of this critical juncture, offering both critical analysis of the barriers to progress and examining strategies beyond law and rights for moving America down the road toward racial reconciliation.

NOTES

1 Stephen Balkaran, "Post Racial America in the Age of Obama," *Huffington Post*, May 27, 2015, www.huffingtonpost.com.

2 Rev. Al Sharpton, "What Ever Happened to Post-racism?" *Huffington Post*, May 23, 2015, www.huffingtonpost.com.

3 Jennifer Berry Hawes, "Racial Divides Remain Deep After Emanuel AME Church, Walter Scott Shootings," *Post and Courier*, June 11, 2016, www.postand-courier.com. See also Louis Nelson, "Dallas Shooting Stokes Tensions over Race, Cops," *Politico*, July 8, 2016, www.politico.com.

4 Alice O'Connor, Charles Tilly, and Lawrence Bobo, eds., *Urban Inequality: Evidence from Four Cities* (New York: Russell Sage Foundation, 2003).

5 Sonali Kohli, "Modern Day Segregation in Public Schools," *Atlantic*, November, 18, 2014, www.theatlantic.com.

6 Sharon Noguchi, "Report: California among Worst in the Nation in School Segregation," *Mercury News*, May 14, 2014, www.mercurynews.com. Noguchi states, "The average black student in California attends a school that is 82 percent students of color." See also Rajini Vaidyanathan, "Why Don't Black and White Americans Live Together?" *BBC News*, January 8, 2016, www.bbc.com.

7 See Ericka Frankenberg, Chungmei Lee, and Gary Orfield, "A Multiracial Society with Segregated Schools: Are We Losing the Dream?" (Cambridge, MA: The Civil Rights Project, 2003). Also see Rachel Cohen, "New York City Tackles School Segregation," *American Prospect*, December 9, 2015, http://prospect.org.

8 Noguchi, "Report."

9 Gary Orfield and Erica Frankenberg with Jongyeon Ee and John Kuscera, "Brown at 60: Great Progress, a Long retreat and an Uncertain Future" (Los Angeles: The Civil Rights Project, 2014), www.civilrightsproject.ucla.edu.

10 *Id.* at 5.

11 See Laura Shin, "The Racial Wealth Gap: Why a Typical White Household Has 16 Times the Wealth of a Black One," *Forbes*, March, 26, 2015, www.forbes.com.

12 Mark Gongloff, "45 Million Americans Still Stuck below Poverty Line: Census," *Huffington Post*, September 16, 2014, www.huffingtonpost.com.

13 Sam Lin-Sommer and Sebastian Łucek, "The Dangerous Mind: Unconscious Bias in Higher Education," *Brown Political Review*, April 11, 2015, www.brownpolitical-review.org.

14 Lauren Camera, "The College Graduation Gap Is Still Growing," *U.S. News and World Report*, March 23, 2016, www.usnews.com.

15 Hazel Rose Markus, "Pride, Prejudice, and Ambivalence: Toward a Unified Theory of Race and Ethnicity," *American Psychologist* 63, no. 8 (November 2008): 651–670.

16 See "Are We Talking Enough about the Black Middle Class?" *Pacific Standard*, April 13, 2015, https://psmag.com. See also Khalilah Brown-Dean, Zoltan Hajnal,

Christina Rivers, and Ismail White, "50 Years of the Voting Rights Act: The State of Race in Politics" (Washington, DC: Joint Center for Political and Economic Studies, January 12, 2015).

17 "Are We Talking Enough?"

18 Abigail Thernstrom and Stephen Thernstrom, "Black Progress: How Far We've Come, and How Far We Have to Go" (Washington, DC: Brookings Institution, Spring 1998), www.brookings.edu.

19 See A. J. Robinson, "The Two Nations of Black America," *Frontline*, February 1997, www.pbs.org. Robinson states that "the Black middle class is not only larger than ever, but that it is the fastest growing and largest segment within the Black community." Also see Mary Pattillo-McCoy, *Black Pickett Fences: Privilege and Peril among the Black Middle Class* (Chicago: University of Chicago Press, 1999).

20 Sarah Dutton, Joseph DePinto, Anthony Salvanto, and Fred Backus, "50 Years after Civil Rights Act, Americans See Progress on Race," *CBS News*, July 1, 2014, www.cbsnews.com.

21 Today "sixty-nine percent of Americans say race relations are generally bad." See Giovani Russonello, "Race Relations at Lowest Point in Obama Presidency, Poll Finds," *New York Times*, July 13, 2016, www.nytimes.com.

22 Hazel Carby, "Can the Tactics of Cultural Integration Counter the Persistence of Racial Apartheid? Or the Multicultural Wars, Part 2," in *Race, Law, and Culture: Reflections on* Brown v. Board of Education, ed. Austin Sarat (New York: Oxford University Press, 1999).

23 Carol Greenhouse, "A Federal Life: *Brown* and the Nationalization of the Life Story," in Sarat, *Race, Law, and Culture*.

24 Parts of the following few pages are taken from Austin Sarat, "Introduction: The Civil Rights Story/The American Story," in *Civil Rights in American Law, History, and Politics*, ed. Austin Sarat (New York: Cambridge University Press, 2014).

25 Alexis de Tocqueville, *Democracy in America*, trans. Henry Reeves (Boston: John Allyn, 1976), ch. 18.

26 Kimberlé Williams Crenshaw, "Race, Reform, and Retrenchment: Transformation and Legitimation in Antidiscrimination Law, *Harvard Law Review* 101 (1988): 1331–1387.

27 Gunnar Myrdal, *An American Dilemma: The Negro Problem and Modern Democracy* (New York: Harper, 1944).

28 See Glenn Tinder, *Tolerance and Community* (Columbia: University of Missouri Press, 1995). Also see D. A. Carson, *The Intolerance of Tolerance* (New York: Eerdmans, 2013).

29 Robert Paul Wolff, Barrington Moore, and Herbert Marcuse, *A Critique of Pure Tolerance* (Boston: Beacon Press, 1997).

30 William Connolly, *Identity, Difference: Democratic Negotiations of Political Paradox* (Ithaca, NY: Cornell University Press, 1991).

31 See also Myriam Gilles and Risa Goluboff, eds., *Civil Rights Stories* (New York: Foundation Press, 2007).

32 See Martha Minow, *In Brown's Wake: Legacies of America's Educational Landmark* (New York: Oxford University Press, 2010).

33 Teresa Godwin Phelps, "The Evolving Rhetoric of Gay Rights Advocacy," in *Rhetorical Processes and Legal Judgments*, ed. Austin Sarat (New York: Cambridge University Press, 2016).

34 J. Harvie Wilkinson, *From Brown to Bakke: The Supreme Court and School Integration: 1954–1978* (New York: Oxford University Press, 1979), 6.

35 Charles Black, "The Lawfulness of the Segregation Decision," *Yale Law Journal* 89 (1960): 421.

36 Michael Klarman, "*Brown*, Racial Change, and the Civil Rights Movement," *Virginia Law Review* 80 (1994): 10.

37 Gerald Rosenberg, *The Hollow Hope: Can Courts Bring about Social Change?* (Chicago: University of Chicago Press, 1991), 23.

38 See, for example, Drew Days, "Brown Blues: Rethinking the Integrationist Ideal," *William and Mary Law Review* 34 (1992): 53.

39 What follows is taken from material prepared by John Malague for inclusion in this book.

40 Gordon Allport, *The Nature of Prejudice* (Garden City, NY: Doubleday Anchor Books, 1954), 267. See also Susan Fiske, "Interdependence and the Reduction of Prejudice," in *Reducing Prejudice and Discrimination*, ed. Stuart Oskamp (Mahwah, NJ: Lawrence Erlbaum Associates, 2000), 117.

    Allport's hypothesis led other scholars to empirically evaluate the relationship between contact and prejudice. A review of the literature performed by Pettigrew and Tropp found that 94 percent of studies showed face-to-face interactions to be related to reduced prejudice. See Thomas Pettigrew and Linda R. Tropp, "Does Intergroup Contact Reduce Prejudice? Recent Meta-analytic Findings," in Oskamp, *Reducing Prejudice and Discrimination*.

41 David Johnson and Roger Johnson, "The Three Cs of Reducing Prejudice and Discrimination," in Oskamp, *Reducing Prejudice and Discrimination*, 240.

42 Frances Aboud and Sheri Levy, "Interventions to Reduce Prejudice and Discrimination in Children and Adolescents," in Oskamp, *Reducing Prejudice*, 272–275. See also Mary Jackman and Marie Crane, "Some of My Best Friends Are Black . . .": Interracial Friendship and Whites' Racial Attitudes," *Public Opinion Quarterly* 1 (December 1986): 476.

43 Marilynn Brewer, "Reducing Prejudice through Cross Categorization: Effects of Multiple Social Identities," in Oskamp, *Reducing Prejudice and Discrimination*, 353.

44 Antonia Darde and Rodolfo Torres, *After Race* (New York: New York University Press, 2004), 5–12.

45 Richard Alba, *Blurring the Color Line: The New Chance for a More Integrated America* (Cambridge: Harvard University Press, 2009), 114.

46 Malcolm Gladwell, *Blink: The Power of Thinking without Thinking* (New York: Back Bay Books, 2007).

47 Mahzarin R. Banaji, *Blindspot: Hidden Biases of Good People* (New York: Delacorte Press, 2013).

48 John Dovidio, Kerry Kawakami, and Samuel Gaertner, "Reducing Contemporary Prejudice," in Oskamp, *Reducing Prejudice and Discrimination*, 144.

49 Roy Brooks, *Atonement and Forgiveness* (Berkeley: University of California Press, 2004), 145.

50 See Emily Swanson, "Americans Can't Even Stomach an Apology for Slavery, Much Less Reparations," *Huffington Post*, June 3, 2014, www.huffingtonpost.com.

51 Brooks, *Atonement and Forgiveness*.

52 Ta-Nehisi Coates, "The Case for Reparations," *Atlantic*, June 2014, www.theatlantic.com.

53 J. Angelo Corlett, *Heirs of Oppression* (Lanham, MD: Rowman & Littlefield, 2010), 94. See also Coates, "The Case for Reparations."

54 See Corlett, *Heirs of Oppression*. See also Jon M. Van Dyke, "Reparations for the Descendants of American Slaves," in *Should America Pay? Slavery and the Raging Debate on Reparations*, ed. Raymond A. Winbush (New York: Amistad, 2003), 59. See also Robert Fullinwider, "The Case for Reparations," Report from the Institute for Philosophy and Public Policy (College Park: School of Public Affairs, University of Maryland, 2000).

55 Boris Bittker, *The Case for Black Reparations* (Boston: Beacon Press, 1973), 20. See also George Schedler, *Racist Symbols and Reparations* (Lanham: Rowman & Littlefield, 1998), 109–113.

56 Roy L. Brooks, "The New Patriotism and Apology for Slavery," in *Taking Wrongs Seriously*, ed. Elazar Barkan and Alexander Karn (Stanford, CA: Stanford University Press, 2006), 221.

57 *Id.* at 155–163.

58 *Id.* at 168.

59 Charles Ogletree, "Repairing the Past: New Efforts in the Reparations Debate in America," *Harvard Civil Rights–Civil Liberties Law Review* 38 (2003): 299–300.

60 *Id.*

61 Robert Westley, "Many Billions Gone: Is It Time to Reconsider the Case for Black Reparations?" *Boston College Third World Law Journal* 19 (1998): 469.

62 Armstrong Williams, "Presumed Victims," in Winbush, *Should America Pay?* 165–167.

63 John McWhorter, "Against Reparations," in Winbush, *Should America Pay?* 182.

64 Kathy Reincke and Michael K. Frisby, "WKKF Leads Broad Coalition to Launch Truth, Racial Healing and Transformation Process Aimed at Addressing Centuries of Racial Inequalities in the United States" (Battle Creek, MI: W. K. Kellogg Foundation, January 28, 2016), www.wkkf.org. See also Rob Corcoran, *Trustbuilding* (Charlottesville: University of Virginia Press, 2010), 1–17.

65 Randall Robinson, *The Debt: What America Owes to Blacks* (New York: Penguin, 2000), 208.

66 Much of what follows is taken from material prepared by Lorenzo Villegas for inclusion in this book.

67 Dorr quotes from Ruth Wilson Gilmore, *Golden Gulag: Prisons, Surplus, Crisis, and Opposition in Globalizing California* (Berkeley: University of California Press, 2006), 28.

68 Wilkinson, *From Brown to Bakke*, 6.

1

Racial Fakery and the Next Postracial

Reconciliation in the Age of Dolezal

MATTHEW PRATT GUTERL

If you don't fit into one box and if you don't stay there your whole life, being identified from birth as who you are—what does that look like?
—Rachel Dolezal, interviewed on *Today*, April 12, 2016

This is, in brief, the story of two images, representing two very different contexts and, by extension, a pair of radically different Rachel Dolezals. These are images you've probably seen, but they are also easily found online.

In the first—widely circulated by the press after her "outing"—a teenage Rachel Dolezal sits on the ground, surrounded by the racially variegated, adopted family her parents had assembled. She has blond hair and pale skin. She is dressed, coiffed, and curated as white, presented as a complement to the blackness of her adopted siblings.

In the second, contradictory image, Dolezal is in the foreground, her hair wrapped, her fist raised, surrounded by her students at Eastern Washington University. At the time it was taken, this second image was meant as an erasure of the first, which was well hidden and kept from the public. If the earlier photo of the adopted family emphasized—as many such families and many such photos do—juxtaposition in a diverse ensemble, the later image deployed skin color and fashion and politics in support of a big, bold deception. It was meant to mobilize a particular kind of racial sight, to encourage the eye to see her as black, to correlate the hair wrap and the skin and the wardrobe with the politics and the semi-fictional backstory, to lead the eye to make a great, half-thought assumption.

What is the relationship between these two visions of Rachel Dolezal? Does one contradict the truth of the other, revealing a history of subterfuge and deception? Or do they mark plot points on a private narrative of racial passage and personal transformation? Do they capture, as well, a unique chapter in the national history of racial passing?

There is a long history of white folks passing for black. Most of this history involves some kind of elaborate disguise—makeup or blackface; attention to hair, clothing, and manner—but it also usually emphasizes a certain degree of transcendence. During a trip to Spartanburg, South Carolina, in the early 1920s, Jean Toomer made it possible for Waldo Frank to pass as black so the older writer's evocative descriptions of African American life in the deep Jim Crow South would be more accurate. Frank found the experience utterly moving. In *Black like Me*, the 1961 memoir of a politically purposeful trip across the color line, John Howard Griffin recounted his dawning awareness of racial prejudice in the deep South. In the 1987 film *Soul Man*, the character Mark Watson donned blackface so he could accept a minority scholarship to Harvard. In much of this history, the emphasis is on white feelings, on the discovery of empathy, having "walked a mile in someone else's shoes." In this way, as Baz Dresinger notes, white-to-black racial passing rests on physical proximity, and on a comforting narrative of "awakening," envisioning the forsaking of racial privilege as noble self-sacrifice, and acknowledging it as a precondition, perhaps, of reconciliation and justice.[1]

These two images and this long history are the context for the "postracial" subject position of Rachel Dolezal, the great fake of the summer of 2015, whose existential wanderings across the color line, uncovered dramatically in a live television interview and explained in the weeks that followed, were widely seem as a distraction from much more serious matters. Her decision to claim blackness, and the charged, provocative subterfuge of her performance, provoked media attention and public outrage and was read as an ironic reminder that even in the aftermath of Ferguson, blackness could still be seen as a vehicle for self-aggrandizement. Throughout all the high comedy and the melodrama, though, Dolezal consistently saw herself as an avatar for a racially reconciled future and defended her right to "be" black.

With the benefit of two years' reflection, I'd like to take up the story of Dolezal and her "trans-racial" subject position. I'd like to read it, as she did, through the experiences of Caitlyn Jenner, the transgender sports figure. I'd like to ask what it means to celebrate racial self-fashioning as if it were akin to gender transitioning, and I'd like to think about the broader cultural responses to Dolezal's story of passing and subterfuge. "I am always a sort of 'bridge' between white and black worlds," she told a student reporter, stressing her role as a reconciling figure, long before she was uncovered by the local press.[2] In light of this volume's collective discussion of reconciliation as a meaningful practice, rooted in sincere and meaningful movements toward a more just future, I'd like to reflect on Dolezal's positions, and also on what it means that her passage into blackness was punctuated by the death of so many in Charleston, by the reminder of the structural real world. More than anything, I'd like to move back and forth between this rather existential story about one woman's quixotic quest to re-make the racial self and the everyday, violent truths of modern America. Big, general questions leap out: In a moment where whiteness is afforded great structural advantage, where dark skin color can make you a literal target, is there an odd, offbeat lesson here in the story of a woman born to racial privilege who choses to "become black"? Does "meaningful" or "progressive" racial reconciliation require, as she has suggested, a rejection of race? An assumption of someone else's race? Does it allow for an abridgment of the gap between categories? Does it allow for subterfuge and insincerity? In our responses to Dolezal, are we obliged to naturalize race? To reject Dolezal's crossings because we imagine, bio-politically, that white-to-black crossings are never permanent? And to suppose that her work, rooted in years of deception, must therefore be suspect?

In the end, while I appreciate her arguments about the fluidity and contingency of race, I have serious reservations about Dolezal's project, which draws, as I see it, on long-standing, exclusive associations of blackness with suffering and which fits a disturbing pattern, historically, of white women gaining access to the gains of Affirmative Action. There is more, too: Whatever else she hopes to accomplish, I conclude, Dolezal surely wants to profit from her proximity to blackness and from the empathy she archived in her years lived as a woman of color. That should trouble us all.

* * *

Making sense of Rachel Dolezal requires, first, that we narrate the events of the summer of 2015, that we trace her rise as an object of public fascination and her subsequent descent into relative obscurity.

The interview that started it all lasted eight minutes.[3]

Dolezal wore a smart black-and-white patterned suit, the light background peppered with random, dark-colored geometric shapes, a striking metaphor for her subject position, a woman born white masquerading as black, deploying tiny pieces of evidence—darkened skin, a kinky hairstyle, photographs of mythic family, and, above all else, her determined commitment to justice—to establish a new racial position. As the camera rolled, she never once referred to herself as black, as African American, as a woman of color; instead, she called herself, repeatedly, "a mother with a black son," working the ancient lines of matrilineal descent in reverse.

The cameraman tucked her into the right side of the screen, allowing the day-to-day of life of downtown Spokane to be reflected in the black marble backdrop on the left. She stood across the street from the downtown mall, in front of a Starbucks, framed by that wall of polished stone, fielding questions about a series of local hate crimes and threatened mailbox bombings. Meanwhile, cars and pedestrians, bright and shiny, and the outline of the corporation's mermaid logo, were reflected behind her, a distracting background swirl of late capitalism.

KXLY4's Jeff Humphrey had reached Rachel Dolezal, president of the Spokane branch of the National Association for the Advancement of Colored People (NAACP), after leaving a business card at her residence. He was trying to get to the bottom of a long-simmering story about hate mail sent to the local branch, purportedly from Coeur d'Alene. Just a few decades earlier, that small Idaho city—twenty or so miles east of Spokane along Interstate 90—had been home to a white supremacist compound. A recent surge in bomb threats, all received through the mail, had led Dolezal to push for an investigation, but journalists in eastern Washington were finding it hard to substantiate any serious threat. Postmarks were missing from envelopes. There were no witnesses to comment on the receipt of the mail. It seemed like an inside job, which meant that someone had used a key, circumventing the usual process and placing the offending letters directly in the NAACP's box. Only a few people could have done that, and everything seemed to swirl around Dolezal.

The start of the interview, then, was about hate mail and a post office box key, about the presumption that something weird was going on, and that the local head of the NAACP was, rather strangely, behind it all.

At six minutes, the interview changed. The camera zoomed in, and the cameraman switched to a shotgun mike. Dolezal's face got larger, then, and her voice got louder, but she was still determinedly off center, and the polished façade behind her continued to reflect back to the camera the mall's traffic. Watching the raw footage now, her off-centered-ness is fascinating, as is her ability to twist Humphrey's questions to generate sympathy. Asked about the mailbox key, she invoked her motherhood and wondered how anyone could ever suggest that the mother of a black child could have schemed up a fake threat. Asked about her determination to stand up for racial justice—a leading question, designed to reveal egomania—she deftly critiqued the very notion that publicity could be a positive good. "*That*," she admitted, "is not the kind of publicity anyone wants." When Humphrey asked her whether her father had ever made it up to Spokane, she got a sad look in her eye for just a moment and then referred to her dad's ongoing battle with lung cancer and suggested that it wasn't going well.

Finally, Humphrey, an avuncular news personality, held up a printout of a picture posted on Dolezal's Facebook feed, and asked, with a slight note of incredulity: "This man right here is your father?"

The image revealed a smiling Dolezal, dressed in white, standing next to a dark-skinned man, who was also smiling. His arm was around her, and they evinced a certain kind of intimacy and familiarity. Before posting the image to social media, she had added a few words of text: "Special Guest Jan 19." The intimate affect and shared smile linked the two together, presumably, as father and daughter:

"Yes he is," she replied slowly. "You have a question about that?"

"Yes, I do, ma'am." "Are you African American?"

She looked perplexed. "I don't understand the question." Then she recovered. "I did tell you that that was my dad." She gestured to the paper, to the representation of blackness, to the simple idea that intimate proximity was proof of family relations, proof of her own blackness.

Then her eyes faded a little.

And when Humphrey started to ask her if she had two white parents, Dolezal simply walked off camera.

In Spokane, the news media had been acutely aware for months that something unusual was happening. Online stories about Dolezal routinely got anonymous comments questioning her race. Rumors had circulated for years—Melissa Luck, the manager of KXLY4, remembered that Dolezal had been less than truthful about her racial background. As the press struggled to verify the details of the hate mail inquiry, it commenced a parallel—and very quiet—investigation into Dolezal's personal life story.

That day, the camera crew had been driving all over town looking for her, leaving those business cards at every stop. Dolezal had called Humphrey to let him know that she was meeting someone for coffee at the downtown Starbucks at 5 o'clock and that she could spare a few minutes for an interview. They set up hastily on the street right outside the shop, and Dolezal set her purse and her phone down in a small planter against the wall. At the close of the interview, as the final question about her racial provenance hung in the air, she tossed the wireless mike to Humphrey, but absentmindedly left her purse and the phone behind.

Ernie, the cameraman, followed her into the dress shop next door, where she'd retreated, to return them.

He found her on the store phone, animatedly talking to someone. By his own admission, Humphrey was simply too embarrassed to go in.

Defined by the interview, Dolezal appeared in that month as an icon of self-invention just ten days after Caitlyn Jenner appeared on the cover of *Vanity Fair*—re-imagined by Annie Leibovitz—and released her new name to the public.

Soon, Dolezal's fantastic, fictional biography had been partially unearthed. She'd been born in a teepee and had lived in South Africa, where she'd been lashed with a baboon whip by cruel parents. She'd been selling greeting cards to pay for her own clothes since she was a child and hunting for her own food, too. Those same parents had determined the severity of punishment based on the skin tone of their offspring, and their cruelty ultimate led to her escape—and her assumption of parental responsibilities over some of her siblings. She'd married an abusive man, gotten sick with cancer, and survived both. Moving to Idaho with her dark-skinned son, she'd taken up a job at a human rights institute, but they'd been subject to racial taunts and threats of violence. Through it all, she maintained a steady performance rooted in her vast knowledge of African American history and American racial politics. "She opened the door and looked at me," once student reporter remembered, "with unexpected green eyes, a caramel skin complexion, and a warm smile." Rumors spread, too, about a deeper truth, about her white past, the adopted black siblings passed off as her own children, and her tumultuous, formative years at Howard, where she'd once sued the university for reverse discrimination after it had attempted to withdraw its offer of a full scholarship to a master of fine arts program.[4]

At first, a sympathetic passing narrative took hold. "Dolezal's view of herself," wrote Allyson Hobbs, author of the first social history of racial passing, "reveals an essential truth about race: It is a fiction, a social construct based in culture and not biology. It must be "made" from what people believe and do." "Race is performative," Hobbs continued, "It is the memories that bind us, the stories passed down to us, the experiences that we share, the social forces that surround us. Identities are never entirely our own, but does that mean that we should lose all control in determining who we are?"[5]

Jelani Cobb, excoriating the phenomenon of the "white Negro" and itemizing the long list of offenders from Norman Mailer to Iggy Azalea, paused to wonder whether Dolezal represented something new and different. Faddish racial appropriation was revoltingly self-serving and, in the end, only reinforced the whiteness of the ego in the spotlight at the center of the act. "The white Negroes," he reminded his readers, adopt "an identity as impermanent as burnt cork, whose profitability rests upon an unspoken suggestion that the surest evidence of white superiority is the capacity to exceed blacks at even being black." "Dolezal's transracialism," Cobb mused, "was imbued with exactly the opposite undertaking. She passed as black and set about shouldering the inglorious, frustrating parts of that identity—the parts that allocate responsibility for what was once called 'uplifting the race.'" Still, he concluded, "race, in this country, functions like a faith, in that the simple profession of membership is sufficient [and] we are not in the business of checking membership cards."[6] Dolezal knew all of this, he wrote in closing, and knew that she'd crossed the line with the intent to deceive, even if not to profit.

Dolezal, though, rejected the charge of passing. Less than a week after her stumbling, awkward interview with the KXLY4 news crew appeared on television, she went on the now tragically defunct Melissa Harris-Perry Show to declare, with great conviction, that she was not white.

"Are you black?" Harris-Perry asked. "What does that mean?"

Using Jenner's language of self-expression, Dolezal invoked a "visceral, spiritual" connection to a personal blackness, a sense that she knew from a young age that she was not white but something else. "Nobody really got it," she remembered, "and I didn't really have the personal agency to express it."[7]

The more she spoke, the harsher the public reaction. On stage with Matt Lauer, she defined herself as "trans-racial," saying, "I identify as black."[8] When she told NBC's Savannah Guthrie that she wept when she read Caitlyn Jenner's story in *Vanity Fair* and professed that "nothing about being white describes who I am," *Slate's* Jamelle Bouie joked that, "with the fake father and the fake children, it seems like she's deceiving people for the sake of an *à la carte* blackness, in which you take the best parts, and leave the pain aside."[9]

Time passed. One day after Dolezal appeared on the Melissa Harris-Perry Show, the young white supremacist Dylann Roof entered the Emanuel African Methodist Episcopal Church in Charleston, South Carolina, and murdered nine members gathered together in prayer, and the conversation about Rachel Dolezal as a humorous object came to an abrupt end.

"The existential question of who is black," Jelani Cobb then concluded, "has been answered in the most concussive way possible: The nine men and women slain as they prayed last night . . . in Charleston, South Carolina, were black. The people for whom this new tableau of horror is most rooted in American history are black as well. The people whose grief and outrage over this will inevitably be diminished with irrelevant references to intra-racial homicide are black people."[10]

As the month closed out, the murders at Charleston dominated media coverage. When Bree Newsome scaled a flagpole in front of the South Carolina State House in Columbia, removed the Confederate Battle Flag, and was taken away in handcuffs, the media turned to the symbolisms of white supremacy, a grimmer and—by some measures, more pressing—concern than the bildungsroman of Rachel Dolezal. Newsome's spectacular ascent and descent—her profound disrespectability politics—extinguished whatever energy the public had left for Dolezal. We'd witnessed a serious tragedy—and a serious sort of radicalism.

Two weeks later—roughly one month after her interview in front of that shimmering Starbucks façade—Rachel Dolezal was out of office, stripped of her positions, and making a living braiding African American hair.

Allison Samuels, a veteran African American journalist, contacted Rachel Dolezal almost as soon as the KXLY4 interview went viral. As Dolezal faded from public view, Samuels traveled to Spokane. Dolezal, Samuels came to believe, was a "new type of white woman," one who sought to "pass for black" and was "bold and brazen enough to claim ownership over a painful and complicated history she wasn't born into." Recalling the moment she first saw the interview with Humphrey, Samuels described the look on Dolezal's face with perfect clarity: "the look of a white woman who tanned for a darker hue, who showcased a constant rotation of elaborately designed African American hairstyles, and who otherwise lived her life as a black woman, being asked if she is indeed African American. It is the look of a cover blown."[11]

Visiting her after Charleston, Samuels found Dolezal stripped of her teaching position and her leadership of the NAACP, impoverished and worried about August rent payments. "And yet," she described, with a tinge of wonderment, "Dolezal's claim on black womanhood still seems to be non-negotiable. Even in conversation with an actual black woman on the other end of the line or sitting in her cozy home, Dolezal unequivocally identifies as black." Samuels expected that once things got tough, Dolezal might have relinquished her claims. But she hadn't.

"It's not a costume," Dolezal told Samuels. "I don't know spiritually and metaphysically how this goes, but do know that from my earliest memories I have awareness and connection with the black experience, and that's never left me. It's not something that I can put on and take off anymore. Like I said, I've had my years of confusion and wondering . . . but I'm not confused about that any longer. I think the world might be—but I'm not."[12]

* * *

Hearing the narrative of one month in the summer of 2015, some might argue that Dolezal's fakery was a trivial distraction from the structural real and that Charleston snapped us back to a focus on what really matters: on the movement against white supremacy and economic injustice and on the critique of racialized policing policy and its inverse, the permissive gun culture of the United States. We could think about the broader cultural responses to Dolezal's story of passing and subterfuge. We could reflect, as well, on what it means that the illumination of her passage into blackness was punctuated by the death of so many in Charleston, by the reminder of the structural real world. We could read her subterfuge as an act of derangement, as a racial passing tale told out of sync with nation time, offered up in a moment when, as Allyson Hobbs might put it, the act itself has become a vestige of history.

These interpretations are powerful, but they don't do the intellectual work they should. They reduce Dolezal to a forgettable triviality. We should be thinking about her racial fakery—and especially the dissonance that preceded its reveal—as evidence of something bigger. On the one hand, her masquerade's unraveling is a signifier of the police state's determination to sniff out what it calls reality, to identify what it labels as fraud and call our collective attention to it. And, on the other, the unraveling of the masquerade itself—and the public outcry—reveals our commitment to the maintenance of baroque categories and taxonomies and our maudlin obsession with those who circumvent them, too. We are now, as Jelani Cobb might put it, in the business of checking membership cards, and that should give us great pause.

Most of all, I think we've let one particular argument about Rachel Dolezal lie fallow: We've too readily accepted the idea that there is no profit for her in this bit of racial fakery. We should see Dolezal as an entrepreneur, with an obvious (if misunderstood) financial motive for her crossing of the color line, a financial motive that tells us a lot about the contemporary political economy of race and class. But we should also see our fascination with her as rooted in the same structural set of circumstances, as a reflex of our desire to understand how race and class work together and to map out a set of "real" social positions on a grid.

Dolezal's story is not, of course, directly about the gap between the very rich or the very poor. Nor is it bout the much-celebrated middle of America, increasingly pinned between those two great extremes. Set in the inland west, in a small city, it doesn't directly reveal anything about the uneven landscape of cities and suburbs, about group advantage or disadvantage, or about the structures that make it harder and harder with each passing year to merely find the social ladder, let alone climb it. It doesn't tell us much about the extraordinary challenges faced by women, by people of color, by immigrants, by the working poor, and by many others when they attempt to secure a good job, or step up that social ladder, or hold onto the gains of yesterday. At least not on the surface. Instead it cuts sideways across these histories, attentive to their shape and outline but not re-tracing what we already know of the struggle to live in the new Gilded Age. It is about an elusive figure—an avatar of racial capitalism's intentional failure—who can't be bothered to wait patiently and play by the rules, to build a great fortune, or even just to establish a modest foundation over generations and who, instead, reinvented herself, using subterfuge and disguise and guile to jump over everyone else, to frame herself as the expert with the unbelievable life story, and to land at the top of the heap. Or even just a little further up. In its own way, it is about the disconnections between our fascination with class and race and gender and our uncertainty, in this moment, about how to fix them into our firmament.

Rachel Dolezal did many things, but she also most certainly draped herself in blackness to escape her small-town life. Her interest in black art—which was reportedly and mistakenly taken as a sign of African descent—earned her a scholarship to college and a full ride for an master of fine arts. From that point, her blackness paid the bills. It generated newspaper attention, cameras, and student adulation. It put her in the center of the spotlight in the interior of the Pacific Northwest, where the African American population was small. She did what she did, in part, because, in such a relatively small place, she saw blackness as a route to greater success and fame. The surest proof of this is the simplest proof: She never planned to give it up. If white-to-black passing is inevitably, historically temporary, then that isn't exactly what Dolezal was doing.

To label this as "passing" is to situate it in a particular interpretative context, one that directs our attention away from her racial capital gains—one that puts this conversation on terms that Dolezal herself surely wants. The "passing figure" is sympathetic, escaping punishment. But fakery, instead, is a bigger category, one with a sharper critical edge.

Let's walk away from Rachel Dolezal for a few paragraphs here. Clark Rockefeller, another great fake, arrived in the United States with a thoroughly German name: Karl Christian Gerhartsreiter. Soon, though, he adopted a series of more American, more ingratiating identities to accelerate his social climbing. He first became Chris Gerhart, part-time student at a branch campus of the University of Wisconsin. Then, heading westward, he became the salubrious boarder and Hollywood hanger-on, Christopher Chichester of California. After several years (and a handful of murders), he moved east and became Clark Rockefeller, a New England aristocrat imprinted with a recognizable brand, his affect and accent derived from repeated viewings of the character Thurston Howell III on *Gilligan's Island*.[13]

This sequence of identities reveals the syllabus for his careful study of American culture. Moving from immigrant to student to West Coast houseguest to New England aristocrat, Gerhartsreiter basically enacted the metaphor of assimilation over the course of one lifetime, becoming more American—and whiter—with every step. His final masquerade—his pretension to be a member of one of the world's most famous wealthy families—was his boldest crossing of the class line, but it also signaled his move to claim the most elite sort of whiteness imaginable. His over-the-top performance was a kind of nation drag and even, in some moments and times, a sort of racial transition.

As was true with Rachel Dolezal, this clever subterfuge reminds us of the stories of racial passing, of melodramatic tales of light-skinned African Americans slipping quietly over the color line, adopting new family histories, new names and identities, and forever masquerading as white. One thinks, of course, of James Weldon Johnson's *Autobiography of an Ex-Colored Man*, of Nella Larsen's *Passing*, or of Phillip Roth's *The Human Stain*, and of the more recent historical work of Martha Sandweiss, Daniel Sharfstein, Allyson Hobbs, and especially that of Karl Jacoby.[14] Whatever the backdrop, the passing narrative almost always included an assumption that the color line was intersected by the class line at a right angle so that passing for white was a matter simply of maintaining a consistent class position and simply slipping over into whiteness. Then, over time, the privileges of pale skin would enable a gradual upward mobility. Not only does this assumption establish, in its own way, the hegemony of social status—because it assumes that whether one was a stevedore or a banker, one could only move, in that first extraordinary performance, laterally across the color line—it also focuses most of our attention on the very well off, whose melodramatic complaints, abundantly represented in our archive, about the absence of elite privilege led them, occasionally, to cross. The subjects of real and fictional accounts of passing were willful chameleons engaged, it seems, in a high stakes act of racial reassignment that was meant, in the end, to enable access to long-denied class privilege. What Jacoby's tale of William Ellis reveals, for instance, is how centrally connected are the issues of racial passing and class mobility, with the former making the latter possible.

The man who went from Christian to Chris to Christopher to Clark was doing something similar. He was class passing, but also altering his national position. He was playing at being American, pretending not to be foreign, softening the harsh tones of his accent, enhancing his public commitment to a very particular kind of elitist whiteness. Re-settled in New England, he accumulated a vast, largely forged art collection, a reflected consequence of his falsified biography, which presumed that the ubiquitous and nonchalant consumption of high culture was a sure marker of status. "His fabulous name had credentialed the phony art," his friend Walter Kirn remembered, "and the art had returned the favor, credentialing him."[15] There were always a few doubts, though. Members of the Rockefeller family let it be known that they wouldn't authenticate his claims. His near-constant renovation of the home in Norwich struck many as gauche, the shroud of plastic sheeting and concrete blocks scattered around the foundation standing as reminders that something was wrong. Kirn, visiting the man, recalled his great hunger, as afternoon became evening, and the absence of hospitality, as they stood in the house and talked while no offer of a modest repast was made.[16] Like Dolezal, Rockefeller was able to manufacture fame but not wealth. Kirn, and others, took note. Something seemed off.

This dissonance is the thing to watch out for. It alerts us not just to the historical act of passing—happening right in front of us all the time—but also to the social phenomenon of seeing, hearing, and imagining what "race" and class" are and how they work and to the broader cultural definitions of what it means to "make" both. That dissonance marks the purportedly real and the presumably authentic. It is an indicator that we see, feel, and sense class and race. It alerts us that something doesn't look or sound correct. It encourages us to take a closer look and to make a note to ourselves about the evidence.

The fakery of Clark Rockefeller—like that of Rachel Dolezal—was shaped by the apocalyptic economic circumstances of the day, in which the wealthiest get richer by the day, the middle class is rapidly shrinking, and the numbers of the angry, working, and often disenfranchised poor are growing. In these times, perhaps not surprisingly, the counterfeit rich abound. The top-ranked television program among the most desirable demographic—eighteen- to forty-nine-year-olds—isn't a sitcom or a drama but the *Real Housewives* franchise on Bravo, featuring a cast of scrambling, ambitious women, all of them clinging to the fringe of the 1 percent and battling each other to promote cookbooks, workout videos, and cheap wine. An unofficial prescriptive literature on "acting rich" proliferates, enabling the rapid acquisition of cultural literacy in the ways of the truly well off—but not, precisely, the full bank account. Google reveals thousands of entries for "How to Act Rich," a telling revision of "how to *get* rich."

We obsess, in this context, over the absence of sincerity in race and class. After all, as any student of the *Real Housewives* franchise can tell you, what makes the show so appealing is the constant failure to keep up appearances, to act appropriately. Curses are hurled. Tables overturned. Slanderous accusations are thrown like lightening bolts. Everywhere there is that dissonance, that sense that these are wealthy people who are not performing their proposed class position accurately.

Maybe that is because faking it isn't really faking it, after all. Maybe it is real. Real in the same sense that Truman Capote referred to Holly Golightly as a "a phony, but a real phony." Or real in the way that the "fake Rockefeller" accumulated art and property and access, despite his fictive name and over-the-top backstory. Maybe the line between mobility and trickery is blurry. The ever-popular Emily Post's etiquette guide, after all, wasn't written for the girls of elite private schools like Spence, Choate, and Brearley; it was written for girls who want to be *like* those girls or to become them, after careful study. Is the scrupulous student of the ways of the truly rich any less "real" than the legacy child born knowing where, exactly, to place that silver spoon at the table?

My point is that I don't think that we should be in the business of adjudicating who is real and who is a phony. We shouldn't be doing the indexical work of racial capitalism. Instead, the index itself should be our object. And by index I mean this taxonomic sense—that we have breathed in—of whose claims on race and class are real, or honest, or verifiable and, again, this keen awareness that some claims are read, or seen, or assessed as somehow dissonant or offbeat. How does that get made? What works does it do? Rachel Dolezal manufactured signs that she was racially "real," but she also left behind trace signs that something wasn't "right." Instead of verifying her intent, we should be thinking about how some of what she did was marked as an indication of "real" blackness and some of it as an obvious sign of fakery.

This may all seem rather abstract, but that is the merely a reminder of the alchemy of commodification—a reminder, that is, that "real" and "phony" aren't useful terms for anyone scrutinizing race and class in late capitalism. The great danger inherent in any history of passing, again, is that you might establish a fixed point from which every act of subterfuge and self-making must depart and that, by doing so, you harden identity and underscore the work of power. That, in order to demonstrate passing, you have to double down on the idea that race or class is natural or real and fixed. That the membership card matters.

Maybe Rachel Dolezal, then, has more in common with Clark Rockefeller than she does with Waldo Frank, or John Howard Griffin, or even Normal Mailer.

* * *

Once the interview with KXLY4 broke, simple Internet searches revealed a haphazardly constructed biography that broke with all conventional narratives. Dolezal had grown up far from others, she remembered, living in a teepee, and killing game with a bow and an arrow. She recalled moving to South Africa and being punished on the basis of skin tone—punished with a baboon whip, that is, and by her own parents. Her dreadlocks, she admitted, were a wig, but they were also a reminder of what her real hair had been like before a struggle with cancer led to chemotherapy. She let the reporter know that she'd gone to school in Jackson, Mississippi, letting the reader (and the paper) assume that she went to a historically black college, an assumption underscored by her decision to go to Howard for her master of fine arts. After moving to Coeur d'Alene, she broke away from an abusive husband and struggled against racism as the director of the Human Rights Institute before white supremacist groups threatened to kidnap her son and before someone broke into her home to hang a noose. Seeking peace but committed to racial justice, she moved across the state line to Spokane in 2012, where she took her job, eventually, with the NAACP. The list of challenges she claimed to have confronted—parental and spousal abuse, date rape and cancer, and bomb threats—was extraordinary.

What we learned since is worth summarizing here, too. Her parents were white Christian missionaries. When she was sixteen years old, they began to adopt children marked as black—two from Haiti, and two domestically from within the United States. She attended a fundamentalist Christian university—Belhaven, in Jackson, Mississippi—and, while there, was involved in "racial reconciliation" work and lived in an integrated setting. She received a master of fine arts from Howard but sued the school in 2002, claiming that her artwork had been displaced from an exhibit because she was white. She settled in Coeur d'Alene after her divorce and lived there for a time as an artist. Only after she moved to Spokane in 2009—only after a decade's internal struggle—did she identify herself as black, begin teaching Black Studies classes, and struggle for the leadership of the local NAACP.

If we were searching for a biographical rationale, we might think about her adopted family. Multi-racial adoptive families are, by design, racially complicated, dependent on especially elastic notions of kinship, and drawing sharp attention to the racial difference manifested in every family photo. They have an over-determined significance in terms of national race relations and international foreign relations and a history of myriad significations along these lines that dates back to the advent of the Cold War, if not even earlier. All of this is especially true of multi-racial adoptive families that are bigger, bolder, and built with an explicitly political or religious purpose. The Doss family and the DeBolt family, for example. Or the rather different "Rainbow Tribes" of the African American superstar and civil rights activist Josephine Baker and the progressive, religious cult leader, Jim Jones. In these dramatic, publicly spotlighted ensembles, racial identity is simultaneously—and obviously—in flux and under constant public maintenance, and the juxtaposition of racial variety is the point. Dolezal comes from one of these bigger ensembles, created later in her life, and under the presumably intense circumstances of a fundamentalist home run by missionaries.[17]

Setting the biographical narrative aside for a moment, it is also clear that at every step of her life, her appropriation and navigation of blackness—first black art and then a black identity—had made a material difference of some kind. Most important, her public assumption of a black identity corresponds to her acquisition of a certain kind of fame in Spokane. The heavy stress placed on Dolezal's modest life—before and after her unveiling—misses all of this, though, and asks only that we assess her commitment by counting the dollars in her checkbook. The notion that "bad" white-to-black passing is a form of profiteering, that its success is measured in dollars, is useful only if we construe value in the narrowest, most pecuniary terms and suggests that, if a simple payout isn't reasonably easy to attain as a consequence of the act of passing, then nobler reasons must make more sense. Such a notion also misunderstands the relationship between race and capital, erasing the work of decades on the subject of racial capitalism generation and white privilege specifically. To recall Du Bois's formulation from *Black Reconstruction in America*, in addition to the tangible, material benefits of the racial caste system in the United States, whiteness and white privilege paid an extraordinary "psychological wage."[18] Fakery, once more, gets us away from the melodrama of passing and centers us on both material and psychological compensation.

That "psychological wage" has a history, too, in which its value has shifted over time. As numerous studies have shown, real structural power continues to adhere to whiteness, offering those defined as "white" a wide variety of multi-generational economic and political benefits. Still, there is, in some quarters, the perception of a declining or diminished symbolic value to whiteness, a perception that can be traced back to the 1970s and to what the historian Matthew Frye Jacobson has described as the re-fracturing of the singular white race into ethnicities, a movement away from the category "white" as somehow less meaningful, or less accurate, than national or regional classifications. As a sign of this "ethnic revival," at the close of his extraordinary *Whiteness of a Different Color*, Jacobson recounts a survey of his classroom, at first divided up by color but then, after everyone had qualified their privilege by invoking more politically de-centered ethnic identities, it was suddenly without anyone to represent whiteness at all.[19] Far more of this recent history is rooted in the conservative counterrevolution and specifically in the emergence of the idea of "reverse racism" that percolates in rightwing think tanks, news channels, and new media. Many people, these days, believe—despite all of those measurable benefits and despite a thousand points of evidence that disprove it—that whiteness brings only a greater disadvantage.

And so, in an age of mass incarceration and widespread racial profiling, where black bodies are victimized and brutalized at dystopian rates, we find ourselves, ironically, surrounded by people born "white" who chose to reposition themselves as persons of color. People like Michael Derrick Hudson, the middling poet from Indiana who styled himself as "Yi-Fen Chou" and managed to get himself included in the 2015 edition of *Best American Poetry*, hoodwinking the Native American writer Sherman Alexie along the way. Or like Andrea Smith, the scholar activist who accepted the racially identifying moniker of "Cherokee" and circulated publicly as "Indian" for years, only to have a group of native scholars publicly reveal her to be otherwise. Or the actress Mindy Kaling's brother, who changed his name to "Jojo" and altered his CV so that he could gain entry to medical school. "Blackness seems to pay," writes Marcia Dawkins, "except if you're black."[20] So, too, it seems, do other markers of marginalization.

If blackness—and color—seem to pay, to borrow from Dawkins, they do so only in a very limited number of circumstances: in roles where the symbolic value of race can actually be marshaled, by some very few, to create capital; in industries that require some degree of celebrity, fame, and self-promotion; and in spotlighted professions, where blackness connotes access, or popularity, or the avant-garde, where it has a draw on mass culture. Even there, the durable structures of white supremacy would seem to ensure that such wealth doesn't easily gain mass and volume, that it doesn't always produce an inheritable concentration or make a dent in the long-term capital disadvantage forced upon black bodies.

And then there is the matter of that "psychological wage." It is much harder to measure that payout, given all of this backstory, to Rachel Dolezal. But it was surely, and in some strange fashion, considerable.

* * *

In December 2015, Mitchell Sunderland of *Broadly*, an online magazine, sat down to interview Dolezal. Six months had passed since she'd become infamous for her racial passage, when the revelation of her secret whiteness during an interview with a news crew had gone viral. Cheekily titled "In Rachel Dolezal's Skin," Sunderland's piece was a melancholy exoneration and recuperation, in a way, of the infamous icon's political position.[21]

The occasion for the interview was a baby shower. Dolezal was pregnant, and the child—to be named Langston Attikus Dolezal, after the poet—was (then) due in February. A dozen of her long-term friends and clients came together in a modest hotel for a baby shower, and Sunderland tagged along for what he presented as an "exclusive" interview.

The accompanying photos of the event are hardly celebratory, but they also aren't a joke. Indeed, they seem to document Dolezal's sad failure, as Oprah scholar Katie Lofton might put it, to incorporate her brief infamy into something durable.[22] The lighting is harsh, the contrast between light and dark is too sharp, and all of the earth tones are gone. Collectively, they capture the quotidian experience of a has-been hosting a party in the rented private domesticity of a decent hotel in a small city in the middle of the region known as the Palouse.

Without any reference to the events of the summer, Sunderland reminded his readers of Dolezal's misfortune. She had lost her position at the NAACP and had not been renewed to teach at Eastern Washington University. She'd been unable to land a book contract for her memoir. She'd made some recent daytime talk show appearances, but those had gone badly. She'd lost all of her local friends but seemed determined to stay in Spokane. She was still a hairdresser. Her failure to capitalize on her infamy looms over the hardscrabble spectacle at the Davenport

Hotel, and the event itself reads like a latch-ditch effort to create something big out of nothing much.

"In Rachel Dolezal's Skin" is a profoundly sympathetic portrait, though. Dolezal is re-defined as a single mother—moved politically by her parent's wild-eyed adoption of children of color, by their assemblage in a dirt-poor town, and by their radical lifestyle—to see herself as something other than white. A young woman inspired to attend a historically black university, to adopt a child of color, to attend to her son's physicality—his hair and his skin—just as she'd done for her adopted siblings. Siblings, we later learn, that she'd rescued from abusive parents, over whom she now claimed guardianship, who call her "mom." One could say—if one wanted to be macabre—that Dolezal's uniqueness lies in her remaking of white matriarchy.

But that isn't what Sunderland says at all.

As extensively as possible, he reveals just how poor his heroine, Rachel Dolezal, is right now—and always has been. She has lost everything, but she never had much to lose anyhow, and she'd do it all over again, if she had a chance. Her martyrdom, as the piece defines it, insulates her from the charge that she'd passed as black for pecuniary gain. "You don't get money for being black," a local man and friend identified as a "Spokane-based Black Lives Matters activist" says; "You get shot. You get stereotyped. You get no funding."

Our long-standing interest in racial passing, and in discerning the truth beneath the performance of a false surface, is a part, once more, of a more widespread fascination with identifying fraud—with doing, in short, the indexical work of capitalism. This, in the end, is why Sunderland labors in the *Broadly* essay so very hard to establish the certainty of Dolezal's financial position and to frame what flows from her relative poverty as a philosophical, historical question: Why would a white person pass as black, if not because of some deeply held political belief, some political belief we should, one supposes, be bound to respect? In the end, it is her financial position that assures the sincerity of her political beliefs and that gives much-needed gravity to her re-imagined racial subject position.

Twice Sunderland notes that her weave is not quite right. He comments on her skin tone, on her creation of a black-themed children's book, on her adopted children's unusual relationship to blackness. The dissonance, again, is everywhere. He dwells on her invocation of Langston Hughes as a muse. He invokes queer theory as a heuristic, concluding that Caitlyn Jenner and Rachel Dolezal might, in fact, be doing the exact same thing. He confesses, in the end, that what he is witnessing is something new. There is quite a lot of precedent for the story of a small-town girl, desperate for a life with meaning, willing to change her name, her look, and her politics, willing to transform herself for fame and celebrity. But "there is," he decides, looking to enfranchise Dolezal as the very first, "no historical precedent for someone being transracial."

There isn't, of course. Especially not in the literal, biological way that Sunderland means it—and maybe not even in the more imaginative way that Dolezal means it when she invokes her own journey of self-discovery. (Although a more informed ear might hear in her narrative of racial expression an under-theorized echo of Jean Toomer's inventive deployment of the "bloods" in his veins, his capacity to "feature" any given "type" or "stock.") In her longer treatment of this subject, Marcia Dawkins suggests that "passing" is in the midst of a renaissance, and she connects this revival to "updated" identity categories with more inherent flexibility. Passing, in this context, is a signifier of the breaking down of old categories and a symbol of a new multiraciality and biraciality.[23] And this, of course, is exactly what Rachel Dolezal would say.

Few, though, are still listening to her. Less than a year after that fateful June, Rachel Dolezal's prevarications and outright falsifications are the object of global derision. The mere invocation of "a Dolezal" brings to mind a catalog of deceptive falsehoods related specifically to race. The essential narrative remains bound up in concerns about her sanity, about her refusal, as Allyson Hobbs put it last June, to confess to her deception. A Dolezal is a racial faker—not just a passing figure, but also something worse. A Dolezal is a liar. A Dolezal is deceptive. A Dolezal is a joke.

Our inability to theorize Rachel Dolezal as anything more than a cheap amusement is a problem. Inevitably, the language of racial passing is used to explain—and dismiss—what she set out to do. The downside of that language isn't just that it wants us to believe that race is a hard, material thing, or that it conceptualizes all movement across the color line as subterfuge, but also that as a historical concept it too narrowly defines why anyone might seek to move from one color-coded, class-bound position to another—establishing a pretty straightforward escapist rationale, from disempowerment to privilege, and from black to white—and little else. It relies on a too-narrow conception of "profit," eschews much of what we know of racial capitalism, and positions Dolezal in the narrative as a victim, aggrieved by society, seeking her best self. Conceived in this manner, the invocation of "passing" enlists us in projects we might wish to question. And our laughter about Rachel Dolezal, in turn, makes it hard for us to hear what is profoundly unsettling here: that we have reached a new strange moment in the political life of whiteness and white privilege, and the end result has made a certain kind of racial fakery perhaps just slightly more appealing as a permanent, profitable enterprise. If Dolezal is understood as the "first," it will become a part of her corporate brand, with consequences.

This cavalier approach to our own backstories challenges our efforts at reconciliation. Cross-racial progressive movements aimed at many of the great questions of the day—policing and punishment, poverty and inequality—would seem to require an "honest" or "sincere" sense of one's own subject position, an acknowledgment of where each of us fits in our intersectional racial histories. This personal accounting is serious business, and it is the first step we take when we move toward action and understanding. Dolezal doesn't treat this practice that way, though. Her willingness to re-write her racial life, to re-imagine where she came from, gets us to a place where inconvenient facts are dropped, revised, or buried beneath a wall of half-truths and lies. It is possible to reject the simple, hard line between whiteness and blackness—a hard line that supports charges that she "passed"—while also holding her accountable to the weird, fascinating, relevant details of her racially complicated life.

NOTES

1 See Cynthia Earl Kerman and Richard Eldridge, *The Lives of Jean Toomer: A Hunger for Wholeness* (Baton Rogue: Louisiana State University Press, 1989), 90; and John Howard Griffin, *Black like Me* (New York: Houghton Mifflin, 1961). More comprehensively, see Baz Dresinger, *Near Black: White-to-Black Passing in American Culture* (Amherst: University of Massachusetts Press, 2008).

2 See Shannon Beddell, "Professor Interprets Racial Differences," *Easterner*, February 26, 2014, http://easterneronline.com.

3 Rachel Dolezal, interview with Jeff Humphrey, *KXLY4 News*, June 11, 2015, on YouTube, www.youtube.com. Much of the information below also comes from a telephone interview with Humphrey, conducted on January 19, 2016, and from

executive producer Melissa Luck's account, "Rachel Dolezal: The Story behind the Story," *KLXY4 News*, June 16, 2015, www.kxly.com.

4 See Beddell, "Professor Interprets Racial Differences"; Shawntelle Moncy, "A Life to Be Heard," *Easterner*, February 5, 2015, http://easterneronline.com. For a catalog of Dolezal's many statements about her past life, see Margaret Hartmann, "Everything Rachel Dolezal Has Said about Her Identity," *New York Magazine*, June 17, 2015, http://nymag.com.

5 Allyson Hobbs, "Rachel Dolezal's Unintended Gift to America," *New York Times*, June 17, 2015, www.nytimes.com. Hobbs is the author of the extraordinary book, *A Chosen Exile: A History of Passing in American Life* (Cambridge, MA: Harvard University Press, 2015).

6 Jelani Cobb, "Black like Her," *New Yorker*, June 15, 2015, www.newyorker.com.

7 Melissa Harris-Perry Show, June 17, 2015, www.msnbc.com.

8 Rachel Dolezal, interviewed by Matt Lauer, *Today Show*, June 16, 2015, www.today.com.

9 Jamelle Bouie, "Is Rachel Dolezal Black Just Because She Says She Is?" *Slate*, June 12, 2015, www.slate.com.

10 Jelani Cobb, "Murders in Charleston," *New Yorker*, June 18, 2015, www.newyorker.com.

11 Allison Samuels, "Rachel Dolezal's True Lies," *Vanity Fair*, July 19, 2015, www.vanityfair.com.

12 Ibid.

13 Mark Seal, *The Man in the Rockefeller Suit: The Astonishing Rise and Spectacular Fall of a Serial Imposter* (New York: Plume, 2012).

14 Hobbs, *A Chosen Exile*; Martha Sandweiss, *Passing Strange: A Gilded Age Tale of Love and Deception across the Color Line* (New York: Penguin, 2010); Karl Jacoby, *The Strange Career of William Ellis: The Texas Slave Who Became a Mexican Millionaire* (New York: Norton, 2016); and Daniel Sharfstein, *The Invisible Line: A Secret History of Race in America* (New York: Penguin, 2012).

15 Walter Kirn, *Blood Will Out: The True Story of a Murder, a Mystery, and a Masquerade* (New York: Liveright, 2014), 211.

16 Ibid., 147.

17 For more, see Arissa Oh, *To Save the Children of Korea: The Cold War Origins of International Adoption* (Palo Alto, CA: Stanford University Press, 2015); and Matthew Pratt Guterl, *Josephine Baker and the Rainbow Tribe* (Cambridge, MA: Harvard University Press, 2014).

18 W. E. B. Du Bois, *Black Reconstruction in America, 1860–1880* (New York: Harcourt Brace, 1935). For a more recent formulation, see George Lipsitz, *The Possessive Investment in Whiteness: How White People Profit from Identity Politics* (Philadelphia: University of Pennsylvania Press, 2006).

19 The anecdote is in the epilogue of Matthew Frye Jacobson, *Whiteness of a Different Color: European Immigrants and the Alchemy of Race* (Cambridge, MA: Harvard University Press, 1999).

20 Quoted in Melanie Eversley, "Whites Pass for Black to Gain Empathy, Experts Say in Wake of Dolezal Case," *USA Today*, June 14, 2015, www.usatoday.com.

21 Mitchell Sunderland, "In Rachel Dolezal's Skin," *Broadly*, December 7, 2015, https://broadly.vice.com.

22 Kathryn Lofton, *Oprah: The Gospel of an Icon* (Berkeley: University of California Press, 2011), 17–25.

23 Marcia Dawkins, *Clearly Invisible: Racial Passing and the Politics of Cultural Identity* (Houston, TX: Baylor University Press, 2012).

2

Race and Science

Preconciliation as Reconciliation

OSAGIE K. OBASOGIE

I. Introduction

Many of the racial antagonisms that existed in the United States from slavery up through the end of World War II were based largely upon a single idea: biological race, or the essentialist notion that folk categories of race reflect innate biological differences. From scientific racism to phrenology to the eugenics movement and more, science and medicine played central roles in creating and sustaining the belief that racial differences and disparities are natural phenomena. It is largely thought that this idea was debunked after World War II as the Holocaust revealed the ghastly outcomes that can result from thinking about race in biological terms. Social constructionism emerged in this post-war period as a popular rearticulation of race in its suggestion that the meanings that come to attach to human bodies are not natural but are instead created by social, economic, and political forces. Although this approach has become prominent throughout the academy, social constructionist understandings of race have remained widely contested in the very fields that their development was intended to influence—that is, the life sciences and medicine. It is no secret that mainstream scientific and medical research continues to promote biological understandings of race to describe racial differences and explain racial disparities.

As a nation, we have yet to fully reconcile or appreciate how modern forms of racism and discrimination gain legitimacy from long-standing notions of biological race. This idea, in turn, remains salient through past and ongoing forms of scientific and medical research. This enduring sensibility not only hampers efforts at racial reconciliation in the areas

of science and medicine but also has cascading impacts on reconciliatory efforts in other areas of social life. For example, notions of biological
race fueled by research in the life sciences provide justification for the
discriminatory perception and treatment of people of color in fields such
as education, employment, and the criminal justice system, where it is not
uncommon for observers to link disparities in outcomes to seemingly intrinsic shortcomings. Thus, racial reconciliation in science and medicine
is central to any broader overall strategy concerning racial justice.

This essay briefly reviews how notions of biological difference became the cornerstone of modern understandings of race. It also explores
the extent to which science and medicine are both complicit and proactive in providing the misleading empirical foundations for social categories of race to be thought of and experienced as differences created by
nature, ultimately obscuring the social and structural ways in which racial hierarchies are perpetuated. Thus, reconciliation of these historical
moments with their ongoing implications means a collective endeavor
at acknowledging and atoning for these material and psychic harms. Yet,
how does one do this in light of health care and research industries that
see themselves (and their histories) as saving and sustaining lives, not as
political actors implicated in creating the false empirical foundations for
racial ideologies? Conceptually influenced by Congress's enforcement
powers under Section 5 of the Fourteenth Amendment to the U.S. Constitution, I propose *preconciliation as reconciliation*—that is, the best way
to atone for past wrongs in the areas of race, science, and medicine is to
proactively and aggressively seek out those situations in which harms
similar to those inflicted in the past by faulty notions of biological race
are likely to manifest themselves in modern times and to provide preventative remedies *before* any harm might actually occur. I conclude by
providing an example of how such preconciliation might play out in
modern times through the development of race impact assessments.

II. Biological Race: Emergence, Moments of Reconciliation, and Hypocrisy

Emergence

Historians of science offer numerous accounts of how biological understandings of race have shaped the ways that professionals and laypersons

perceive human differences and the causes of disparate social and health outcomes. Evelynn Hammonds and Rebecca Herzig's *The Nature of Difference* offers a comprehensive overview of how racial difference has been measured and quantified over hundreds of years to give the impression of scientific precision to mapping out the physiology of human distinctions—skin color, anatomical variations, distribution of genetic variations, and so forth—and rooting group ability/disability in these "natural" differences.[1] Thus, inequality and racial hierarchy become justified as the natural order of things—what God wanted or, in an increasingly secular society dominated by professions like medicine, what nature commands. We see this in the earliest efforts of eighteenth- and nineteenth-century scientific racism, when researchers like Samuel Morton compared the skulls of racial groups to offer a physiological basis (head size) for mental ability; the larger the average head, the more the group was thought to be naturally inclined towards intelligence.[2]

Quantifying racial differences and drawing connections to the existing social order became a hallmark of scientific racism during this period. Anatomical differences—everything from sexual organs to ears[3]—became a basis from which to draw distinctions between groups that ultimately served the goal of giving the appearance of empirical backing to racist ideology. Moreover, such practices became the epistemological basis from which physicians began using race as a lens through which to treat patients differently, under the premise that physiological differences between races explained the cause of certain diseases.

With the emergence of the eugenics movement in the late nineteenth and early twentieth centuries, these practices concerning the measurement of bodies to assess inherent ability became part of a broader global effort to promote the reproduction of the "strongest" while discouraging—even eliminating—those thought to be "unfit." Eugenics, as a practice, touched all races. But it had a disproportionate impact on vulnerable populations whose structural marginalization became reconceptualized as an intrinsic part of who they were, leading governments to enact policies like forced sterilization to limit their growth and therefore contain what was perceived as their burden on society. These strategies disproportionately affected the poor, disabled, people of color, and other minority groups at society's fringes.

Moments of Reconciliation

A global recognition of these practices' brutality emerged after World War II, as the world came face to face with the most horrific iteration of scientific racism and eugenic state policy: the Holocaust. As stories and evidence from Nuremberg about state-level practices of exterminating entire populations converged with narratives concerning physicians' and researchers' complicity in such gross cruelty in the name of science, people paused for a moment to consider the unspeakable harm that biological race as an ideology inflicted on the world. This led to what can be considered the first of at least three major reconciliatory moments, in which there was an attempt at public atonement for the profound damage caused by embedding biological race in the professional work of physicians and scientists. This first moment of reconciliation came with the Nuremberg Code in 1947 after the Doctors' Trial (*United States v. Karl Brandt et al.*), where gruesome testimony concerning Nazi experiments on Jewish people and other stigmatized populations were revealed in detail. Nazi researchers subjected prisoners to horrific treatment, such as high altitude experiments to determine the conditions in which people would die under rapidly changing air pressure, freezing experiments in which subjects were forced to stay unclothed in the cold or sit in a tank of ice water for multiple hours, and experiments in which subjects were forced to consume mustard gas or drink seawater to determine their effects on the human body.[4] These, among many other gruesome experiments, were justified by the idea that Jewish people and other prisoners were not fully human and therefore could be treated callously in the name of advancing science.

The Nuremberg Code set forth ten principles affirming the humanity of human subjects and establishing the conditions upon which all future research on human subjects should move forward. These include obtaining voluntary consent, avoiding unnecessary harm and injury, and placing responsibility on staff to stop experiments if they become dangerous. These basic principles have had a tremendous impact on the ethics of human subject research and have created the baseline sensibility that researchers should acknowledge and affirm their shared humanity with human subjects. This idea affirmatively rejects the notion that biological difference—real or perceived—can ever justify inhumane treatment.

A second reconciliatory moment came a few years later in 1950 with the first of a series of statements by UNESCO on race. It is important to note that although physicians and researchers in the life sciences played a particular role in providing biological and physiological justifications for scientific racism and eugenic state policies, social scientists and researchers from other academic fields also contributed to the perceived intellectual credibility of biological race during this period. While acknowledging the presence of human populations—a "horizontal" differentiation between humans that is different from the "vertical" nature of racial hierarchy embedded in ideologies concerning biological race—the UNESCO statements represent a collective moment across disciplines in which the academy ostensibly rejected biological race as both a descriptive and normative matter. The 1950 statement begins with "Scientists have reached general agreement in recognizing that mankind is one: that all men belong to the same species, homo sapiens."[5] This original statement received heavy pushback, to say the least, and subsequent revisions were made. Nonetheless, the UNESCO Statement on Race remains, to this day, an important moment of reconciliation, in which the harms of biological race were acknowledged and (mostly) discredited as a way to signal that science admitted its wrongdoing and that the academy and other professionals would no longer tolerate such ideas.

A third major moment of reconciliation came several decades later in 2000 with the announcement of the completion of the first draft of the human genome—a "map," so to speak, of all of the genes that make up humankind. Then President Clinton noted in his public remarks that the findings from the Human Genome Project show that

> all human beings, regardless of race, are more than 99.9 percent the same. What that means is that modern science has confirmed what we first learned from ancient fates. The most important fact of life on this Earth is our common humanity. My greatest wish on this day for the ages is that this incandescent truth will always guide our actions as we continue to march forth in this, the greatest age of discovery ever known.[6]

Francis Collins, then director of the National Human Genome Research Institute, followed Clinton, saying "I'm happy that today, the only race we are talking about is the human race."[7] The announcement marked an important reconciliatory moment by framing this monumental scientific advancement as conclusive evidence that there are no biological demarcations in our genes that align with folk notions of race. The idea of biological race, at that moment, was now officially dead. Or so many thought.

Saying One Thing and Doing Another

Despite these moments of reconciliation in which science appears to openly refute[8] the idea of biological race, a closer look at the research shows that biological race continued to shape scholarly agendas. I recently co-authored an article in the *Fordham Law Review* that provided the first large-scale empirical assessment of how researchers conceptualized race in the post–World War II period (1950–2000)—the moment when racial reconciliation in science allegedly began—to see if notions of biological race dissipated in this period as the standard reconciliatory narrative suggests.[9] Our qualitative and numerical review of 291 articles in four major journals in medicine and genetics (*New England Journal of Medicine, JAMA: The Journal of the American Medical Association, American Journal of Human Genetics,* and *Annals of Human Genetics*) showed that biological race as an ideology clearly persisted. We found three themes: (1) that multiple theories of race—including biological race—co-occurred and motivated research projects; (2) a general search for racial purity, or drawing upon biological and other conceptions of race to identify "pure" or "real" groupings of humans; and (3) the use of typological categories of race to understand disease and disease patterns. The trends identified by our qualitative assessment highlight how residual notions of biological race remained in the literature after World War II and subsequent public articulations of reconciliation, contrary to conventional wisdom suggesting that researchers were moving away from such thinking. Our numerical assessment also shows that such conceptualizations were not uncommon; the overall number of articles using these framings increased over time. While this examination stops at 2000—the year the Human Genome Project announced its results—there is ample evidence that this trend continues in present times. For example, Duana Fullwiley points out that just as the findings of the Human Genome Project were used to make certain public pronouncements about the insignificance of race due to the 99.9 percent genetic commonality among all humans, certain research teams after 2000 began mining this less than .1 percent variation for clues on how race might be meaningful in research and clinical settings.[10]

What we begin to see is a blatant inconsistency that verges on hypocrisy. That is, as a gesture of reconciliation, medicine and science have made expressive commitments to move away from biological race. Yet, they have substantively maintained this theory of race in research and practice. And this matters in terms of the content of the scientific knowledge base and the services provided by medical professionals. In her remarkable sociological study of how scientists understand race, Ann Morning concludes that contrary to espoused reconciliatory narratives, "constructivism and anti-essentialism have hardly conquered the academy . . . [and that] the essentialist proposition that races are biologically grounded entities remains a compelling view for many contemporary scientists."[11] John Hoberman's work shows the profound consequences that essentialist understandings of race and biology can have in producing medical racism, leaving people of color with significantly worse clinical interactions that have meaningful impacts on their health outcomes.[12] For example, a paper published by the *Proceedings of the National Academy of Sciences* recently found that half of the White medical students in the study believed that biological differences led Blacks to feel less pain—a perspective steeped in old-school notions of racial biology that shaped their treatment recommendations.[13] Thus, this inconsistency between reconciliatory expressions from the scientific community and the continued belief in biological race in practice suggests that more serious engagements regarding race and reconciliation are needed.

III. Preconciliation as Reconciliation

Section 5 of the Fourteenth Amendment as Context

The Reconstruction Amendments of the U.S. Constitution were ratified after the Civil War partially as a reconciliatory effort to put former slaves into a position of legal equality and to give them the full rights of American citizenship. The Thirteenth Amendment abolished slavery; the Fourteenth Amendment, most notably, provided for Equal Protection and due process; and the Fifteenth Amendment gave former slaves the right to vote.

The Fourteenth Amendment's Equal Protection Clause is perhaps the most well known part of these amendments, as it has been at the heart of some of the Supreme Court's most important cases on race and equality, such as *Brown v. Board of Education*. In these cases, the Equal Protection Clause serves as a repository of rights that individual plaintiffs can ask a court to enforce, whether it is access to public schools on a nondiscriminatory basis, as in *Brown*, or, as in *Loving v. Virginia*, the right to not have the state interfere in one's decision to marry someone of a different race. The enforcement of these specific rights depends upon individual plaintiffs litigating a matter through the court system.

But the Reconstruction Amendments are not entirely dependent upon the judiciary and individual litigants for the enforcement of their reconciliatory norms. Each of these amendments has a mechanism that allows Congress to enforce their provisions by appropriate legislation. With the Fourteenth Amendment, this is known as Congress's Section 5 powers. Under some interpretations, these powers allow Congress to provide a remedy for a perceived or observed harm related to the provision of the Fourteenth Amendment's notion of equality independent of or before a particular violation of an individual's rights are litigated.[14] For example, Congress might observe that a state is engaging in a practice that it understands to violate the Equal Protection Clause. Typically, an aggrieved party would file suit arguing that the state action in question is an Equal Protection violation, which may delay any resolution due to the possibility of extended litigation. Section 5 of the Fourteenth Amendment gives Congress the authority to, among other things, legislate proactively to remedy this problem, as opposed to waiting until the courts resolve the matter.

One can think of such preventative remedies as a form of *preconciliation*. What I mean by this term is that, whereas reconciliation is largely "backward looking" to resolve a present issue or relationship,[15] preconciliation is anticipatory and "forward looking" to root out likely harms that look eerily similar to old problems that one has an expressed moral commitment to not repeat. So, for example, in *Katzenbach v. Morgan* (1966), Congress enacted Section 4(e) of the Voting Rights Act pursuant to Section 5 of the Fourteenth Amendment to prevent states from using

English language literacy tests as a prerequisite for voting. In this situation, Congress determined (contrary to a previous opinion by the U.S. Supreme Court)[16] that such literacy tests had a discriminatory impact on voting that, in its judgment, violated basic notions of Equal Protection. It therefore passed a federal law preventing states from using them. Now, to be clear, the U.S. Supreme Court has in subsequent years scaled back Congress's ability to proactively legislate in this manner pursuant to Section 5.[17] Nevertheless, *Katzenbach* highlights the conceptual significance and moral clarity of preconciliation in matters of race and reconciliation. That is, race is such a dynamic and structural determinant of everyday life that it is woefully insufficient to burden individuals with the responsibility to initiate reconciliatory efforts that attend to the totality of racial wrongs that have and continue to affect minority groups. As seen in the previous section, race and racism have an elasticity that subverts and eventually overwhelms the good intentions of isolated reconciliatory moments such as the UNESCO Statement, findings from the Human Genome Project, or any other efforts to atone for the past. A more holistic approach to racial justice must encourage state actors to take a preconciliatory standpoint into account—that is, the state must actively seek out remedies to structural problems as part of a moral commitment to not letting the past repeat itself.

Preconciliation in Science and Medicine: Toward Race Impact Assessments

As with Congress's Section 5 powers, there are moments in which law can be used to promote preconciliatory sensibilities with regard to issues of race, science, and medicine. One approach that I previously proposed[18] is race impact assessments. Impact assessments are tools that are utilized in various fields to promote better decision making within regulatory agencies before certain policies are put in place. For example, health impact assessments can be understood as

> a means of evidence based policy making for improvement in health. It is a combination of methods whose aim is to assess the health consequences to a population of a policy, project, or program that does not necessarily have health as its primary objective.[19]

By assessing the available evidence and data, heath impact assessments estimate the effect that a potential policy might have on health at a population level. Health impact assessments attempt to understand policies' otherwise hidden impact on human health in order to develop strategies for mitigating adverse outcomes. Impact assessments have been used in other areas such as human rights and environmentalism as a way to ensure that regulatory bodies take these concerns seriously and proactively get ahead of any challenges when making policy decisions.

Many of the race-related products and practices stemming from scientific research that may be tainted by biological understandings of race fall under the umbrella of specific administrative agencies. Thus, there is an opportunity for these agencies to use race impact assessments to root out claims about racial differences or racial disparities that may be premised upon essentialist notions of biological race. Take, for example, race-based medicines, or pharmaceuticals that claim to work better for particular racial populations. The Food and Drug Administration (FDA) approved the first race-based medicine in 2005 with BiDil, a drug that claims to be particularly beneficial for African Americans suffering from heart failure. Critiques of BiDil have been substantial, and much of the evidence suggests that the drug is more of a marketing scheme than a breakthrough in racial pharmacogenomics.[20] But what is particularly troubling is that the FDA does not have any procedures in place to assess what it might mean for a federal regulatory agency to approve a drug that allegedly responds to the different physiology and biochemical makeup of African Americans, linking such difference to misperceptions regarding Blacks' ostensibly high rates of heart failure. Put differently, by affirming the idea that racial disparities in health outcomes are a natural disposition for Blacks that can be treated with a special pharmacological intervention, the federal government essentially gave legitimacy to nineteenth-century ideas of biological race when a closer look at the data does not support this.[21] Indeed, the creator of BiDil told the Los Angeles Times that he prescribes the generic drugs that comprise BiDil to many of his White patients, noting, "I actually think everybody should be using it."[22]

While BiDil's sales have not been significant, its FDA approval reinforced notions of biological race both within medical and scientific communities and among laypersons. This undermines efforts at reconciliation and further entrenches damaging understandings of racial difference and disparities. Here is where a race impact assessment as part of the regulatory approval process could have been helpful. For example, an independent committee could have been charged to examine how the claims of racially specific treatment might give credence to inaccurate understandings of race. While most FDA reviews of new drug applications focus on granular examinations of statistical data and clinical trial studies, a separate examination of the data in light of the social, historical, and political implications of racial discourses might have facilitated more helpful scrutiny of the claims. This might have allowed the government to avoid its misleading and harmful endorsement of biological race.

Conclusion

Race impact assessments can be an important preconciliatory tool for making sure that our moral duty to not employ biological race translates into everyday anti-racist actions that can further our commitments to racial justice. In my previous writings, I have discussed how race impact assessments can play an important role within administrative agencies beyond the FDA to provide critical pushback against recurring articulations of biological race in science and medicine.[23] This includes the Federal Trade Commission's oversight of genetic ancestry tests that are often marketed as capable of telling consumers what race they are from a cheek swab of DNA. It also involves the Federal Bureau of Investigation's oversight of and influence over criminal investigations using DNA forensic tests, which often use questionable notions of group and population difference that implicate race to capture suspects. Such use of race impact assessments is, in short, what racial reconciliation is truly about: ensuring that the pain and suffering that previous generations endured is not inflicted upon their descendants. Such a commitment requires not simply looking backward to make amends for past harms but also looking forward to ensure that the inertia of structural racism does not re-create the very same problems under different guises. Embracing the preconciliatory sensibilities of race impact assessments is an important step toward this goal.

NOTES

1 Evelynn Hammonds and Rebecca M. Herzig, eds., *The Nature of Difference: Sciences of Race in the United States from Jefferson to Genomics* (Cambridge, MA: MIT Press, 2009).

2 For Morton, see Steven Jay Gould, *The Mismeasure of Man*, 2nd ed. (New York: Norton, 1996).

3 For example, see T. E. Murrell, "Peculiarities in the Structure and Diseases of the Ear of the Negro" (1887), in Hammonds and Herzig, *The Nature of Difference*.

4 Brigadier General Telford Taylor, "Opening Statement of the Prosecution, December 9, 1946," in *Trials of War Criminals before the Nuremberg Military Tribunals under Control Council Law 10*, vol. 1 (Washington, DC: Government Printing Office , 1949–1853), Military Tribunal, Case 1, *United States v. Karl Brandt et al.*, October 1946–April 1949, 27–74.

5 UNESCO, Statement on Race (Paris: UNESCO, July 1950).

6 Remarks made by the President [Bill Clinton] et al., "Text of Remarks on the Completion of the First Survey of the Entire Human Genome Project," the White House (Washington, DC: National Archives, June 26, 2000), www.archives.gov.

7 Francis Collins, quoted at *id.*

8 Jenny Reardon provides an excellent narrative exploration into how claims that biological understandings of race in the post-war era were more complicated than many think. See Jenny Reardon, *Race to the Finish: Identity and Governance in an Age of Genomics* (Princeton, NJ: Princeton University Press, 2005).

9 Osagie K. Obasogie et al., "Race in the Life Sciences: An Empirical Assessment, 1950–2000," *Fordham Law Review* 83 (2015): 3089.

10 Duana Fullwiley, "The Molecularization of Race: Institutionalizing Human Difference in Pharmacogenetic Practice," *Science as Culture* 16 (March 2007): 1.

11 Ann Morning, *The Nature of Race: How Scientists Think and Teach about Human Difference* (Berkeley: University of California Press, 2011), 221.

12 John Hoberman, *Black and Blue: The Origins and Consequences of Medical Racism* (Berkeley: University of California Press, 2012).

13 Kelly Hoffman et al., "Racial Bias in Pain Assessment and Treatment Recommendations, and False Beliefs about Biological Differences between Blacks and Whites," *Proceedings of the National Academy of Sciences* 113, no. 16 (March 2016): 4296.

14 Tracy A. Thomas, "Congress' Section 5 Power and Remedial Rights," *University of California Davis Law Review* 34 (2000): 673–767.

15 Merriam-Webster defines "reconciliation" as "the act of causing two people or groups to become friendly again after an argument or disagreement." See Merriam-Webster, www.merriam-webster.com.

16 See, generally, Lassiter v. Northampton Election Board, 360 U.S. 45 (1959).

17 The Supreme Court has pushed back against the relatively expansive understanding of Congress' Section 5 powers as articulated in *Katzenbach* and has held in

subsequent opinions that Congress cannot expand the scope of rights beyond what has been acknowledged by the Court. In City of Boerne v. Flores, the Court noted that

> the design of the [Fourteenth] Amendment and the test of [Section] 5 are inconsistent with the suggestion that Congress has the power to decree the substance of the Fourteenth Amendment's restrictions on the States. Legislation which alters the meaning of the Free Exercise Clause cannot be said to be enforcing the Clause. Congress does not enforce a constitutional right by changing what the right is. It has been given the power "to enforce," not the power to determine what constitutes a constitutional violation. Were it not so, what Congress would be enforcing would no longer be, in any meaningful sense, the "provisions of [the Fourteenth Amendment]." (City of Boerne v. Flores, 521 U.S. 507, 519 (1997))

See also Board of Trustees v. Garrett, 531 U.S. 356 (2001).

18 For previous discussions on race impact assessments, see Osagie K. Obasogie, *Playing the Gene Card? A Report on Race and Human Biotechnology* (Oakland, CA: Center for Genetics and Society, 2009), www.thegenecard.org, "The Color of Our Genes: Balancing the Promise and Risks of Racial Categories in Human Biotechnology," *Science Progress*, June 15, 2009, and "The Return of Biological Race? Regulating Race and Genetics through Administrative Agency Race Impact Assessments," *Southern California Interdisciplinary Law Journal* 22 (2012): 1.

19 Karen Lock, "Health Impact Assessment," *British Medical Journal* 320, no. 7246 (2000): 1395.

20 Jonathan Kahn, *Race in a Bottle: The Story of BiDil and Racialized Medicine in a Post-genomic Age* (New York: Columbia University Press, 2012).

21 Jonathan Kahn, "Getting the Numbers Right: Statistical Mischief and Racial Profiling in Heart Failure Research," *Perspectives in Biology and Medicine* 46, no. 4 (2003): 473–483.

22 Denise Gellene, "Heart Pill Intended Only for Blacks Sparks Debate," *Los Angeles Times*, June 16, 2005.

23 See Obasogie, *Playing the Gene Card?*, "The Color of Our Genes," and "The Return of Biological Race?"

3

From Perceiving Injustice to Achieving Racial Justice

Interrogating the Impact of Racial Brokers on Racial Antagonism and Racial Reconciliation

CARLA SHEDD

What does it mean to be a conscious citizen in an unequal society? As a sociologist who studies the interactions of people with public institutions that can combat or exacerbate inequality (e.g., schools and courts), I am intrigued by the power of these state-governed structures, watching ever vigilantly how institutional promises are made, sometimes broken, and ultimately, we hope, fulfilled. There are many gulfs that exist in this moment, this iteration, of America. This project to assess whether genuine racial reconciliation can occur is stymied because one can only reconcile that which was once ever connected. In the United States, there are remarkable breaches across the domains of race/ethnicity. This essay focuses on the connections between the people—adolescents specifically—and the social institutions that shape us, betray us, redeem us, and ultimately, we hope, free us.[1]

As schools and neighborhoods have become more securitized during an era of mass incarceration, I argue that certain young people end up on a "carceral continuum" that produces daily exposure to hypersurveillance and criminalization at the hands of police in their communities. Police contacts are the most direct link between law enforcement and the public. Adolescents begin to have contacts with police during a formative period that simultaneously shapes their lifelong attitudes and life trajectories, and much of the contact occurs in places that are not overtly penal—such as urban public schools and neighborhoods.

Urban (high) schools play a major role in either ameliorating or further reinforcing adolescents' racially divergent social worlds, particularly their perceptions of and experiences with authoritative figures (e.g., teachers in school and police officers on the street). For some kids, especially those in our nation's biggest cities, attending a well-resourced school in a well-resourced neighborhood is the only way out of an existence where citizens become "subjects" whose every move, inside and outside the home, is subject to police control. And we've even transported the policing from the neighborhood realm into the schools via "zero tolerance policies." Thus it is necessary to move beyond micro-level analyses of police contacts to better understand the larger nexus of state-based interventions in the lives of urban youth.

More specifically, I argue that the state plays a critical role in delivering the "embryonic citizen to the body politic" within the institutional confines of its most formative and reformative institutions, public schools and juvenile justice, respectively.[2] Based on the concept of *parens patriae*—the legal framework through which the state acts as the surrogate parent of the country—governmental actors are allowed to intervene in the lives of individuals and their families with the ultimate goal of building better citizens. But how do these actors who operate along the carceral continuum—particularly public schoolteachers, police officers, and judges—use these powers? Do they bring us together across the lines of race, place, and experience toward this idea of racial reconciliation? Or do they act to further antagonize the relationships and to stratify the outcomes of racially stigmatized bodies via their interactions with these state actors?

Each of these institutional agents plays a major role in shaping the trajectories citizens take to and through school and toward or away from the formalized juvenile and criminal justice systems. They serve as brokers that direct the flows of young people toward their ultimate destinies, and I believe it is critical that we start this inquiry about the role of these brokers at the phase of the "carceral continuum" that begins outside the home and is based in our most formative social institution—our public schools.

In contrast to places of reformation, like workhouses and prisons, schools are well established as places of *formation* and socialization. Schools shape their charges by enabling their social, intellectual, and emotional development and (in ways not often defined) prepare them for the experience of being an adult. School is therefore an essential developmental setting, which in many ways purports to serve as a microcosm of the community and the larger social world. However, I argue in my book, *Unequal City: Race, Schools, and Perceptions of Injustice*, that schools do not reflect the world in which we live. Instead, schools serve to further distort social worlds in an unequal society.[3] That is, schools—which should be an equalizing force in American society—are instead likely to reproduce and further distort existing social stratification by race, gender, class, and neighborhood. This is especially true in places like Chicago where the conflicts accompanying changes in educational and residential segregation in that city are played out through the lives of young people and prominently feature encounters with the law.

This essay builds on and deeply explores several themes from my book to examine the roots, structure, and substance of racial antagonism via the perceptions and experiences of marginalized urban youth. More specifically, the measure at the center of my research on the lives of Chicago youth is "perceived injustice," a variable that captures young people's attitudes about social and structural disadvantage. This may include their awareness of "how opportunities for economic or educational success may differ by race, ethnicity, gender, or class."[4] Typically, Whites and Blacks are at the poles of America's long-standing racial spectrum with Asians, Hispanics/Latinos, and Native Americans (when counted) falling somewhere in between.[5] This stagnant racial hierarchy is a form of racial antagonism in itself in that it allows the more advantaged groups to perceive that they are in their "rightful place" (granting them relative gratification in comparison to their lesser-status, extra-racial counterparts), and for the least-advantaged, it can illustrate to them their unequal status to which they can acquiesce or actively fight. The attainment of racial reconciliation will continue to be a social fiction without serious investigation into and subsequent restructuring of racially divergent trajectories to the ends of opportunity, equality, and justice. I submit it is the paths that young people take to and through school that will allow an opening for the achievement of racial justice.

Schools, Neighborhoods, and the Comparative Context

Unequal City: Race, Schools and Perceptions of Injustice examines Chicago public school students' paths between home and school and argues that during those travels youth confront inequality and aim to steer clear of danger from peers, neighbors, and police. *Unequal City* covers three interrelated topics: First, it reveals how students from different backgrounds (i.e., racial, economic, etc.) perceive injustice and experience police contact along a continuum that is stratified by racial and ethnic lines. Second, it explores how interactions with authority figures, such as parents, teachers, and police, shape young people's perceptions of themselves and their social worlds. Finally, it reveals both the impetus behind and the results of policies that connect public schools to other systems that surveil, punish, and incarcerate.

Schools serve as a central, formative social institution that shapes adolescents' understanding of wider social and structural hierarchies. Further, they provide a frame for understanding the world that can be "expanded" for youth who cross lines of race, class, neighborhood, and/ or gang each day or more "restricted" for those who remain in more homogeneous contexts. These comparative frames, whether narrow or wide ranging, shape youth perceptions of self, opportunity, and mobility. In effect, (high) schools further reinforce students' racially divergent social worlds, or they could play a role in making those teens' lives, and their perceptions of the same, better.

In *Unequal City*, I use the sociologists Ruth D. Peterson and Lauren J. Krivo's analytical framing of the "racial-spatial" divide to buttress my argument about schools operating as more powerful engines of social stratification than neighborhoods in urban America.[6] According to Peterson and Krivo, this racial-spatial divide is characterized by "a social arrangement in which substantial ethno-racial inequality in social and economic circumstances and power in society is combined with segregated and unequal residential locations across racial and ethnic groups."[7] Though the work of Peterson and Krivo does not focus on the locations of schools, I submit that the racial-spatial divide analytical frame powerfully captures the array of resources, opportunities, and diversity available to young people—and these social structures significantly influence adolescents' abilities to understand, encounter, and adapt to discriminatory treatment in various social domains, particularly in housing, education, and employment.

Moreover, schools in America are central to the creation and the corrosion of possibilities for its most vulnerable populations, poor Black and Brown youth, who since the *child-saving movements* of the Progressive Era (1890–1920) were seen as "indispensable in the battle for the nation's destiny."[8] When schools fail to affirm the personhood and democratic status of Black and Brown youth via racial discrimination, paternalism, and denial of full citizenship, it is likely that these young people will encounter, become enmeshed within, and suffer the ill effects of the state's subsequent "manufactory of citizens," the juvenile justice system. My research of and within these two institutions demonstrates the failure of America in its long-standing experiment of achieving the ideals of a true democracy. This failure is largely due to the persistence of racial segregation that sociologists Douglass Massey and Nancy Denton argue is the "institutional apparatus that supports other racially discriminatory processes and binds them together into a coherent and uniquely effective system of racial subordination."[9] I proceed to interrogate how schools and juvenile justice courts deftly intertwine the combined failures of the state to reconcile and redress the corrosive effects of racial subordination.

Crossing Boundaries of Race and Place

The paradox of increasing racial diversity and diminished social integration is an apt foundation for this essay. For some urban students, public school is the only place for different racial/ethnic groups to convene since neighborhood segregation is persistent and far-reaching.[10] The permeability of neighborhood boundaries varies a great deal with regard to racial/ethnic ambiguity (to outsiders) as well as variation by skin shade. To be sure, social integration does not necessarily flow from physical integration. However, social situations allow observation of the strictures of racial transgressions and the strictures of racial segregation. Schools powerfully reflect and sustain difference, but they may also disrupt segregation and racial subordination by moving people across the strict boundaries of race, class, and place. Because of this latter possibility of catalyzing physical and social mobility, they are the optimal sites through which an effort toward racial reconciliation could be achieved.

The following is an excerpt of an interview I conducted with Joaquin (his chosen pseudonym), a ninth grader at Lincoln Park High School in Chicago, who responds to my question of whether he sees divisions among racial/ethnic groups at his school:

JOAQUIN: There's definitely some clear divisions between the groups.

AUTHOR: What about students who live in the neighborhood of the school and those who don't? Can you tell?

JOAQUIN: You can tell, 'cuz Lincoln Park High is a neighborhood school for the Cabrini-Green projects . . . and you have lots of the population of the school coming from higher-class Lincoln Park homes, so you have a clash there. And it also brings out the diversity of the school.

AUTHOR: So when you say "a clash," is it antagonistic or just different?

JOAQUIN: No, it's just when I say "clash" you can see it. When you look out at the crowd after school, you can sit there and you can see the groups moving as, like, two different species of people almost.[11]

I interviewed Joaquin while studying youth perceptions of social and criminal injustice in the Chicago Public School system, and his vantage point has stuck with me for over ten years. As a sociologist who uses both quantitative and qualitative methods to analyze the life(worlds) of urban adolescents, I found that his answers to my questions above graphically convey the same facts I could tell you using school-wide demographic data, but to a more powerful effect. The phrase "two different species of people" is peculiar unless, like me, you were able to observe school dismissals and see distinct groups of students who were White and walking to their homes in the tony Lincoln Park neighborhood, Black and Hispanic and waiting at the bus stop outside the school to head west to the *Brown Line* "El" train on Armitage Avenue, or Black students walking to catch a southbound bus to the (now-demolished) Cabrini-Green housing projects.

Joaquin revealed later in our hour-long interview that he had no idea how isolated he was until he came to Lincoln Park High School from his "predominantly Caucasian and Hispanic" parochial school because its homogeneity didn't force him to think about racial demographics. What is striking is that he is neither Hispanic nor White, but he still did not think about race much until he came to a school with greater racial/ethnic diversity because it was a neighborhood school for students from upper-middle-class-earning families, housing project dwellers, and students who were drawn from across Chicago because of its *interna-*

tional baccalaureate advanced curriculum. Joaquin identifies as Filipino American, but he said that others always perceived him as White Hispanic, so his ability to pass for White Hispanic may have played a role in his lack of attention to race and its effects on social relations until his high school years. The permeability of racial boundaries for students who identified/were ascribed as White Hispanic and students of Asian descent came up several times during my interviews with various students at Lincoln Park High School, and as a biracial (Black and White) ninth grader told me, in a knowing conspiratorial way, these groups are able to "hide in with anybody."[12]

Though Blacks may be found at the bottom of America's racial hierarchy, they typically are at the top of the racial gradient that measures perceptions of injustice. Based on the typology, Blacks are more likely to believe members of their race have a harder time finding a job and a nice place to live; additionally, they are more likely to be unfairly stopped and searched by the police. Even though Blacks are more likely to believe that the world is fundamentally unjust, it does not mean that they have given up.[13] This group is very much committed to education, equity, and opportunity, even though they do not believe that they are given a fair shake at achieving those goals in American society. Thus this is not about aspirational justice, but it is about experiential justice—that is, perceptions of how justice is actually distributed.

In retrospect, I wonder whether my investigations would have had more theoretical power if I had aimed to capture racial democracy via a measure of *racial dis/content* instead of perceptions of racial injustice. As the sociologist Geoff K. Ward argues in his book *The Black Child-Savers*, "If racial identification and stratification are to be reconciled with democratic principles of justice, we must understand how the ideas and practices of justice become intertwined with racial ideologies and structures . . . to diminish and affirm the democratic standing of [B]lack youths and communities in this institutional context [juvenile justice]."[14] I would argue that Ward's analysis of the dialectic of racial oppression, racial domination, and antiracist resistance should not begin at the point of juvenile justice intervention in the lives of Black youth. Instead, we should look at the earlier, persistent failures of social institutions to be racially inclusive (particularly schools and neighborhoods) to the tangible end of democratic exclusion. This is how the state's provision of necessary services (e.g., housing, education, welfare, etc.) fails to achieve its mission of "citizen building," and its corruption renders violence to and on those same vulnerable populations. Racial democracy is not only elusive, as Ward argues; it is also antagonistic. These conditions put us further away from achieving both racial reconciliation and its more substantive outgrowth—racial justice.

Toward a Theory of the Institutional Self

If racial segregation is the institutional apparatus that undergirds White supremacy in America, then I posit that the public domains where racial subordination is manifest (i.e., neighborhoods, schools, and courts) indelibly mark the individuals encased within these spaces. My work thus far has used a "place-sensitive" sociology that maps the terrain of injustice across school and residential contexts as informed by race, gender, and class.[15] My understanding of place, particularly that of public schools, means that I see these institutions as agentic players in our social lives, with measurable and independent effects.[16] Therefore, I could fashion a theory of the "institutional self" that encapsulates both the agency of place and its stasis, paradoxically.

This theory might best build on the work of David Sibley, who writes about "geographies of exclusion" that are the literal mappings of "power relations onto geographic places and their commensurate social spaces, such as schools and neighborhoods."[17] Sibley theorizes how physical terrain becomes imbued with social meaning and markers, which together shape what he calls the "ecological self."[18] An explicit theory of the "institutional self" would also draw on a line of scholarship by Robert Sampson and Dawn Bartusch on "cognitive landscapes" that serves to connect one's ecological and imagined realities by understanding how place *and* physical mobility shape individuals' perceptions of success and mobility.[19] Adolescents' specific social locations, such as their neighborhoods and schools, act as the comparative frames through which they make sense of their place in the reigning social hierarchy by race, age, gender, class, and other components of identity. But at this developmental stage, it is the institution that is shaping the full/holistic self most prominently instead of thinking about the combined effect of a structure onto the individual variants of identity (e.g., race, gender, etc.).

The persistence of racial subordination has tricky implications for mobility, both physical and social, for those who are at the bottom of urban America's social and racial hierarchy. I argue that the most disadvantaged are tasked with offsetting the deficits others (or they themselves) assign to their personhood, homes, communities, schools, and organizations. It is somewhat perplexing that a visible minority of our most needy urban denizens have become guinea pigs in myriad social experiments across the institutional gamut. For instance, they are tasked with "moving to opportunity" instead of being able to "stay in place" to achieve social mobility via more attractive housing; they are given an "expanded portfolio of choice" in schooling that pushes them toward public-private education ventures; they are tasked with surmounting a spatial mismatch in the realm of viable employment; and so much more. Thus accountability to their own democratic aspirations, in addition to state-level mandates about their goals (e.g., welfare-to-work), puts the onus on these individuals to escape from their persistent plight of institutional subordination. That is, they are marked by the deficits of public institutions and, consequently, have to seek help from the same structures to *whiten/lighten* the mark toward a fuller humanity. Racial dignity—which has been beseeched, contested, and denied—becomes the most foundational step toward the achievement of democracy with racial justice, not racial reconciliation, at its center.

There are examples in my data that help illustrate this point in which place becomes as important as the master status category of race. More specifically, deficits that are rooted in race become grounded in place. It is these intersections of race and place that affect the following manifestations of racial antagonism: the false premise of (public) school "choice" and the racially disparate terrain of misdemeanor arrests.

School Choice and Racial Composition of Schools

Over ten years ago, I started doing in-depth interviews and observations at four Chicago public high schools in order to see how varying school structures would shape young people's perceptions and experience. My fieldwork was necessary to supplement the statistical analyses on the same population that gave me the general landscape but did not offer much insight on the dynamics of the findings regarding youth perceptions of social and criminal injustice and police contact as structured by race, gender, age, neighborhood, and school context. I became rather intrigued with the "school effects" that intersected with the race effects, so this is what led me to look more closely at four unique school environments on different sides of Chicago.

The two North Side schools were racially mixed/integrated (per Chicago Public Schools [CPS] guidelines: Mixed schools are 15–30 percent White, and integrated schools are more than 30 percent White), had greater resources, were in great neighborhoods, and had curricular diversity. The other two schools on the South Side, Tilden High and Harper High, were composed of the population of students you might imagine have been "left behind" after their counterparts with "true choices" left for private, parochial, or selective public schools like the two in my North Side sample: Walter Payton Preparatory School and Lincoln Park High School.

Tilden High is a vocational school that is located in a (still) fiercely defended Irish-American neighborhood that has become more diverse in the last few decades after Mexican Americans began moving in (and were not pushed out). Tilden is predominately Black and Hispanic, although the majority of the Black students live at least a mile away from Tilden in more disadvantaged, predominantly Black neighborhoods like Englewood and Washington Park. Max, a freshman at Tilden, is Mexican American and lives in the neighborhood.

Max tells me that he was accepted into two other schools but did not return any of the paperwork to lock in one of those choices; therefore, he was "sent over" to Tilden. Max's grammar school was over 90 percent Hispanic (primarily Mexican); going to Tilden was a huge change for him. The racial composition of Tilden in 2005, when I conducted my first interviews, was less than 2 percent Asian and Native American, 5 percent White, 32 percent Hispanic, and 60 percent African American. Max adapted to Tilden's diverse population by honing his skills as a "cultural straddler"—that is, making friends across and within racial and gang lines at the school.[20]

Unlike Max, his schoolmate Shay, an African American tenth grader, chose to go to Tilden instead of her neighborhood school. She travels to Tilden from her housing project just over three miles northeast of the school. Shay explains that "the people that go to my neighborhood school like picking fights, and I wanted to explore more by meeting new people instead of being around all the people who act bad. Even though I know every place is bad." Shay's estimation that all places are bad reflects a particular brand of cynicism that was rather common among students in my two South Side schools.

Shay goes on to provide details about the bad behavior she witnesses at Tilden. There is the general expectation, according to Shay, that the boys at Tilden will "act bad because they're in a different neighborhood, a much different neighborhood." She likes the neighborhood, however, since "it's quiet most of the time. But they got Kings and Latins [Hispanic gang names] around here." Shay corroborates Max's descriptions of the clashes between the Hispanic gang members and the Black gang members:

> SHAY: Everybody talks to everybody. Latinos talk to Blacks 'cuz we got some Latinos in the Black gang! They talk to each other. They interact with each other. But you know, when it's really time to fight, they'll probably, you know, flip sides or something, just 'cuz of they skin color.
>
> AUTHOR: Do you think your school is pretty diverse racially?
>
> SHAY: What you mean by "diverse"?
>
> AUTHOR: Like a lot of different races.
>
> SHAY: Uh huh [yes], 'cuz we got Chinese, Puerto Rican, Mexican, Latino, Black, Hispanic. I like it. Because one of my friends is Mexican, and he learn a lot from us and we learn a lot from him. He teaches us stuff, we teach him stuff. So, basically we been friends for so long, we know about each other past. Well, you know, we don't dwell on our past; we look at the future and try to help each other go towards a good future and whatnot.

As Shay reveals, the climate at Tilden is not always peaceful, but the cleavages between students are not invariably delineated by race. Gang affiliation, neighborhood, and even language can play a role. For instance, two interviewees describe arguments that escalated into fights because one group thought another group was "cussing them out" when they spoke in their native languages. (Chinese and Spanish were the examples given.)

Although the cross-racial affiliations may be tenuous, other students at Tilden describe positive interactions with students from different racial backgrounds and different neighborhoods. Jackson, a sophomore at Tilden who lives in a majority-Black neighborhood minutes away from the University of Chicago—but a world away in reality—says that he "wants to see different color people and what they like to do, how they have fun." Simply stated, he just gets "tired of being with the same people." That thought is a point of both disagreement and agreement with students a few miles south at Harper High School. Michael, a sophomore at Harper, says that his adjustment to high school was quite easy. Harper is "basically the same": since his grammar school serves as a feeder institution for Harper, Michael made the transition from eighth to ninth grade with the same people.

Despite the easy transition, Michael had fervently hoped to go to a different school because he did not think Harper was "gonna be challenging enough."[21] After his first year, Michael was invited to join the Construction Technology Academy within Harper because he reportedly was "too smart for the regular classes," and that has made him happier to be at Harper, since this is a more challenging track. In contrast to Shay and Max, who crave a broader student body at Tilden, Michael says that he would not choose to attend a school with more Whites or Hispanics. This feeling carries over into his preference for his neighborhood's racial composition. Michael states that he does not go outside often, so "it don't really matter what neighborhood I'm gonna be in, as long as I'm safe. I like my neighborhood just fine because it's quiet. It ain't been no shooting or nothing over there."

His schoolmate Rina also considers her safety when I ask whether she would go to a different school if given the opportunity. She wants to be a lawyer and would transfer in a heartbeat to a school with a program to prepare her for that career. But Rina does not want to travel to another school because she would not feel safe. She explains:

Harper is right around my house, and I don't have a problem because I know people here. Most of my friends I grew up with are here, and I don't want to start over at another school, even though it would be fun. I wanna get to know other people. I like to make friends. It don't matter what race you are. And I'm not really hard to get along with, because I love to talk.

Rina's statement may give pause to readers who care about children's aspirations and know something about what helps them achieve their dreams.

Rina, a petite tenth grader with an open personality and an easy smile, sees herself as trapped in both a school that is not that great and a neighborhood that is limiting because she is too afraid to cross borders. She does not want to push at the geographical boundaries of exclusion by leaving Harper, even if crossing those boundaries would take her out of a low-resource school and a disadvantaged neighborhood and enable her to see and experience different things. Rina and some of her peers have a palpable fear of the unknown that has a simultaneously protective and detrimental effect. Rina is quite clear, however, about the consequences of staying at Harper.

She believes that there is "nothing but problems" in an all-Black school, with "people going against each other for no reason." Rina especially dislikes the gangs. Her schoolmate Chris shares her concerns. He complains about the fights that occur "mostly every day" at Harper. He says that friends would describe him as "kinda smart, and one who don't get down with all that bad stuff like smoking and drinking or talking back to grownups," even though he hangs out with "some bad and some good" kids. Chris estimates that most people at the school are in a gang, and he worries that if someone who is in a gang tries to fight him, he'll "get jumped on by that person and all his boys." Chris especially worries that when he gets off the bus in the mornings at Sixty-Ninth and Wood something will happen to him during his four-block walk to school; he worries even more about the walk back to the bus after school, since "that's when all the drama starts!" Instead of the two or three police cars he sees outside after school, he would prefer to see "ten to fifteen cars" surrounding the perimeter of the school.

Chris's descriptions of his experiences in his immediate neighborhood make it all too clear that he cannot stop worrying about his safety, even on his own block. He describes his neighborhood as clean but says, "The people around there are just bad. Once you walk outside, you'll probably see a group of boys come up to you, and try to jump [fight] you or take something out of your pockets. It happens right on my block, but they don't live on the same block." He wants to move to what he believes would be a nicer environment, a place where "you don't hear a lot of gunshots, it don't be a lot of gangs, and people don't get jumped on and robbed." Chris would also rather go to a school "that got Black and White, or even Mexican, as long as it's not all-Black."

* * *

What emerges from my detailed interviews in all four schools is the central role of race and place in shaping the students' worldviews. While some of them find their homogeneous world constraining, others find it reassuring. But whether or not these students realize it, the narrowness, or breadth, of their frames of reference will have profound consequences for both their experiences and their interpretations of those experiences.

Place and the Perception of Injustice

In parsing the physical worlds in which these students live, and the boundaries they must cross, we gain great—and sometimes depressing—insight into the lived reality of the next generation of America. Again, this long-standing and far-reaching "racial-spatial divide" anchors their divergent social worlds, especially in the realm of education.[22] Even those students who attend relatively integrated schools return home to neighborhoods profoundly divided by race. Together, these two spaces—home and school—play critical roles in shaping adolescents' sense of self, and both of these institutions are deeply rooted in place. Their perceptions of the world are indelibly shaped by their place in that world. It is clear, both from Chicago's school desegregation travails and the many thoughts expressed by the teenagers quoted in these pages, that the racial composition of a school is of vital importance to the resources teenagers can access, their future opportunities, and their perceptions of inequality.[23] But what, then, is the best racial balance in schools for our children to provide both access to resources and exposure to diverse arrays of people and perspectives?

Walter Payton Preparatory Academy is the most selective and the most diverse school in my sample. Each of the students I interviewed at the school offer some variation on the following description of the school by Alex, an African American ninth-grade male who travels nearly six miles from the his Black middle-class neighborhood on the South Side to attend Payton: "Even though it's diverse, it's divided."[24]

Students may "mix in with everybody," but as John, a White ninth grader tells me, "There are a lot of cliques, and to be honest, they're almost completely race-based. It's bad, but it's sort of inevitable, I think. People feel most comfortable with people in their own race." Students at Payton who identify as biracial or multiracial are challenged when deciding which clique to join because clique membership is not as complex as their racial identities. Carmen, another ninth grader, who resents being the "authority on all things Hispanic-themed" at Payton, explains why she would like to go to a school that has more racial diversity (specifically, she wants 25 percent of each race: Hispanic, White, Black, and Asian). Carmen believes, "If you get like a quarter of each [race], then you get to pick out who you want to hang out with. 'Cuz you have a lot of Hispanics and the Hispanics know what you're talking about. And then the Black people that hang out with the Hispanic people know what you're talking about, too. And then, so you kinda assimilate." For Carmen, erasure of one's non-White culture is not assimilation. She sees it as being able to have your [non-dominant] culture *not* define you as a person.

In a city as segregated as Chicago, attending a school with a sizable population of White youth might arguably lend youth of color one of their only opportunities to compare their personal experiences with those of their White peers. Unfortunately, instead of providing opportunities, spending time with people of different races more often seems to leave youth of color perceiving themselves as "deprived" or "subordinated" relative to White youth. Youth of color attending segregated schools experience structural discrimination on a daily basis, but they lack the opportunity to make between-race comparisons on a daily basis. Students who cross boundaries, in other words, are more likely to see discrimination than those who do not make these journeys.

One of the especially interesting students in my study is TB, an African American ninth grader from Harper High on the South Side of Chicago. He is satisfied with his way of life. Asked whether he would move to a different neighborhood if he had the choice, he responds: "I'll probably stay in the neighborhood where I am." He finds it just as unlikely that he would choose to go to a different school because his friends are at Harper and he "prefers to stay around my own kind." In response to the survey questions that deal with social injustice, he disagrees with statements suggesting that members of his race face racial discrimination in hiring and residential choice.

In short, he sees the playing field as level. TB explains, "You can find a nice house where you want to live, and most African Americans are successful in what they do." TB attends a racially segregated school virtually devoid of resources. He lives just north of Harper in Englewood—a neighborhood that is as poor and racially segregated as his school. Although he tells me that he sees "lawyers, assistants, and accountants" doing well in his neighborhood, empirical data from his neighborhood belie his perception: According to census estimates, only 53 percent of the population age sixteen and older are in the labor force, and only 35 percent of those individuals are actually employed, predominantly in sales and service occupations.[25] Even so, TB is confident in his vision of the world. TB and his neighbors live in an "extremely isolated" environment, as the sociologist Alford Young would characterize it.[26] He is at an extensive disadvantage just by virtue of where he lives, one of the dilemmas of place that has been documented in several important sociological works.[27] Individuals in segregated communities are sequestered from job opportunities and housing choices, to name just two of life's necessities. But alongside this grave disadvantage, youth like TB are also sequestered from continuous, unequivocal evidence that they are likely to receive inferior treatment simply because of their race. In other words, because TB lives in a world of so little diversity, it may be easy for him to think that most Black people are doing well; he does not see enough concrete evidence of Black mobility to realize how immobile his world really is.

And though some may find this distressing, I would argue that there is a protective element to this lack of confirmed disadvantage. In the same way that "ignorance can be bliss," less knowledge about structural inequality may be more enabling than paralyzing in the quest for social and economic mobility. Consider, in contrast, the "privilege and peril" that Black middle-class Chicagoans encounter on a daily basis. As the sociologist Mary Pattillo and others have documented, members of the Black middle class are able to gain education and skills, but they still usually operate in the same social circles and spaces as their less advantaged racial counterparts. The families Pattillo studied—and the children in particular—have to reconcile their race and class positions with their social and physical geographies.[28] Nor is this phenomenon limited to those who have actually attained middle-class status: It is especially true for young people[29] who attend more integrated, better-resourced schools but whose family incomes and social status would not be classified as middle class. For these young people, attending better schools may put them on a more upwardly mobile life trajectory compared with their peers left behind in racially segregated, disadvantaged educational institutions, but there is still, to use Pattillo's term, "peril" along the way. Straddling the class fence actually increases adolescents' perceptions of injustice and their sense of relative deprivation.[30]

Consider the following account from Alex, the African American ninth grader at Payton Prep. His response exemplifies the dubious distinction of being exposed to multiple worlds. Alex is privileged because he is at a good school where he has a diverse set of friends. He is also disadvantaged because he not only encounters differential treatment in public spaces but also can confirm it. When our interview turns to the topic of discrimination, Alex reveals a wide variety of thoughts on how discrimination operates in various facets of life. In discussing teacher interactions, he strongly disagrees with the survey statement "Discrimination makes it harder for people from my racial group to get good grades in school." Alex elaborates: "Well, I can't really speak for every school, but for this school, it's all pretty much strictly by the book. And like, when it comes to, like, borderline grades, the teacher pretty much gives you a grade on how much effort you put into it. 'Cuz for the most part, I don't know any teachers who are really racist in any way at this school."

Alex also has strong impressions about criminal injustice, especially as it concerns police unfairly stopping members of his race. He has never been stopped by the police, but he reports, "It's happened to my dad several times while I was with him, especially in, like, certain suburbs." Again, place matters. When I ask Alex about whether racial discrimination is a problem for him or other African Americans, he states, "You just can't blame everything for being Black, but sometimes it is because you are Black." He is quite aware that race and racial discrimination are not the only reasons why people have differential opportunities and divergent outcomes. I therefore ask him: How does he know when racial discrimination is to blame? Alex responds by describing vicarious experiences of discrimination. He also gives the following personal account of discriminatory treatment in the Water Tower Place, a mall located in downtown's Magnificent Mile:

ALEX: When I went to the Water Tower this year, I was with my group of friends. I normally hang out with a diverse group. So I was with Black, White, Asian people, and a Mexican. And one of my friends, he went inside a store and he picked up something, [but] he didn't want it. He walked out. Big Black guy, really big, had a big shirt on. He walked out, and all of a sudden the lady, she like, stops him and she's like, "Oh, you [looking at Alex's Black friend] stole something." So then, like, the security guards at the Water Tower come, and then they pretty much kick all of us out, like, all the Black people out.

AUTHOR: So not your whole group?

ALEX: No, not the whole group. They actually said, "You, you, you, and you [pointing to all of the Blacks in the group], get out." 'Cuz I don't know, maybe they didn't know we were together, but I doubt it.

Although Alex lives in an all-Black South Side neighborhood, he has made friends with a racially diverse group of friends during his first year of high school. Although he tells me that he has heard about discrimination mainly from others' experiences, he also has personally encountered discrimination, as this account makes clear. Alex's peril comes from seeing discrimination operate directly in front of him instead of simply knowing that it exists.[31] I am especially curious to hear from Alex how class intersected with race in the resolution of his experience at the mall. How did his friend react to the store clerk's accusation and the security officers' racism?

AUTHOR: What did your friend say? The one who was specifically targeted?

ALEX: He was quiet about it, and then he was, like, "Oh." At first he didn't know what was gonna happen, so he called, like, his mom and then he called his mom's lawyer. I don't know . . . he called, like, a lot of people.

AUTHOR: Does he go to Payton Prep, too?

ALEX: Yeah, he's a freshman.

AUTHOR: So he was able to call people and let them know what happened?

ALEX: Yeah, he had a cell phone. I don't carry a cell phone, but he had one.

AUTHOR: And what about your friends of other races who were there? How did they process that experience?

ALEX: I don't know . . .

AUTHOR: Did you ask them . . . ?

ALEX: I didn't really ask them about it.

AUTHOR: Did they stay in the mall?

ALEX: Yeah, they stayed, got something to eat, and then left later.

I was also interested in how the students who were not ejected read the episode, but Alex did not discuss it further with them at the time. He only knows that they used their own (racial) privilege to stay in the mall, have a meal, and then leave the premises on their own volition. Alex is only a ninth grader, so this experience may be the first of many in which he is treated differently because of his racial identity—and in which he recognizes that differential treatment.

Even when some youth have police encounters that many would construe as racially discriminatory, they may still insist that the police are fair. A ninth grader at Harper High, TB recounts an incident in which he and his Black male cousins were asked to leave Naperville (a White, upper-middle-class, suburban neighborhood), while a group of White youth was allowed to hang out on the same street:

TB: Like, me and my cousin [were] in the suburbs one time. . . . We used to hang by the pool, and they called the police on us. But when the White kids came, they had the skateboards and stuff talking. They didn't call the police on them.

AUTHOR: So why do you think they treated you differently from the White kids if it wasn't about race?

TB: They probably thought we was gang-related or something like that.

AUTHOR: Do you think if you were out there with skateboards that it would have been different?

TB: Yeah.

AUTHOR: They would have been okay with you being out there?
TB: Yeah.

TB believes that having a skateboard would have diminished any negative racial stigma and lessened his being marked as possibly "gang
related." He saw the skateboard as an objective indicator of innocence,
or perhaps even legitimacy, that would have allowed him to remain in
that space and not be negatively marked by his race, gender, or youthful-
ness. Although TB seems to be able to disaggregate presumptions about
gang affiliation from other central identifying characteristics (young,
Black, male) that might define outsiders' perceptions of him, others may
not be willing or able to grant him the same courtesy. Place indubitably
shapes these young people's experiences and their perceptions of justice
or injustice.[32]

* * *

Alex and TB have some things in common, but they live very different lives. They are both young, Black males who reside on Chicago's
South Side; however, Alex travels outside of that world for school and
sees things that TB might never see and might interpret very differently
if he did. Their different locations on the racial-spatial divide tell us a
great deal about how those factors collide to shape our attitudes and the
ways in which we all read our various experiences. The primary reason
Alex has to cross racial boundaries is to attend Payton Prep. Conversely,
the more I talk with TB, the more I realize that Harper High keeps him
cloistered in a world that he does not even realize is in stark contrast to
the worlds of those with a different hue, class, gender, or zip code.[33]

Coming of Age in an Unequal City

Adolescence is a distinct life stage during which youth, while undergoing
numerous transitions in their personal and social development, are in
flux with regard to society's expectations for them and their adherence to
social norms. One of the major components of this developmental phase
is the greater responsibility that young people are expected to assume for
their behavior, which may subject them to more serious consequences
if they deviate from the norms. The status shift from adolescent to adult

may be prompted by age, experiences, role transitions, or some combination of these factors. A transitional life event such as marriage or parenthood can catapult an adolescent into adulthood, as can being arrested or searched by police.

Adolescence can be seen as a "protected role," while adulthood brings certain vulnerabilities, both legal and social. Premature exits from adolescence and into adulthood have legal effects and life-course implications. One of the reasons why adolescent experiences with the police are important is that negative experiences can derail normative life trajectories (such as moving from high school to college) and disrupt the timing of life transitions (such as school graduation). Official police intervention in the lives of adolescents—particularly police contact that is unwarranted or discriminatory, as may be the case when youth are searched but released—can create an early exit from adolescence.

The life-stage principle holds that individual and social events can differentially affect life patterns, depending on the age at which events occur. "Cumulative criminal continuity" refers to a dynamic process in which delinquent behavior at one point in time has consequences that increase the likelihood of continued delinquent behavior at later points in time. Officially recorded criminal continuity leads eventually to "cumulative disadvantage"—a piling up of negative experiences and failures that make it difficult for a person to succeed.[34] Although this study does not have a longitudinal design, sociologists must consider the possibility that students are at an elevated risk of negative life trajectories as a result of their increased contact with police in their schools and neighborhoods. It is critical that we understand how adolescents' contacts with key authoritative figures, like police officers in their neighborhoods and teachers in their classrooms, can alter the course of their life trajectories. Police have a striking presence and impact on youths' formative experiences and their resultant attitudes about themselves and the world in which they live.

* * *

The formation and transformation of public schools in a city like Chicago powerfully shapes the social and cultural lives of students— constructing their institutional selves in two ways: (1) High school may be the primary reason why they leave their neighborhoods or never leave their neighborhoods, and (2) youth will experience the long reach of the law via the incursion and embeddedness of police officers in schools (which serve as their primary institutional setting at this life stage). Owing to the overwhelming predominance of Black and Brown bodies in these institutional settings, since schools are more segregated now than they were during the Jim Crow era (e.g., Chicago public schools are approximately 10 percent White), it is more likely that the *criminal gaze* is turned inward—onto the students—rather than turned outward onto a purportedly dangerous public.

The Face of Racial Antagonism

Based on the race-based disparities in the frequency and severity of police contact, I argue that this variable is an exemplar of racial antagonism. The presence of police officers, who are trained to surveil and control, in a space that is supposed to be the site of education and nurturing is antagonistic on its face. Schools, such as the public high schools in Chicago, that are mandated to have at least two police officers patrol and punish in its environs, make an indelible mark on the institutional selves of adolescents. This allows the police wide latitude in shaping the worldviews of youth since they are the most direct link between law enforcement and the public (via schools as institutional brokers). These contacts with the police in schools are happening during a formative period in which people's lifelong political attitudes are planted and fomented. Not only are these contacts with police in the institutional setting of a school shaping young people's perceptions, they are also shaping their life trajectories. For some youth, particularly those who are the bottom of the racial/social strata, the contacts with police in school are simply the beginning of what are likely to be repeated contacts with the state and its representatives at deeper and deeper levels of severity.

Interestingly, one of the main findings of the Chicago research is that Black and Hispanic youth who attend more diverse high schools (with more than 15 percent White students—this is in a public school universe that is only 10 percent White and has the majority of White students clustered in its most selective (magnet) public schools) have a significantly higher perception of social and criminal injustice in contrast to their peers who attend more racially segregated schools.[35] Therefore, Joaquin's Black and Hispanic classmates at Lincoln Park would be more likely to negatively assess their life chances because they would have a wider racial comparative frame for their personal-social assessment. These young people who daily cross the racial-spatial divide for the purpose of achieving an education superior to that which is available closer to them in their racially segregated neighborhood undoubtedly have greater chances of success and social mobility by attending a better school. But the exposure to difference would also make them more attuned to noticing stratification at earlier ages than their counterparts who remain in more homogeneous environments. This does not mean that they are more likely to experience the physical elements of racial antagonism, such as police searches and arrests, or even violence from their peers of a different race. Instead, they have to grapple with the symbolic violence of being seen as out of place in these different ecological contexts where the skin color, class status, and even the experiences of their so-called peers are different.

This also means that a Black or Hispanic youth who may be subject to more actual unlawful policing may offer a less negative assessment than someone subject to fewer (or no) violations because the former individual has lower expectations for police and/or a more limited racially comparative frame. A foremost example of racial antagonism was for me to hear the heartbreaking statement by TB, a ninth grader I interviewed who attends the "neighborhood" school in his racially homogeneous South Side Chicago community. He had been searched multiple times but never arrested in the past year. I asked him how the searches made him feel, and he answered me with a more poignant question, "Doesn't it happen to everyone?" What will happen when TB finds the answer to his question is, "No, it does not happen to everyone"?

Racial Reconciliation: Realistic, Idealistic, or Fatalistic?

In the absence of truth, racial reconciliation is a fiction. In the absence of justice, racial reconciliation is nothing more than an ideal. How might the aims of racial reconciliation and justice become a reality? First, we must put truth at the center, and as a researcher, I push for the collection and analysis of data on the range of perceptions, experiences, and outcomes within and across institutional settings in order to uncover these "institutional truths." In this vein, we can empirically capture the ways in which racial antagonism has resulted in inequality at the individual, group, and institutional levels. This goes beyond racial misunderstandings but grapples honestly and deeply with the manifest structural imprint of racial antagonism in the realms of health, residence, education, employment, and wealth, most prominently.

Second, we must look at the long reach of the state in furthering stratification through its many institutional arms. In light of the condition just stated, the public domain is the most fertile domain for nurturing the aim of racial justice. This means that we can look to the individuals who are nested within society's most formative institutions, who operate as racial brokers in their teachings and their interactions, and who are therefore most likely to positively influence the achievement of racial justice. Akin to the racial middlemen who Mary Pattillo names in her book, *Black on the Block*—who she says "put people together, they negotiate subsidies and concessions, they run interference, they relay information, and they mediate disputes"—there are specific institutional brokers who do the same.[36] There is a middle that these individuals occupy that could do much to do the work of racial reconciliation.

And third, in the institutional realm of the home, parents are the primary educators of their children on racial privilege, racial discrimination, and the principles that might lead to racial reconciliation. It is they who will prepare their children to confront injustice when they see it and to check their privilege when it is necessary. Teachers play the next important role in shaping individual ideas of racial justice owing to their imprint on the civic mind of the young people they teach. Police are next in their ability to uphold the principles of justice (without regard to race) and properly exercise their authority toward the ends of social control. In the absence of parents (and great teachers) and via the intervention of the police, judges are the final frontier in their ability to exercise parental authority via the state.

If parents, teachers, police officers, and judges use their positions to attenuate difference and facilitate connections across racial groups, this would vastly reorganize the social conditions that currently leave us more divided. Parents, who sensitize their children to perceiving injustice early on, will prepare them to recognize, confront, and perhaps even change the unequal structures in their communities and their schools. Teachers would then reinforce these teachings from home by acknowledging structural inequality in their curricula and in their interactions with their students to then give young people a language and toolkit with which they might call out and agitate against inequality. For police, they would never take any of their interactions with the public at face value. Instead, they would use their primary mission to serve and protect as the guide for their actions and engagements with the public. Finally, judges have a unique role as institutional middle(wo)men to put people into systems that could restore them, instead of simply furthering the punishment their charges will endure. I see this in my current study of juvenile delinquency courts when young people only get services like counseling and drug treatment because they have formal cases before the court. Judges have great potential to use their positions to confront and redress the deficits that might exist in other institutional realms (such as the home or the school) and work toward connecting young people to resources that will positively affect their lives.

In achieving the goal of racial reconciliation, I still wonder whether the race of the institutional brokers matters in determining their effectiveness/impact. The Black and Hispanic Chicago youth who encountered the police in my study were more likely to give the benefit of the doubt to police officers who shared their race. However, they also believed that race could be a subordinate identity to the officers' occupational identity, which means that a Black officer could meet their low expectations and just be another police officer criminalizing them if they perceived the interaction was tinged with unfairness. This also means that a White officer could potentially exceed their low expectations if the young people felt they were seen and treated as fully human no matter their appearance and/or their "place." Interestingly, there were a couple young people that I interviewed who discussed knowing police officers across institutional realms (e.g., the officer worked the beat in their housing project and in their nearby grammar school), and they had more positive impressions of the officers and were likely to support their work because of those connections across place (but still mostly within race).

These same logics could extend to how we view the impact of race on the enactment of roles and responsibilities accorded to parents, teachers, and judges. Is a White mother able to convey to her adopted Black son an understanding of how the world may view him that would allow him to be sensitized to, but still/also fight against, injustice? Is it necessary for Black/Brown (male) teachers to be the face of education/democracy/opportunity in the public classrooms that are filled with Black and Brown children in order for them to perform their best? Finally, can judges, no matter their race, mete out justice that is truly just? Or do their racial identities need to match that of the individuals who come before them in court? These are all questions that we must answer if we want to achieve racial justice in an unequal society. Racial reconciliation can only be achieved if we upend the social organization of our most formative social institutions and place racial justice at the center.

NOTES

1 A portion of the arguments and evidence contained here are also included in my book, *Unequal City: Race, Schools, and Perceptions of Injustice* (New York: Russell Sage, 2015). Please see *Unequal City* for a fuller discussion of the topic and my findings.

2 Geoff K. Ward, *The Black Child-Savers: Racial Democracy and Juvenile Justice* (Chicago: University of Chicago Press, 2012), 25.

3 Shedd, *Unequal City.*

4 Ibid., 6.

5 Ibid., 8.

6 Ruth D. Peterson and Lauren J. Krivo, *Divergent Social Worlds: Neighborhood Crime and the Racial-Spatial Divide* (New York: Russell Sage, 2010), 132.

7 Ibid.

8 Ward, *The Black Child-Savers*, 32.

9 Douglass Massey and Nancy Denton, *American Apartheid: Segregation and the Making of the Underclass* (Cambridge, MA: Harvard University Press, 1993), 8.

10 Ibid.; and Shedd, *Unequal City.*

11 Shedd, *Unequal City*, 48–49.

12 Ibid., 48.

13 Ibid., 8.

14 Ward, *The Black Child-Savers*, 15.

15 Shedd, *Unequal City*, 8.

16 Ibid.

17 Ibid., 9.

18 David Sibley, as cited in ibid., 9.

19 Ibid., 10; see also ibid., chap. 1, notes 29–30.

20 Ibid., chap. 3, note 9.

21 Ibid., chap. 3, note 10.

22 Ibid., chap. 3, note 12.

23 Ibid., chap. 3, note 13.

24 Ibid., 51–52.

25 Ibid., chap. 3, note 20.

26 Alford A. Young, Jr., *The Minds of Marginalized Black Men: Making Sense of Mobility, Opportunity, and Future Live Chances* (Princeton, NJ: Princeton University Press, 2004).

27 Shedd, *Unequal City*, chap. 3, note 21.

28 Mary Pattillo, *Black Picket Fences: Privilege and Peril among the Black Middle Class*, 2nd ed. (Chicago: University of Chicago Press, 2013); and Shedd, *Unequal City*, chap. 3, note 22.

29 Shedd, *Unequal City*, chap. 3, note 23.

30 Ibid., chap. 3, note 24.

31 Ibid., chap. 3, note 25.

32 For more on being "out of place," see ibid., 144–145.

33 Ibid., 66.

34 Ibid., chap. 5, notes 9–11.

35 Ibid.

36 Mary Pattillo, *Black on the Block: The Politics of Race and Class in the City* (Chicago: University of Chicago Press, 2007), 121.

4

Weaponized Empathy

Emotion and the Limits of Racial Reconciliation in Policing

NAOMI MURAKAWA

Police scanners, Tasers, increased data collecting and sharing, SWAT teams, gang injunctions, stop-and-frisk, "quality of life" ticketing—all of these policing reforms have been taken up to improve the quality of policing in the United States. The dominant school of thought on police reform has suggested that reforms like these make for safer communities and that improving policing will allow us to escape its violence. This orientation toward police reform imagines that documentation, training or oversight might protect us from the harassment, intimidation, beatings, occupation and death that the state employs to maintain social control under the guise of safety. What is missing from this orientation, however, is recognition of the actual function of policing in US society: armed protection of state interests. If one sees policing for what it is—a set of practices sanctioned by the state to enforce law and maintain social control and cultural hegemony through the use of force—one may more easily recognize that perhaps the goal should not be to improve how policing functions but to reduce its role in our lives.
—Rachel Herzing[1]

"Because with an open heart, we can learn to stand in each other's shoes and look at the world through each other's eyes." Thus began President Barack Obama's July 2016 call for perspective sharing between police officers and black people, groups who must "embark on the hard but necessary work of negotiation" and "the pursuit of reconciliation."

Interrupted by bursts of applause, President Obama offered a sanguine hypothetical of an officer who "sees his own son in that teenager with a hoodie who's kind of goofing off but not dangerous." And, because his vision of bridging "the divides of race in America" is a form of emotional labor required equally by all—unmodulated by age, race, professional authority, institutional power, or easy access to legitimate use of batons, Tasers, and guns—President Obama's hypothetical also requires the policed "teenager with a hoodie" to see from the officer's perspective, ideally "see[ing] in the police officer the same words and values and authority of his parents." The fact of racialized policing is leveled down to flat terms of interpersonal misunderstanding. In this logic, there are different but equally valid feelings between symmetrically empowered groups, "an African-American community that *feels unfairly targeted* by police" and "police departments that *feel unfairly maligned* for doing their jobs." In this world of feelings, the decisive question is whether these groups, in President Obama's words, "can ever understand each other's experience."[2]

With this call for reciprocal understanding, President Obama achieved something at once ordinary and obscene: He translated the political economy of policing into an emotional economy, reducing racialized state violence from institutional pattern to personal perspective. Since Black Lives Matter activists successfully reignited national debates over police terrorism in August 2014, the Obama administration has responded as if racialized policing and punishment are problems of mistrust, misunderstanding, and historically accrued bad feelings between police and communities of color.[3]

This essay explores why I have such a bad feeling about all this talk of bad racial feelings. Many activists, especially young and LGBTQ people of color in organizations such as Hands Up United, We Charge Genocide, Million Hoodies March, and the Sylvia Rivera Law Project, are calling for massive redistribution of resources away from the carceral apparatus—articulated, for example, in the hashtag calls of Black Youth Project 100 to #StopTheCops and #FundBlackFutures.[4] My concern is that these well-reasoned demands for carceral divestment are being translated into carceral investments, and I suspect that the falsely egalitarian, deceptively responsive vernacular of feelings enables this mistranslation. By framing racialized state violence as an affective problem, a painful deficit of trust and empathy, the arc of political discourse swings optimistically toward the possibility of reconciliation through more, more, more: more "community policing," more recruitment of police officers of color, more "friendly" enmeshment of police in communities of color, and more funding for police training to reduce implicit bias and enhance communication skills. In short, humane carceral development promises to bridge racial divides.

Within this vernacular of humane policing, I am centrally concerned with the dangers of empathy. Empathy—the ability to see through another's eyes—is a calling card of social grace and social status, a marker of sophistication and smarts ("emotional intelligence"), of being cultured and cultivated ("emotional literacy"). Empathy is almost universally considered a positive trait, but, as the anthropologists Nils Bubandt and Rane Willerslev point out, the "dark side of empathy" appears when Casanovas, con artists, or military strategists see through another's eyes for the purpose of seducing, misleading, or ambushing.[5] In line with their analysis, I examine policing's dark side of empathy, where increasingly officers train in "tactical empathy" and police leadership advocates reciprocal empathy between police and black communities. Without reducing the scale, scope, and racial concentration of policing, empathy operates as a form of political distraction that masquerades as emotional validation. In effect, tactical empathy promotes "racial reconciliation" in one terrible sense: It attempts to "reconcile" racially marginalized populations to their reality of being over-policed, as if resistance can be subdued by police who are courteous to those they stop, frisk, handcuff, arrest, injure, and kill.

* * *

Given that controversies over racialized policing pivot on mistrust, misunderstanding, and miscommunication, it is perhaps not surprising that many trainings aim to improve police communication skills and their "tactical empathy" for those they police. This section focuses on tactical empathy as it is taught in one training framework called "Verbal Judo," created by George Thompson, who earned a Ph.D. in English from the University of Connecticut in 1972 and held black belts in Judo and Taekwondo. Thompson, who told people to call him "Doc Rhino," combined his expertise in rhetoric and martial arts to produce the Verbal

Judo model of "tactical communication," which, in Thompson's words, uses "the gentle art of redirecting my opponent's energy to achieve my own goal." Thompson elaborated the Verbal Judo framework in four books published between 1983 and 2007. The first three books share the same pre-colon title, *Verbal Judo*, and the fourth book is titled *The Verbal Judo Way of Leadership*.[6] In 1983, George Thompson founded the Verbal Judo Institute.

Verbal Judo is regularly taught in police academies and incorporated into in-service training, and its popularity, or at least public announcement of its use, seems to be increasing. Indeed, a July 2016 *Guardian* subhead announced that Verbal Judo is "making a comeback in the face of high-profile police shootings."[7] It is difficult to ascertain the popularity of Verbal Judo for a number of reasons. Police academy curricula are decentralized, and there are only irregular and undetailed surveys of them. One 1994 peer-reviewed journal article asserts that "verbal judo is the most widely used police training program in interpersonal communication" and that "verbal judo is now taught in most police academies across the USA."[8] (Given the lack of footnotes or citations in this peer-reviewed article, however, it is unclear to me how the author came to this conclusion.) According to the Verbal Judo Institute, more than one million police officers have been trained in the techniques of Verbal Judo. (I have no way to confirm this number.) A search of "Verbal Judo" mentions in local newspapers in 2014 and 2015 reveals that no less than twenty-seven cities are currently, or on the precipice of, training city police in Verbal Judo, including Dallas, Texas; Santa Fe, New Mexico; Denver, Colorado; Las Vegas, Nevada; Modesto, California; Carson City, Nevada; Detroit, Michigan; Wichita, Kansas; Philadelphia, Pennsylvania; and Washington, DC.

It is also difficult to pinpoint the popularity of Verbal Judo given that public officials announce its use as if it were new. For example, New York City's police academy introduced Verbal Judo to its in-service training program in 1995, and it was subsequently adopted for use in training new recruits. In February 2014, despite the fact that Verbal Judo had been a two-decade staple for the New York Police Department (NYPD), Mayor Bill de Blasio announced that all New York City police officers would be trained in the "Seven Steps to Positive Community Interactions," which he referred to as "Verbal Judo."[9] (These seven steps are that the officer [1] "politely introduces himself [*sic*] and provides name and rank"; [2] listens actively; [3] should "keep an open mind"; [4] should "be patient"; [5] should know the resources of the NYPD and other agencies that are available "to help people with their problems"; [6] should "make every effort to address the needs of the people that have asked for help"; and [7] should end every encounter on "a positive note.")[10] Police Commissioner William Bratton also claimed credit for introducing and reintroducing Verbal Judo to the NYPD. "Last time I was here in '94, we brought it to the department, a concept that was newly emerging at the time called verbal judo," he said, which entailed "teaching officers how to communicate in a way that they didn't alienate the people that they were dealing with because of their language, because of their attitude."[11] Similarly, the Baltimore Police Department announced "new" de-escalation and use-of-force policies in the wake of heightened public scrutiny over the murder of Freddie Gray, whom the Baltimore police arrested, put in the back of a police van, and subjected to a "rough ride" that killed him. Baltimore's "new" 2016 emphasis on de-escalation through verbal acumen is indistinguishable from the 2000 in-service training in Verbal Judo, which was purportedly designed to teach communication tactics as alternatives to violent force.[12]

Perhaps another reason for the popularity of Verbal Judo is that empathy trainings deflect lawsuits, or at least police legal officers anticipate as much. A 2015 article in *Police Chief*, the monthly magazine of the International Association of Chiefs of Police (IACP), announced the utility of empathy in a bold section heading: "Empathy Training as an Affirmative Defense." In the lineage of "failure-to-train" case law, courts have deemed inadequate training a matter of conscious choice; thus, a plaintiff who shows "failure-to-train" might clear that high legal bar of proving "deliberate indifference."[13] The article elaborated: "The occupational benefits of training blocks that address the nuances of empathy on the job, in relation to respect and integrity, have proven to be a valuable insurance measure as part of proffered affirmative defenses to allegations of unconstitutional policing, providing that 'benefit of the doubt.'"[14]

The Verbal Judo training framework interests me in part because of its rising popularity, but more fundamentally I am interested in the way that Verbal Judo seems to mimic the sensibilities of sweeping calls for racial reconciliation in policing. The goal of Verbal Judo is to generate voluntary compliance, achieved by deploying what Thompson calls, without a shred of irony, "tactical empathy."[15] Giving the etiology of empathy, Thompson writes: "'Em' is Latin for 'to see through,' and 'pathy' is Greek for 'eye of other.'" From this definition, Thompson clarifies, "Empathy means *to understand*, it does not mean to agree or to sympathize with."[16] Instead of reacting "naturally" with sympathy or aggression, the student of Verbal Judo learns to respond "tactically," engaging in measured and deliberate communication informed by understanding of the other.[17]

Seeing, whether through surveillance cameras or through another's eyes, is a technology of control. Thompson writes, "The ability to see as others see is the source of your power."[18] Witness a police officer using "tactical empathy" to "generate voluntary compliance" in this example from *Verbal Judo: The Gentle Art of Persuasion*:

> I was on the street for a ride-along in California one night when Ron, the police officer I was with, arrested a subject on a minor felony warrant. The perpetrator was about sixteen years old. At about 3:00 a.m., the boy's mother was standing on her porch, shouting obscenities. The officer, one of the most skillful I've ever seen, put the kid in the car, turned to me in the front seat, and said, "I'll be with you in a moment, George."
>
> Frankly, I wished he'd jumped into the patrol car and we were gone because the woman's yelling had attracted more than a dozen angry neighbors. Their sleep had been interrupted by these cops, who had, in their minds, hassled some innocent kid they'd seen grow up on that street. They came out sniffing the air like Doberman pinschers. It was as if they were asking themselves, "Is there something here for me? Anything I need to stick my nose into? What's going on here?"
>
> I was tense because those people were surrounding the car. They weren't saying anything, and it was an uneasy, potentially explosive situation. Suddenly, Ron walked up to the woman, took off his hat, put it under his arm as if he had all night, reached into his pocket for a business card, and said, "Ma'am, listen to me. My name is Officer Ron——, and I'm with the——Police Department. I'm arresting your boy because I have to. I have a warrant. If I don't arrest him, they arrest me. But it's a minor warrant, ma'am.
>
> "I don't blame you for being upset, because I have a son about your boy's age, and I'd be upset too. But he'll be out in the morning. Listen,

don't stand out here tonight. Get some rest. Come on down to the police department in the morning, bring your friends, bring a lawyer if you want. Your son will have been processed by then and you'll be able to talk to him.

"And look, if anyone gives you any trouble down there, you call my number, and I'll take care of it. You don't deserve any more problems. You have a good night now."

He turned and walked away, putting his hat back on, and we drove off while the woman was thanking him! Her son was cuffed in the back of that car, and she was grateful![19]

Here it is worth stating the obvious: Tactical empathy reduces resistance to police power without reducing police power. With Verbal Judo, police adjust the manners and mannerisms by which they exercise their powers without adjusting the scale, scope, or racial concentration of policing. Indeed, the above scenario demonstrates that certain speech acts and gestures can neutralize charged, potentially "explosive" crowds. Further still, tactical empathy can pave the road for further "cooperation" between communities and police. Officer Ron predicts that the mother's gratitude for her son's arrest will become eagerness for additional arrests:

That woman is apt to call me a year from now and say, "Officer Ron, you remember me? You arrested my boy last October on that minor felony warrant? Why aren't you out here cracking down on these people selling drugs right out the back door of number one-twelve every day between four and five in the morning?"

Well, I thank her, and I get on it, and usually these people are right. Their leads are good. The cards have helped me cultivate a beat.[20]

There are four features of Verbal Judo that I want to highlight. The first is that tactical empathy is teachable as a set of gestures and phrases. In the scenario above, the officer's gentlemanly hat removal and professional business card distribution are key gestures, and, according to the teachings of Verbal Judo, there are "hundreds of techniques" to "project understanding."[21] Verbal Judo gives an inventory of phrases "never to say to anyone" and "how to respond if some idiot says them to you." There are eleven verboten phrases: "Come here!"; "You wouldn't understand";

"Because those are the rules"; "It's none of your business"; "What do you want *me* to do about it?"; "Calm down!"; "What's your problem?"; "You never . . ." or "You always . . ."; "I'm not going to say this again"; "I'm doing this for your own good"; and "Why don't you be reasonable?"[22]

While certain phrases are to be avoided, there is one key sentence that serves as "the sword of insertion," a "wedge into the [other's] harangue." This sentence, Thompson instructs, is "the ultimate empathic sentence: 'Let me be sure I heard what you just said.'" As a way "to interrupt somebody without generating further resistance," the ultimate empathic sentence helps the officer to "magically" take "control" ("because you're talking and he is listening"). If your paraphrasing is incorrect, then "he can correct you" and "that fills your pockets with ammunition." Gathering more information about the speaker—"his emotions, his prejudices, and his assumptions"—is useful for generating voluntary compliance.[23] The "basic tools to generate voluntary compliance" are presented as the acronym LEAPS, shorthand for listen, empathize, ask, paraphrase, and summarize.[24] Of these, empathy is the cornerstone. "There may be a hundred different ways to calm people," Thompson explains, but there is "only one principle that underlies all those techniques. It consists of three words—Empathy Absorbs Tension."[25]

The observable gestures and sounds of empathy matter more than the unobservable cognitions and feelings of empathy. When explaining the L of LEAPS, Thompson clarifies that "you've got to look like you're listening." Thompson declares that people do indeed say things "not worth hearing," and some people "may not even make sense." But "the moment your eyes glaze over as if you're uninterested or don't care, conflict can erupt. So it's even more important to *look* interested than to *be* interested."[26] In other places, Verbal Judo underscores the importance of maintaining steady eye contact, not dropping one's eyes down in resignation or rolling them up in disgust; of nodding and showing open body language; of setting one's voice to the appropriate tone, pace, pitch, and modulation; and, generally, of learning "to look good on the outside—to reinforce what you're saying with a face and a demeanor that fits the situation." Simultaneously, officers have to read the gestures of all those around them.[27]

Reading this list of gestures calls to mind Laleh Khalili's account of "the uses of happiness in counterinsurgency," in which reading the affective stance of "the natives" was required "to administer conquered and colonized populations in ways that preempted the possibility of revolt."[28] The focus on eye contact also calls to mind General David Petraeus's twenty-four-point counterinsurgency guidance of August 2010, when he directed soldiers in Afghanistan to "take off your sunglasses. Situational awareness can only be gained by interacting face-to-face, not separated by ballistic glass or Oakleys." These gestural commands were nested in Petraeus's grander aspirations. "Earn the people's trust, talk to them, ask them questions, and learn about their lives. . . . Be aware of others in the room and how their presence may affect the answers you get. . . . Spend time, listen, consult and drink lots of tea."[29]

This brings me to the second observation, which is that Verbal Judo transparently calls on U.S. counterinsurgency tactics, showing its affinity for the doctrine that, in the words of Edward Lansdale, "counterinsurgency is another word for brotherly love."[30] Note that George Thompson co-authored the last two of his four books on Verbal Judo. (Thompson co-authored his third book, *Verbal Judo: The Gentle Art of Persuasion* [1993], with Jerry Jenkins, the self-described author/co-author/ghostwriter of some 186 books. In addition to his contributions to the "autobiography" of southern evangelist Billy Graham, Jenkins is best known for his series *Left Behind*, in which Christ's true believers are raptured to Heaven and Earth's remaining sinners are organized by an anti-Christ figure who runs the United Nations.) Thompson's fourth book, *The Verbal Judo Way of Leadership*, was co-authored by Gregory Walker, a combat veteran of counterinsurgency warfare in El Salvador and Iraq. Walker was awarded the Global War on Terrorism Expeditionary Medal.[31] Building on the theme of tactical empathy, Thompson and Walker outline the "core belief system" that must be inculcated into every soldier and police officer: They must understand that they "are first and foremost protectors," and they must "exhibit the belief that all people are equal on the basis of how they value their lives and the lives of their loved ones."[32]

The logic of this "core belief system," one of guardianship coupled with equal worth, is explicated through a circuitous story that begins in a working-class bar near the NYPD's training academy and ends in a "Third World country" conflict zone. Thompson explains that he "had been exploring a solid core belief system for years" but "found it in the most unexpected of places—a blue-collar bar in New York City, not far from the New York City Police Academy where I was teaching Verbal Judo to 400 officers each day." In the bar Thompson met Jack Hoban, "a former Marine captain and martial arts instructor in Ninjitsu." In Thompson's telling, the bar filled with "raucous, noisy people," "scummy people" who distracted Thompson from his conversation with the admirable captain. But Hoban, a sixth-degree black belt trained under Grandmaster Hatsumi of Japan, maintained equanimity and answered Thompson's agitation in self-congratulatory terms: "'Well, George,' he said, '*at least they were safer because of our presence!*'" Under a new section heading ("People Should Indeed Be Safer Because of Our Presence!"), Thompson explains that Jack Hoban learned his creed from his former commanding officer Robert Humphrey, author of the "marvelous book" *Values for a New Millennium*.[33] Thompson and Walker write:

> The following is an excellent example of what I learned from Jack and Professor Humphrey. Professor Humphrey and some army soldiers were out hunting wild boar in a clearly Third World country. Listen to what he says:
>
> > *As usual, on this trip, the sight of ragged, destitute villagers drew comments from one or another American. A young airman proclaimed: "Look at them; they are like a bunch of animals. What have they got to live for? They might just as well be dead." I sat in chagrined silence, but this day, in response to those familiar words, the old sergeant drawled out his answer between spits of tobacco juice. He said, "You better believe they got something to live for, Jack. If you doubt it, let me see you jump down there and try to kill one of them with your hunting knife. They'll fight you like no one ever heard of. I have fought beside them in heavy combat and I don't know either, why they seem to value their lives so much. Maybe it's them women in them pantaloons, or maybe it's them dirty faced kids; whatever it is they seem to value their lives as much as we do ours, even with all of our money. In fact, both in combat and in freezing prison camps, they hung in there after a lot of Americans were yelling quit."*
>
> The sergeant in this account stepped in and began conducting an immediate intervention. He pointed out "equality of life" to not only the

errant and ignorant airman in question, but to those others traveling with him. He did not yell, swear, or put the airman down. He used solid communication skills based on his years of training and experience as a combat proven veteran to correct and then educate his men, as well as his commanding officer.[34]

Humphrey's *Values for a New Millennium*, the only source to warrant a block quote in Thompson and Walker's book, emphasizes the value of nonverbal communication for soldiers in those "Third World" countries, where

> *you got to be able to jump down off the truck into the sheep manure, go over there into that village of mud huts, walk down those narrow streets, and pick the dirtiest, stinkin'est village peasant that you meet; and as you walk past him, you got to be able to make him know, just with your eyes, that **you** know that he is a man who hurts like we do, and hopes like we do, and wants for his kids just like we **all** do. That's how you got to be able to do it. Nothin' else ain't going to work.[35]*

From this follows my third observation: The only way to teach "humane" policing is to construct dehumanized policed subjects. Pedagogically, training police to be empathic is possible only when the patrolled subject provokes reactions of disgust and contempt. If police and soldiers automatically felt equality of worth with their patrolled subjects, then no training would be necessary. Officers are said to find themselves in "places where there seemed no redeeming value, human or otherwise. Rats, dirt, bugs, and filthy kids and nasty people invade our senses and trouble us to the point of anger and hostility, as well as disdain and arrogance." In Verbal Judo's textbook examples, police interact with filthy people ("ragged" villagers, "dirty faced kids"), beasts ("Doberman pinchers," "a bunch of animals"), or reactive chemical elements ("explosive" crowds). But of course the philosophy of Verbal Judo is to recognize that "despite all the measurable differences between people today there is one common connection we all share: '**We are equal in the most basic and profound respect: My life and the lives of my loved ones are as important to me as yours are to you.**'"[36] If policed subjects are debased, dirty people, then the "empathic" police officer truly demonstrates virtue and virtuosity. In fact, the more dehumanized the policed subject, the more magnanimous, skilled, and wise the officer.

Here I want to emphasize a fourth feature of tactical empathy: It is propped up by an Orientalist notion of the "self-mastered man." References to Sun Tzu, Bruce Lee, and unnamed samurai warriors litter the Verbal Judo series, standing as emblems of self-disciplined and stoical strength. Verbal Judo tells trainees that true strength emanates from a particular "habit of mind" known as *mushin*, "the still center" characteristic of "a samurai warfare state of mind." The still center, also described as disinterestedness, impartiality, and non-defensiveness, gives one "the ability to stay calm, read your opponent, and attempt to redirect his aggression in a more positive way." Self-mastery is pivotal here, as *mushin* means having the discipline to resist one's "natural, defensive" reaction to insults and attacks.[37] The "natural" reaction is inefficient and self-indulgent, potentially counterproductive to Verbal Judo's goal of winning voluntary compliance. To underscore the cunning skill required for Verbal Judo, Thompson and Jenkins offer this pearl of wisdom: "As the Confucian philosopher Sun-tzu put it, 'To win one hundred victories in one hundred battles is not the highest skill. To subdue the enemy without fighting is the highest skill.'"[38]

The figure of the wise Oriental warrior serves a specific purpose for police training, preempting the criticism that communication skills are "soft" skills, feminine and therefore weak. (After Mayor de Blasio announced "new" training in Verbal Judo, an article in New York City's *Gothamist* wrote simply, "NYPD officers will be trained not to be such dicks, as part of a new 'Seven Steps to Positive Community Interactions' protocol being introduced at the Police Academy." Perhaps crassly essentialist, the colloquialism reveals the counter-masculinist connotations of communication training.)[39] Similarly, in the traditions of imperial policing and colonial governmentality, reading the feelings of "the natives" created, in Khalili's explanation, "the illusion that this affective approach is softer, more feminine, more imbued with an understanding of the native. This gendering insists on specifically cultural forms of knowledge about making the colonized visible and legible for the purposes of colonial administration but doing so through humane means."[40]

Orientalism is ensconced in the genre of self-help and self-improvement books, whether in the form of Feng Shui, Buddhist mindfulness, or Japanese minimalism to tidy up the Marie Kondo way.[41] Here it is notable that the third book of the Verbal Judo series, *Verbal Judo: The Gentle Art of Persuasion*, is marketed in the category of "Self-Help/Personal Growth." The uses of Verbal Judo extend beyond law enforcement into retail customer service, corporate management, and any "contact profession" that might benefit from a dose of *mushin*. Those who advocate bringing Verbal Judo to retail customer service, for example, emphasize the "philosophical" underpinnings of "the oriental martial art of judo," which "means a *gentle way*" and "emphasizes gentleness, softness, suppleness, and even easiness."[42] Importing a kind of "gentle" Orientalism, these advocates write, "The word judo also has a more spiritual meaning of *road* or *path*, which suggests a philosophical way of life so that its practitioners seek higher levels of skill and harmony of mind in all areas of life." From this imputed philosophical stance, the advocates conclude that Verbal Judo "fits well with the worldview of the services marketing framework: respecting opponents, using indirect actions to influence others, and a more basic search of mental harmony. All of these are valuable goals in service encounters." Tactical empathy enhances customer satisfaction, as customers are "more satisfied and less likely to complain while they are treated with empathy."[43]

While I have focused specifically of Verbal Judo, it is important to underline that "tactical communication" and "tactical empathy" are central to other training modules, including Tactical Social Interaction training, the Good Stranger framework, the Unconditional Respect model, and the LEED philosophy.[44] The *New Yorker* and National Public Radio have praised the empathic, guardian-style curriculum spearheaded by Sue Rahr, executive director of the Washington State Criminal Justice Training Commission. Rahr's curriculum is based on the so-called LEED philosophy, "listening and explaining with equity and dignity," which "draws heavily from the psychology of procedural justice" and ensures that "citizens feel heard and that they understand the reasons behind police behavior." In Rahr's view, empathy is "a safety strategy that gives officers a tactical advantage" because "when you know why someone is acting in a certain way, you also know how to best react."[45] For a philosophy marked by words such as *dignity* and *equity*, it is remarkable that empathic police speech is like talking to a child: Police officers explain their decisions, they do not modify their decisions based on what they learn from listening. Moreover, behind "voluntary compliance" is the violent force of the law. One instructor at the Verbal Judo Institute, a former NYPD officer named Joel Francis, underscored that tactical communication is a supplement, not a replacement, for violence, saying: "We know that we can always use the strong arm of the law to make them comply, but we're trying to give our officers tools that will generate voluntary compliance."[46]

* * *

We should situate tactical empathy training within larger reforms for what James Kilgore has called "carceral humanism," the recasting of criminal justice administrators as caring social service providers.[47] Carceral humanism takes many forms and has a long history, which includes institutionalizing service provision behind bars, adding mental health services (without supplementing health services in communities), and building "gender-responsive" jails. In his important study of "progressive punishment," Judah Schept documents the carceral humanism of self-identified liberals who supported construction of a new juvenile detention facility in Bloomington, Indiana. Eschewing tough-on-crime rhetoric, local politicians and activists justified the new facility in the name of family preservation (so parents could more easily visit their imprisoned children) and in the name of averting subsequent incarceration (humanely imprison children now to stop adult incarceration later).[48] "Carceral humanism" has a long history within policing in particular. The 1975 publication of *The Iron Fist and the Velvet Glove* captured the dynamic by which more "community" and team policing complement rather than counteract aggressive paramilitary policing.[49] As community policing spread across the country, so did SWAT teams and paramilitary units, both often funded by the Law Enforcement Assistance Administration.[50]

My concern is not that "carceral humanism" and "tactical empathy" encourage emotional artifice, teaching police officers to pantomime compassion. Our first impulse may tell us to question authenticity, to do a close reading of police actions, and to find external clues to the real internal feelings.[51] But evaluating the "realness" of police empathy is a task both interminable and irrelevant. It is interminable because "true feelings" and true intentions are unknowable (perhaps even to the doer). More crucially, the sincerity of police empathy is irrelevant to the violence of policing. The problems of policing should be understood, I believe, by reference to the scale and scope of policing; the demographic distributions of policing, notably the racial and spatial concentration of policing; and the quotidian damages of being subject to suspicion, surveillance, citations, and arrests. In terms of the scale and scope of policing, each year police make roughly between eleven million and thirteen million arrests. Violent crimes account for about 5–6 percent of all arrests, and property crimes for 12 percent of all arrests. Each year, there are about four hundred thousand arrests for public drunkenness, another four hundred thousand for disorderly conduct, about two hundred thousand for vandalism, and about fifty thousand more for loitering and curfew violations. Because police arrest primarily for misdemeanor offenses, non-traffic misdemeanor cases account for 80 percent of state court caseloads.[52] By one estimate, states and localities in 2006 prosecuted 10.5 million misdemeanor cases—double the number of misdemeanor cases prosecuted in 1972.[53] Much of this can be explained by the rise of "broken windows policing" and its now commonsense logic: To prevent a climate of lawlessness that breeds major criminality, police must clamp down on small infractions like littering, vandalism, and panhandling, all of which, if left unchecked, become signs of the decline into disorder. Scholarship disconfirms the efficacy of broken windows policing, but the hundreds of pages of multicity studies and large-N regression analyses that show "no effect" simply cannot dislodge faith in the oh-so-intuitive logic of broken windows policing, emblematic in the Cinderella story of New York City's "turnaround" in the 1990s, when Mayor Rudolph Giuliani, Police Commissioner William Bratton, and the neoliberal think tank the Manhattan Institute advocated "zero tolerance" for every infraction from public urination to street vending. New York City's "success" enabled the exporting of Bratton-style broken windows policing to Baltimore, Los Angeles, London, San Juan, San Salvador, and beyond.[54]

In terms of demographic concentration, consider that nearly one third of arrestees in the United States each year are black. Each year the police make eighteen million traffic stops, such that about 12 percent of all drivers are stopped by police each year. But fully 24 percent of all black drivers are stopped by police each year.[55] Arrests for low-level misdemeanors are especially raced and classed because they are tied to neighborhood policing tactics, and non-white communities experience higher levels of surveillance. In one study of misdemeanor arrests in 2012 in New York City, for example, blacks were arrested for misdemeanor offenses at a rate of about 6,500 per 100,000, compared to whites, who were arrested for misdemeanors at a rate of about 1,200 per 100,000.[56]

In terms of the quotidian, the damages of policing include mass citations, summonses, and arrests, which diminish life chances and economic stability. With our eyes locked on the bloodletting of "extreme" police force, we might miss the death by a thousand cuts through paradigmatic policing, namely the policing of misdemeanors. As the legal scholar Alexandra Natapoff puts it, "Rarely recognized as such, the misdemeanor is in fact the paradigmatic U.S. criminal case: most cases are misdemeanors, most of what the system does is generate minor convictions, and most Americans who experience the criminal system do so via the petty offense process."[57] Misdemeanor offenses are "special" in the sense that there is no Sixth Amendment right to counsel for many minor offenses.[58] Nonetheless, misdemeanants might serve up to six months of jail time, endure years of probation, and even face deportation. Moreover, misdemeanants increasingly shoulder costs for their convictions. In 2004, 80 percent of misdemeanants were assessed fees and fines by the courts (compared with two-thirds of those convicted of felonies and sentenced to prison). Fees and fines for misdemeanor offenses are seemingly small burdens that tend to compound over time, sometimes bringing inescapable debt and heightened surveillance that makes new arrests all the more likely.[59]

In short, even without "profiling" and "brutality," policing is racialized and destructive. Many people are rightly outraged by police use of lethal force. I worry, however, that we minimize the violence inherent in routine acts of policing. Here we should heed the warning from Ruth Wilson Gilmore and Craig Gilmore that outrage against police murders and militarization "enables a strange displacement (often unintended, yet also often cynically co-opted) of political focus from the necessarily systemic character of organized violence." Rather than witnessing murders and militarization as policing "gone too far," we must ask about the preconditions of visibly "extreme" police violence. These include "widespread arrests, the issuance of massive numbers of citations, and the political culture of perpetual enemies who must always be fought but can never be vanquished. These preconditions, and the violence enabled and required to maintain them, will not change if an officer or two is indicted and a few tanks are dismantled for scrap metal."[60]

What happens when the routine racism of policing—the quotidian, non-newsworthy physical and financial taxation of black bodies and the racialized poor—is addressed as a matter of mistrust, perceptions, and feelings? To begin with, a trust-centered framework allows for *agnosticism* on the existence of racialized state violence. When political elites acknowledge that marginalized groups fear police brutality or perceive racial profiling, too often they validate the feelings but sidestep judgment on the conditions that generate such feelings. It is as if political discourse operates by the clinical maxim that "feelings are facts." When the existence of racialized state violence becomes a matter of opinion and personal feelings, and if all opinions and feelings hold equal weight in both their validity and their contribution to community-police "mistrust," then there is an easy equivalence of power. At work here is the false egalitarianism of feelings: All individuals have feelings, all feelings hold equal weight as "fact." From here, what does the transitive property suggest? Is the next step that all individuals hold equal weight in creating the institutional world where some bodies are held in cages while others give televised speeches about bodies held in cages?

The slipperiness of "mistrust" and misperceptions is evident, for example, in the International Association of Chiefs of Police's "National Policy Summit on Community Police Relations: Advancing a Culture of Cohesion and Community Trust." Issued in January 2015, the summit report explains its origins: "In response to events in Ferguson (MO), New York City (NY), and Cleveland (OH), the IACP held a National Policy Summit on Community-Police Relations in October 2014 to open dialogue regarding ways to build and sustain trusting community-police relationships."[61] Note the basic ambiguity in identifying what precisely is so distressing about the events in Ferguson, New York City, and Cleveland. Is it troubling that police killed Michael Brown, Eric Garner, and Tamir

Rice? Is it troubling that people protested in large numbers? The IACP maintains agnosticism: "True change in the area of *perceived or real social injustice* will take time and commitment from the police profession and their communities."[62] Indeed, the IACP continually references "real or perceived" police injustice, an ambiguity maintained by referencing a "history" of discrimination, never clarifying if the past is truly past.

Because communities of color are plagued by suspicions about "real or perceived mistreatment by police," it is possible to create the reality-defying position that the police and their targets are equally responsible for a set of collectively generated ills, some communal property of mutual distrust and misunderstanding. As explained by the IACP, "Unfortunately, in many communities, particularly communities of color, prior decades of real or perceived mistreatment by police and the justice system has led to underlying fear, resentment, and anger, culminating in distrust. This history of tensions has at times led to clashes with police, further intensifying the community's feelings of marginalization and mistreatment by police and other governmental entities, including the entire criminal justice system."[63] In this logic, feelings become causal agents. Fear, resentment, anger, and distrust in communities of color have "led to clashes with police." At its base, the message is this: The way black people feel causes police to shoot them.

Here, the IACP is actually fulfilling the popular recommendation that police leadership should acknowledge "past injustices." Obama's Task Force on 21st Century Policing advises that "law enforcement agencies should acknowledge the role of policing in past and present injustice and discrimination and how it is a hurdle to the promotion of community trust."[64] Many police departments are explicitly taking up the call to acknowledge their "civil rights wrongs." The San Francisco Police Department's (SFPD) self-review, written in response to the Task Force on 21st Century Policing, states that the department agrees with the recommendation to "acknowledge the role of policing in past and present injustice and discrimination." As proof, it cites SFPD's Chief of Police Greg Suhr's monthly column in the *San Francisco Peace Officers Association Journal*: "Let's begin this difficult conversation by being honest enough to acknowledge that much of law enforcement's history in this country has not been pretty. At many points in American history," police enforced a "status quo" that "was often brutally unfair to disfavored groups." Later in the column, Chief Suhr calls this unpretty history "our cultural inheritance. We need to remember our mistakes, and we need to learn from them. Those without a knowledge of history are destined to repeat it. One reason we cannot forget our law enforcement legacy is that the people we serve cannot forget it either."[65]

The emotion-centered perspective lends itself to policy interventions that "correct" bad feelings by *increasing* police presence in communities of color. From a perspective that prioritizes "trust" and downplays the racial concentration of policing, a logical remedy to high enforcement contact in communities of color is to advocate even *higher* non-enforcement contact. In this vein, Obama's Task Force on 21st Century Policing advises police to "actively promote public trust by initiating positive non-enforcement activities" in "communities that typically have high rates of investigative and enforcement involvement with government agencies."[66] Examples of interactions that are "positive and not related to investigation or enforcement" include informal social gatherings like Coffee with a Cop, or Sweet Tea with the Chief, or more structured conversations such as Students Talking It Over with Police.[67]

* * *

By giving officers scripts to generate compliance, trainings in "tactical empathy" do not constrain police power; rather, they license police power with superficial imprints of courtesy and understanding. It is tempting to conclude with Saidiya Hartman's analysis of "the repressive effects of empathy," located in the long-standing desire to don blackness as "sentimental resource" and the facile intimacy that actually obliterates the other.[68] But I want to end by going to the more fundamental call in Hartman's work, which is the call to identify racial terror where it is perhaps least discernible.

There is a brutality to policing that enables and exceeds the well-known hashtag obituaries—Michael Brown; Walter Scott; Freddie Gray; and for those who have learned to say her name, Sandra Bland, Natasha McKenna, Rekia Boyd; and for those who recognize the deep intersectional vulnerability of black transgender women, Mya Hall, Kayla Moore, Nizah Morris.[69] From the quotidian violence of policing, activists weave together a structural critique that is continually unraveled despite itself, reduced to a collection of "incidents" gone awry, repackaged from institutional critique into interpersonal laments about whether, in President Obama's words, black people and police "can ever understand each other's experience." Such calls for reciprocal understanding feed the popularity of police trainings in communication and empathy, as if the right curricula can transform policing into another word for brotherly love.

But it is precisely in these blueprints of "humane policing" that we must identify domination. In the context of policing, recognition of another's perspective operates as a form of weaponized empathy, a tool to dull resistance to the routine racial terror of policing—racialized suspicion and the processing of mass citations and arrests. In this sense, trainings for "humane policing" are borne of the hollow hope that improving policing will allow us to escape its violence. But the core function of policing is armed protection of state interests, and therefore, as Rachel Herzing reminds us, "the goal should not be to improve policing but to reduce its role in our lives."

NOTES

1 Rachel Herzing, "Big Dreams and Bold Steps toward a Police-Free Future," in *Who Do You Serve, Who Do You Protect? Police Violence and Resistance in the United States*, ed. Maya Schenwar, Joe Macaré, and Alana Yu-lan Price (Chicago: Haymarket Books, 2016), 111.

2 Barack Obama, "Remarks by the President at Memorial Service for Fallen Dallas Police Officers," July 12, 2016, www.whitehouse.gov; emphasis added.

3 Examples of the "mistrust" perspective abound. In his remarks at the Congressional Black Caucus Awards Dinner on September 28, 2014, seven weeks after white Ferguson, Missouri, police officer Darren Wilson shot and killed eighteen-year-old black Michael Brown, President Obama portrayed the state of policing in emotional terms that might be used to describe a marriage turned sour. "The anger" following Michael Brown's death showed that "a gulf of mistrust exists between local residents and law enforcement." See Barack Obama, "Remarks by the President at Congressional Black Caucus Awards Dinner," September 28, 2014, www.whitehouse.gov. Likewise, Attorney General Eric Holder visited Ferguson and said he understood "mistrust" of the police, with his Justice Department investigation "a critical step in restoring trust between law enforcement and the community, not just in Ferguson, but beyond." See "Many Communities Still Mistrust Police," *New York Times*, August 19, 2014; and "Holder Says He Understands Mistrust of Police," *New York Times*, August 20, 2014.

4 Black Youth Project 100, "#StopTheCops and #FundBlackFutures," http://byp100. org; and The Movement for Black Lives, "A Vision for Black Lives: Policy Demands for Black Power, Freedom, and Justice," https://policy.m4bl.org.

5 Nils Bubandt and Rane Willerslev, "The Dark Side of Empathy: Mimesis, Deception, and the Magic of Alterity," *Comparative Studies in Society and History* 57 (January 2015): 5–34.

6 George Thompson, *Verbal Judo: Words as a Force Option* (Springfield, IL: Charles C. Thomas, 1983); George Thompson and Michael Stroud, *Verbal Judo: Redirecting Behavior with Words* (Albuquerque, NM: Communication Strategies, 1984), subsequently reprinted as George Thompson, *Verbal Judo: Redirecting Behavior with Words* (Auburn, NY: Verbal Judo Institute, 2012); George Thompson and Jerry Jenkins, *Verbal Judo: The Gentle Art of Persuasion* (New York: Quill, 1993; reprint, New York: William Morrow Paperbacks, 2013), citations are to the 2013 ed.; and George Thompson and Gregory Walker, *The Verbal Judo Way of Leadership: Empowering the Thin Blue Line from the Inside Up* (Flushing, NY: Looseleaf Law Publications, 2007).

7 Tom Dart, "'Verbal Judo': The Police Tactic That Teaches Cops to Talk before They Shoot," *Guardian*, July 21, 2016.

8 Richard Johnson, "Citizen Expectations of Police Traffic Stop Behavior," *Policing: An International Journal of Police Strategies and Management* 27 (2004): 487, 489. See also Rick Bradstreet, "Reducing Citizen Complaints," *Journal of Police and Criminal Psychology* 9 (October 1993): 34.

9 Azi Paybarah, "Bratton: Police Officers to Be Taught 'Verbal Judo,'" *Politico*, February 27, 2014.

10 New York City Office of the Mayor, "Transcript: Mayor de Blasio Visits 25th Precinct with NYPD Commissioner Bratton," February 27, 2014, *NYC: The Official Website of the City of New York*, www1.nyc.gov.

11 Ibid.

12 Michael Wood, "Baltimore Police Department's 'New' Use of Force Policy Is Actually Old," *Baltimore Sun*, July 6, 2016; and Mike Farabaugh, "Officers Learn to Defuse Violence with 'Verbal Judo,'" *Baltimore Sun*, August 22, 2000.

13 Thomas Martinelli, "Unconstitutional Policing: Part 3—A Failure to Train Is Compensable Liability," *Police Chief* 82 (November 2015): 56–60; emphasis in original.

14 "Educating officers in the significance of empathy on the job can prove beneficial on so many differing levels in police-community relations and peer interactions, as well as in jury deliberations." See ibid., 59–60; and Thomas Martinelli, "Unconstitutional Policing: Part 1—Redefining the Police Ethics Paradigm," *Police Chief* 82 (September 2015): 72–77.

15 The goal of Verbal Judo is to achieve order not through overt coercion but through what is often referred to as the "generation of voluntary compliance": "In the basic Verbal Judo class we teach that the goal of law enforcement is to bring Order out of Disorder and to generate voluntary compliance." Thompson and Walker, *The Verbal Judo Way of Leadership*, 33; emphasis (and odd Hobbesian-style capitalization) in original.

16 Ibid., 110; emphasis in original.

17 The tactical is presented as the rejection of the natural. "The real enemies are the people who get to you for they make you react rather than respond; they make you act 'naturally' rather than tactically." See ibid., 50.

18 Ibid., 110.

19 Thompson and Jenkins, *Verbal Judo: The Gentle Art of Persuasion*, 140–141.

20 Ibid., 142.

21 "If you can project understanding, empathy, you will absorb like a sponge the tension of your child, your spouse, or anyone else you're dealing with." See ibid., 139–140.

22 Ibid., 37–44.

23 Ibid., 70–71.

24 Ibid., 153.

25 Ibid., 139–140.

26 Ibid., 154.

27 Ibid., 66, 80–82, 100, 114–117, 177–178. Another training module, the so-called Good Stranger model of policing, also emphasizes the importance of gestures and eye contact. One crucial "rapport-building" behavior is called "using the social gaze—maintaining eye contact as a sign of connection except in cultures where prolonged eye contact creates discomfort or is seen as rude." See Gary Klein et al., "Police and Military as Good Strangers," *Journal of Occupational and Organizational Psychology* 88 (June 2015): 245.

28 Laleh Khalili, "The Uses of Happiness in Counterinsurgencies," *Social Text* 118 (Spring 2014): 27.

29 Quoted in ibid., 32. The original is from David H. Petraeus, "COMISAF's Counterinsurgency Guidance," memorandum from Commander, International Security Assistance Force / United States Forces–Afghanistan, "For the Soldiers, Sailors, Airmen, Marines, and Civilians of NATO ISAF and US Forces–Afghanistan," August 1, 2010, Stars and Stripes, www.stripes.com.

30 Quoted in Khalili, "The Uses of Happiness in Counterinsurgencies," 23.

31 Thompson and Walker, *The Verbal Judo Way of Leadership*, ii, viii.

32 Ibid., 30.

33 Ibid., 27–29; emphasis in original. See also Robert Humphrey, *Values for a New Millennium* (Maynardville, TN: Life Values Press; Stockton, CA: WIN Publications, 1992).

34 Thompson and Walker, *The Verbal Judo Way of Leadership*, 28–29, quoting Humphrey, *Values for a New Millennium*, 68; emphasis in original.

35 Thompson and Walker, *The Verbal Judo Way of Leadership*, 29, quoting Humphrey, *Values for a New Millennium*, 69; emphasis in original.

36 Ibid., 30; emphasis in original.

37 Thompson and Jenkins, *Verbal Judo: The Gentle Art of Persuasion*, 62.

38 The Sun Tzu quote is used twice. See ibid., 24, 194.

39 John Del Signore, "NYPD Will Train Officers in Art of 'Verbal Judo,'" *Gothamist*, February 28, 2014, http://gothamist.com.

40 Khalili, "The Uses of Happiness in Counterinsurgencies," 26.

41 Sara Ahmed, *The Promise of Happiness* (Durham, NC: Duke University Press, 2010), 3.

42 Teemu Kokko and Marko Mäki, "The Verbal Judo Approach in Demanding Customer Encounters," *Services Marketing Quarterly* 30 (June 2009): 220.

43 Ibid., 220–221.

44 Ruth Zschoche, Tony Anderman, and Steve Lettic, "Tactical Social Interaction Training: Innovation in Multi-cultural Adaptation and Communication Programs," *Police Chief* 82 (June 2015): 44–-47; Klein et al., "Police and Military as Good Strangers"; Jack L. Colwell and Charles "Chip" Huth, *Unleashing the Power of Unconditional Respect: Transforming Law Enforcement and Police Training* (Boca Raton, FL: CRC Press, 2010); and Sue Rahr and Stephen K. Rice, *From Warriors to Guardians: Recommitting American Police Culture to Democratic Ideals*, New Perspectives in Policing Bulletin (Washington DC: National Institute of Justice, 2015).

45 Jamil Zaki, "When Cops Choose Empathy," *New Yorker*, September 25, 2015.

46 Dart, "Verbal Judo."

47 James Kilgore, "Repackaging Mass Incarceration: The Rise of Carceral Humanism and Non-alternative Alternatives," *CounterPunch*, June 6, 2014, www.counterpunch.org.

48 Judah Schept, *Progressive Punishment: Job Loss, Jail Growth, and the Neoliberal Logic of Carceral Expansion* (New York: New York University Press, 2015), 98–100.

49 Anthony M. Platt et al., *The Iron Fist and the Velvet Glove: An Analysis of the U.S. Police* (Berkeley, CA: Center for Research on Criminal Justice, 1975).

50 Matthew T. DeMichele and Peter B. Kraska, "Community Policing in Battle Garb: A Paradox or Coherent Strategy?" in *Militarizing the American Criminal Justice System: The Changing Roles of the Armed Forces and the Police*, ed. Peter B. Kraska (Boston: Northeastern University Press, 2001), 82–101.

51 See Matthew Pratt Guterl, "Racial Fakery and the Next Postracial: Reconciliation in the Age of Dolezal," in this volume.

52 Amy Lerman and Vesla Weaver, *Arresting Citizenship: The Democratic Consequences of American Crime Control* (Chicago: University of Chicago Press, 2014), 8.

53 Robert Boruchowitz, Malia Brink, and Maureen Dimino, *Minor Crimes, Massive Waste: The Terrible Toll of America's Broken Misdemeanor Courts* (Washington, DC: National Association of Criminal Defense Lawyers, 2009), 11. The estimated number of misdemeanor cases is based on data gathered in twelve states by the National Center for State Courts.

54 Jordan Camp and Christina Heatherton, "Introduction," in *Policing the Planet: Why the Policing Crisis Led to Black Lives Matter*, ed. Jordan Camp and Christina Heatherton (New York: Verso, 2016), 3, 5; and Neil Smith, "Giuliani Time: The Revanchist 1990s," *Social Text* 56 (1998): 1–20.

55 Charles Epp, Steven Maynard-Moody, and Donald Haider-Markel, *Pulled Over: How Police Stops Define Race and Citizenship* (Chicago: University of Chicago Press, 2014), 2.

56 Jenny M. Roberts, "Why Misdemeanors Matter: Defining Effective Advocacy in the Lower Criminal Courts," *UC Davis Law Review* 45 (2011): 277–372; Citizens Crime Commission, "Trends in Misdemeanor Arrest Rates in New York" (New York: New York Citizens Crime Commission, October 2014).

57 Alexandra Natapoff, "Misdemeanor Decriminalization," *Vanderbilt Law Review* 68 (2015): 1055–1116, quote at 1063.

58 Ibid., 1078; and Issa Kohler-Hausmann, "Managerial Justice and Mass Misdemeanors," *Stanford Law Review* 66 (March 2014): 611–693.

59 Alexes Harris, Heather Evans, and Katherine Beckett, "Drawing Blood from Stones: Legal Debt and Social Inequality in the Contemporary United States," *American Journal of Sociology* 115 (May 2010): 1753–1799.

60 Ruth Wilson Gilmore and Craig Gilmore, "Beyond Bratton," in Camp and Heatherton, *Policing the Planet*, 176.

61 International Association of Chiefs of Police, "IACP National Policy Summit on Community-Police Relations: Advancing a Culture of Cohesion and Community Trust" (Alexandria, VA: International Association of Chiefs of Police, 2015), ix.

62 Ibid., ix.

63 Ibid., 4.

64 There is a corresponding "Action Item" following the recommendation to acknowledge discrimination: "The U.S. Department of Justice should develop and disseminate case studies that provide examples where past injustices were publicly acknowledged by law enforcement agencies in a manner to help build community trust." See the President's Task Force on 21st Century Policing, "Final Report of the President's Task Force on 21st Century Policy" (Washington, DC: Office of Community Oriented Policing Services, 2015), 12.

65 Greg Suhr, "Chief's Corner," *San Francisco Peace Officers Association Journal*, April 2015, 9, as quoted in San Francisco Police Department, "Review and Response of the 'Final Report of the President's Task Force on 21st Century Policing'" (San Francisco: San Francisco Police Department, September 15, 2015), 3.

66 President's Task Force on 21st Century Policing, "Final Report," 14.

67 Ibid., 15. Other examples include the Obama administration's launch of the National Center for Building Community Trust and Justice, which is currently funding six cities to enact pilot programs to improve police procedural justice, reduce implicit bias, and foster racial reconciliation (Birmingham, Alabama; Fort Worth, Texas; Gary, Indiana; Minneapolis, Minnesota; Pittsburgh, Pennsylvania; and Stockton, California).

68 Saidiya Hartman, *Scenes of Subjection: Terror, Slavery, and Self-Making in Nineteenth-Century America* (New York: Oxford University Press, 1997), 19–21.

69 Kimberlé Crenshaw and Andrea Ritchie, *Say Her Name: Resisting Police Brutality against Black Women*, with Rachel Anspach, Rachel Gilmer, and Luke Harris (New York: African American Policy Forum, 2015).

5

Black Deaths Matter, Too

Doing Racial Reconciliation after the Massacre at Emanuel AME Church in Charleston, South Carolina

VALERIE C. COOPER

There is a remark often attributed to Martin Luther King, Jr., decrying the "sad fact" that "eleven o'clock on Sunday morning" is the "most segregated hour of America."[1] In the more than fifty years since King proclaimed his dream that "one day . . . sons of former slaves and sons of former slave-owners will be able to sit down together at the table of brotherhood,"[2] little has changed. Churches in the United States remain overwhelmingly segregated, and very little progress has been made in transforming communion tables around the country into tables of real, interracial communion. According to figures compiled by the Lilly Endowment–funded Congregations Project at Rice University, where "a 'mixed' congregation [is defined] as one with at least 20 percent of its members providing racial or ethnic diversity," "mixed churches are a rare breed in America—counting for only 8 percent" of all U.S. congregations.[3]

On June 17, 2015, Dylann Roof, a white supremacist, entered Emanuel African Methodist Episcopal Church (AME), a historically black church in Charleston, South Carolina, and after sitting with the parishioners for some time during a Bible study, pulled out a gun and opened fire, killing nine blacks, including South Carolina state senator Clementa C. Pinckney, who was also the pastor of the church. Based upon comments the shooter had made to friends or posted online, law-enforcement officials speculate that his intention was to ignite a race war.

To start that race war, white supremacist Dylann Roof went to a black church.

Racial segregation in America's churches is neither accidental nor benign but instead is the result of racist policies and theologies that whites have ruthlessly applied and maintained. Black-only congrega-tions have tended historically to be the consequence of blacks' reactions to whites' actions to expel them, to control them, or to relegate them to subservient status in church and in society. Despite the progress Ameri-cans have made in desegregating other sectors of society, churches re-main rigidly segregated by race. Whites have resisted integrating their churches throughout most of American history, and blacks have re-sponded to this rejection by creating their own separate religious insti-tutions. Although the nation would prefer not to notice this division, incidents like the shooting at Emanuel AME force us to pay attention to the conflict between race and religion that has played out throughout our history.

The massacre at Emanuel also points to a major consequence of at-tempts at racial reconciliation of the sort that Emanuel AME's members practiced when they welcomed Dylann Roof into their worship service: Even the most benign of these engagements are not exercises in equality. Blacks bear the social and theological costs disproportionately.

At Emanuel AME, Roof's black victims paid the ultimate price for reaching out to an angry white supremacist,[4] but in racial reconciliation efforts it is often the case that blacks bear a greater share of the burden of reaching out to and accommodating whites, who are less willing to be inconvenienced and often less committed to integration as a goal.[5]

The stark contrast between the hate-filled white nationalist shooter and the innocent black victims who had unknowingly welcomed a murderer into their midst invites consideration of the continuing racial divide in American churches. In this essay, I explore the origins, condi-tions, and consequences of the racial divide between black and white churches and black and white Christians in America, ending with the murders at Emanuel and their potential significance to future efforts at racial reconciliation.

Although Americans rarely acknowledge our shared legacy of racism, Emanuel's contrasts between the white maniac and the black martyrs were too stark to ignore. For a brief moment in popular discourse, it be-came almost impossible to turn away from the hatred of the shooter or the horror of his victims' deaths. Indeed, it became almost impossible to ignore the white supremacist hatred that unfolded during a Bible study one Wednesday evening in a black church. As we evaluate the continuing costs and consequences of segregated worship and the limited success of efforts at racial reconciliation, the murders at Emanuel remind us that black Christians have born a disproportionately painful burden and paid a disproportionately high cost.

One last point: As the murders at Emanuel and the murderer's motive speak most directly to the painful history of black/white division in the United States, this essay focuses primarily on that divide between blacks and whites in Christian congregations, and most particularly in Protestant churches,[6] where congregations and denominations with shared origins and theologies nonetheless have divided along racial lines.

Just How Segregated?

In their book, *People of the Dream: Multiracial Congregations in the United States*, Michael O. Emerson and Rodney M. Woo compare the racial segregation found in American neighborhoods to the racial segregation typically found in American churches using an "index of dissimilarity."[7] According to this index, Emerson and Woo identified "an extremely high level of segregation" in American churches. Comparing residential racial segregation in cities to racial segregation in churches, they note that church segregation exceeds that of America's most segregated residential areas:

> As a basis for comparison, in research on neighborhood segregation, cities with indexes of dissimilarity greater than .60 are considered highly segregated. . . . [By comparison,] the value for Catholicism is .81; for mainline Protestantism, .85; and for conservative Protestantism, .91. . . . These values indicate more than high segregation; they indicate *hyper-segregation.*[8]

Emerson and Woo further observe that the residential segregation of the most segregated American cities required "laws, discriminatory lending and real estate procedures, threats, and other racially unequal practices" but that

> Catholicism and mainline Protestantism approach these extreme values [of the most segregated American cities] and conservative Protestantism actually exceeds those values. . . . In the context of millions of people

making choices year after year about which congregations to attend, such segregation values are astonishing.[9]

As a result of these findings, the authors conclude that "congregations in the United States are hyper-segregated. The average level of racial diversity in congregations is near zero, and the average level of segregation between congregations is nearly perfect." In answer to those who would blame segregated neighborhoods for the segregation found in churches, they add that "nearly all congregations are substantially more segregated than the neighborhoods in which they reside."[10] These findings suggest that the levels of segregation in churches in the United States cannot be accidental but must have been enforced by mechanisms at least as consistent and coercive as those that produced patterns of residential segregation in the nation's cities.[11]

Historically, residential segregation and school segregation have decreased in response to public engagement, advocacy efforts, and legislative changes.[12] Churches, in contrast, are voluntary associations protected by the Bill of Rights from the sorts of legal interventions that interdict segregation elsewhere in society. It is not possible to force a church to desegregate using the legal tools presently available. Even congregations that wish to desegregate voluntarily find the going hard. One of the best examples of how difficult it is to desegregate a Christian congregation is found in the phenomenon of the "kneel-in." Once a fixture of the Civil Rights movement of the 1950s and 1960s, these nonviolent integration efforts were forgotten in favor of the more successful attempts to integrate lunch counters, local busses, or interstate transit. Documenting the multiracial groups of students who attempted to integrate white churches in Memphis in 1964 and 1965, Stephen Haynes's *The Last Segregated Hour: The Memphis Kneel-ins and the Campaign for Southern Church Desegregation* details why the efforts have been forgotten: They were forgotten because they failed.[13]

Although the kneel-ins generated the same sorts of horrifying news reports and incendiary white supremacist rhetoric as other aspects of the Civil Rights movement that succeeded in pricking the conscience of the nation, they did not produce successfully integrated worship in Christian churches in the United States. Beyond the confrontations with protesters and the descriptions of whites refusing others entrance to their churches, the kneel-ins failed because, even if you could get black bodies inside a segregated white church, you could not force that church's white members to treat those blacks like Christians, nor could you do anything to make so openly racist a congregation a desirable place for blacks or anyone committed to interracial fellowship to want to worship there.

When Haynes went, fifty years later, to interview witnesses of the ten-month campaign that took place in Memphis between 1964 and 1965 to desegregate Second Presbyterian Church (SPC), he found that people and institutions were "still not over it." For one white student participant in the kneel-ins, Haynes surmised that even half a century later, "the root of his religious trauma was the sobering recognition that men whom he had regarded as spiritual mentors were driven by racist convictions."[14]

Second Presbyterian Church had refused to admit integrated groups of students to its worship services. In fact, the presence of whites attempting to help blacks gain entrance seems to have been a particularly provocative point for SPC. As a result of the negative publicity and controversy, the church's denomination, the Presbyterian Church in the US (PCUS), put pressure on SPC to admit the students. At the time, "church spokesmen said" that "the determination to exclude what the local papers were calling 'biracial groups' . . . had nothing to do with race. Rather, it was based solely on the visitors' intention to 'demonstrate.'" To this day, church members declare that "visitors who sought entry to the church in mixed [race] groups were not 'true worshippers.'"[15]

Eventually, the most unrepentant segregationists left SPC to form the Independent Presbyterian Church (IPC) in Memphis in 1965. Haynes argues that although members of IPC still seek to "veil the church's racist origins in the myth of a noble quest to defend Christian orthodoxy" and to resist theological "liberalism," the myth mainly "salves the wounds of institutional dishonor by suppressing the uncomfortable fact that IPC was founded by dedicated segregationists."[16]

Race Discrimination . . . without Subterfuge of any Sort

Too little has changed since H. Richard Niebuhr's stunning indictment of Christian churches, first published in 1929 in *The Social Sources of Denominationalism*: "Christendom has often achieved apparent success by ignoring the precepts of its founder."[17] For Niebuhr, although some may call themselves Christians while building tall steeples and wealthy institutions, they have not done as Christ commanded them. Divisions of race, class, and nationality are among such Christians' worst failings:

> The division of the churches closely follows the division of men into the castes of national, racial, and economic groups. It draws the color line in the church of God; it fosters the misunderstandings, the self-exaltations, the hatreds of jingoistic nationalism by continuing in the body of Christ the spurious differences of provincial loyalties; it seats the rich and poor apart at the table of the Lord, where the fortunate may enjoy the bounty they have provided while the others feed upon the crusts their poverty affords.[18]

According to Niebuhr's analysis, the social divisions found in Protestant churches constituted a heresy that denied the truth and power of the Gospel and contradicted the life and mission of Jesus.

The persistent patterns of racial segregation in American Christian congregations support the supposition that the Christianity Niebuhr encountered in 1929 continues without significant change into the present. Niebuhr went further in his condemnation of mainline denominational churches, noting with sadness that "the organization which is loudest in its praise of brotherhood and most critical of race and class discriminations in other spheres is the most disunited group of all, nurturing in its own structure that same spirit of division which it condemns in other relations."[19]

Michael Emerson, who was also a lead researcher for the Congregations Project, which studies congregational segregation, agrees with Niebuhr's conclusion: "When we had interviews with pastors, we often heard them say, 'The church ought to lead the way on this.'"[20] Rather than leading the way, however, churches fall far behind their stated goal of integration. "Ironically, the poorest record on diversity—only 2 to 3 percent mixed on average—belongs to historic Protestant churches, which were among the first to trumpet the ideal of integrated congregations" in the wake of the Civil Rights movement of the 1960s.[21]

How can it be that a nation dissatisfied with a racially segregated army or government is content with single-race churches? Niebuhr complains, "But, on the whole, the sufficient reason for the frankness with which the color line has been drawn in the church is the fact that race discrimination is so respectable an attitude in America that it could be accepted by the church without subterfuge of any sort."[22] People who would be ashamed to admit that they had sent their children to a school without a single person of color, that they worked in an office without a single black, Latino/a, or Asian co-worker, or who would be offended if their workplace only had co-workers of color on the janitorial, cafeteria, or landscaping staff, for example, nevertheless attend churches where minority members are startlingly few, without apparent qualms. Although they state that integration is a congregational goal, little or no change ever takes place.

Further, when interviewed about these churches, not a few whites overestimate the minority membership, as though they had not noticed how overwhelmingly white their own churches actually were. Indeed, the Congregations Project found fewer integrated churches than have some other surveys, apparently because "on-site checks of the estimates [of integration rates] given by churchgoers and church representatives" found that these rates were often inflated by survey respondents.[23] Churchgoers tended to overestimate the percentage of minority members in their own churches. When researchers asked congregants if they worshiped in integrated congregations, "11 percent of whites said they did. But when investigators visited these reputed multiracial churches, they found many respondents had exaggerated the amount of racial integration."[24] Further, when surveyed, church members say they prefer their churches as they are—with their current racial and ethnic mix. That is, they prefer their churches to be homogeneous with regard to race and ethnicity, as most churches are. If they make note of the segregation at all, it is only to admit that this is the way they like it.[25]

Church members often perceive influxes of people of different racial or ethnic groups as a kind of cultural assault—an assault on their comfortable ways of worshiping and being in church. One pastor recently described his black congregants' anxiety about becoming a racially mixed congregation:

The Rev. Paul Earl Sheppard had recently become the senior pastor of a suburban church in California when a group of parishioners came to him with a disturbing personal question.

They were worried because the racial makeup of their small church was changing. They warned Sheppard that the church's newest members would try to seize control because members of their race were inherently aggressive. What was he going to do if more of "them" tried to join the church?

"One man asked me if I was prepared for a hostile takeover," says Sheppard, pastor of Abundant Life Christian Fellowship in Mountain View, California.[26]

A hostile takeover? Perhaps that is how it feels. "Integrated churches are rare because attending one is like tiptoeing through a racial minefield. Just like in society, racial tensions in the church can erupt over everything from sharing power to interracial dating."[27] When the demographics of a church change, members of the previous racial or ethnic majority fear the loss of comfort and control. "Consultants who advise churches in transition say . . . resentments surface when these new groups ask for a stronger voice in how the church is run." The battle over which culture prevails may focus on the music used in worship or the sermon topics. Whites, for example, frequently complain that the music is too African American or that racism is discussed too often. Blacks, however, may fear the loss of black cultural or worship norms.[28]

Blacks sometimes experience the loss of a black-majority membership as the loss of one of the last places where it is safe to be black. Because they often work and live in integrated spaces where they are expected to conform to what they perceive as white cultural and behavioral norms, black churches function as some of the last social spaces outside of their homes and families where blackness is normative and even celebrated and where black leadership and culture are nurtured and developed. Eboni Marshall Turman, former director of the Office of Black Church Studies at Duke Divinity School, put it this way: "Many black churches are not particularly enthused about forming multiracial congregations, either. . . . There are black bodies that assimilate into white culture," she said, "but there is an erasure of black Christian tradition."[29]

So Who Is Really in Charge Here?

Buried deep in a recent study on attempts to diversify predominantly white congregations in a predominantly white mainline denomination—in this case, the Evangelical Lutheran Church of America (ELCA)—is the unsurprising news that increasing the diversity of the congregation tends to result in the loss of members. While the study's authors never explicitly state what type of members left the diversifying congregations, the data suggest that it was whites who left as members of other races joined. This effect is intensified among older congregations, where the loss of members is more severe.[30] However, what is interesting about this study is that it validates what Brad Christerson, Korie L. Edwards, and Michael Emerson found, that "whites are more likely than racial minorities to leave interracial religious organizations if their particular preferences and interests are not being met."[31]

Given that Jesus taught his followers to "love their enemies" (Matthew 5:43–44; and Luke 6:27, 35), it is not a little disturbing that, with regard to blacks and whites, racial integration is happening more slowly, and with greater difficulty, in churches than elsewhere in society. One reason why integrating congregations is difficult is because "interracial religious organizations are inherently unstable."[32] Members in the numerical minority are likely to leave the congregation if they are unable to build satisfying relationships. More important, if the members in the numerical majority are white, their commitment to integrated worship is weaker than that of other racial or ethnic groups because they are unwilling to sacrifice their own power or comfort to maintain it. "Whites are accustomed to being in control in social contexts. . . . However, whites are not necessarily aware of their privileged status as the dominant racial group, nor are they aware how their own actions perpetuate it."[33] Whites' efforts to maintain control over the nature of worship or the levers of congregational and denominational power will appear to non-whites as just that: efforts to maintain control, even as they are invisible to the whites seeking to maintain that control. Whether through finances, polity, or indirect pressure, whites' efforts to maintain control of congregational life can offend or anger non-white members.

Worse, conflict in integrated religious settings can be more difficult to resolve than it is in settings that are more homogeneous. Church members tend to interpret conflict in terms of their own cultural and personal preferences, superimposing that culture and those preferences onto larger theological issues and describing them in absolutist terms of right or wrong. Such superimpositions make it much more difficult to see from other people's perspectives, and much easier to conflate one's own perspective with God's. "Interracial religious organizations have higher levels of conflict than interracial nonreligious organizations because cultural differences tend to be given absolute and transcendent meanings, making compromise more difficult."[34] For whites, whose cultural values are constantly validated by wider society and reinforced economically, politically, and socially, seeing their cultural values resisted by newcomers to their churches often becomes too much to bear, and they flee the congregations for more comfortable, more racially homogeneous settings elsewhere.

What about when whites join predominantly black congregations? It happens with far less frequency and has not been widely or rigorously studied. Such studies are desperately needed.[35] Some large or historically significant black churches (like Abyssinian Baptist Church in New York City) are accustomed to tourists and other non-black visitors and have established practices for dealing with and showing hospitality to them. Black churches frequently have set rituals for greeting visitors— irrespective of the visitors' race—that may include the opportunity for the visitors to introduce themselves, to receive a small gift or welcome package, or to hear a special welcome song or recitation. These rituals often end with an invitation to feel at home while in worship and to feel free to visit again. Indeed, this was certainly the case when Dylann Roof went to the historic Emanuel AME Church in Charleston, South Carolina; he was greeted warmly and invited into worship.[36]

A Historical Problem

How did churches became so segregated in the first place? Throughout history in churches and denominations (as it was in the broader society), whites attempted to control their black members and to treat them as inferior to whites or, if unable to control them, to evict black members entirely.[37] The oldest predominantly black church and the oldest predominantly black denomination both emerged in response to pressure from whites. The oldest independent black congregation, a Baptist church, was founded in Silver Bluffs, South Carolina, in the early 1770s, just prior to the American Revolution. Although initially somewhat integrated, white slave owners prevented other whites from preaching to the predominantly slave congregation for fear that they would tell the enslaved converts of British offers of freedom to those who sided with and fought for the loyalists. "Brother Palmer," a white man, had been preaching to and baptizing blacks in the area in and around Silver Bluffs:

> A church was built at Silver Bluffs. . . . When the [Revolutionary] war came to the low country of rice and swamp, the masters stopped ministers such as Brother Palmer from coming to the blacks in case they got ideas. So there was nothing for it now except for David [George, a slave] to minister to his flock of more than thirty souls.[38]

When Mr. Galphin, a white patriot who owned many of the slaves in the nascent congregation, fled at word of the approaching British, David George led the believers, "now numbering 50" toward the British.[39] The congregation settled at Yamacraw, South Carolina, where David George and another slave, George Liele, pastored the congregation until 1779, when the approach of American and French troops forced them to relocate to Savannah, Georgia. Eventually, the American recapture of the area forced David George to flee with his congregation to British-held Nova Scotia and eventually to relocate to the British colony of Sierra Leone. Caught between loyalist and patriot forces, this church of escaped slaves persisted despite the actions of whites (intent upon keeping them in bondage as slaves) and because of the actions of blacks (intent upon keeping them together as a worshiping and believing congregation).

Similarly, the first independent black Christian denomination, the African Methodist Episcopal (AME) Church, was also the product of white efforts to expel or control black members and black efforts to worship freely and autonomously. In Philadelphia in the late eighteenth century, free blacks Absalom Jones and Richard Allen led the Free African Society (FAS), a benevolent society organized for the purposes of supporting the blacks of the area. From the FAS sprang two black congregations, both in Philadelphia, the African Episcopal Church of St. Thomas, pastored by Absalom Jones, and Bethel African Methodist Episcopal Church, pastored by Richard Allen. While St. Thomas maintained its relationship with the Episcopal Church, Bethel severed its ties to the Methodist Episcopal Church (which is known today as the United Methodist Church), and became the founding congregation of a new denomination, the African Methodist Episcopal Church. (Emanuel AME in Charleston, South Carolina, is one of the oldest congregations of this denomination.)[40]

Although the story of the founding of the two black congregations (Bethel and St. Thomas) has often centered on a racist incident in 1792 at St. George's, a predominantly white but mixed-race Methodist Episcopal Church in Philadelphia, the FAS had begun discussions about producing an all-black congregation as early as 1787. While the incident at St. George's, where whites tried to relegate blacks to a segregated section of the sanctuary, has often been highlighted as the motivation for the founding of the AME denomination, it is also clear that the leaders of the FAS sought autonomy from patronizing white control. The incident at St. George's only emphasized what the FAS had already discovered: that in order to be free people of color—people who were truly free to worship a God who acknowledged their full humanity—they would have to separate from their white co-religionists.[41]

Part of the difficulty is that American religious organizations developed alongside chattel slavery, Jim Crow segregation, and the like, and often provided theological justifications for them. Churches and denominations even split over these issues. Church members did not leave their attitudes about race at the sanctuary door but brought them with them into worship. Ironically, American churches may have been most integrated during the antebellum period, when slave owners could mandate where their slaves worshiped and slaveholders thought it was a good idea for them to keep an eye on how their slaves worshiped, lest those same slaves get ideas about freedom from their religious instruction.

In the period following the end of the Civil War, tensions between blacks and whites often focused on how blacks would be treated: These debates in civil society were echoed in society's churches. Would former slaves be welcomed as full members of the congregations, or would they be forced to endure treatment meant to signal their perceived inferiority? These tensions were most marked in the recently defeated South, where the overwhelming majority of African Americans still lived alongside congregations and denominations that had supported slavery and the former Confederacy.[42]

Blacks fled these southern congregations, but did they choose to leave, or were they pushed out? The founding of the CME (formerly "Colored Methodist Episcopal" and now "Christian Methodist Episcopal" Church) in Jackson, Tennessee, in 1870 suggests that some blacks chose to leave while others were forced out. By 1866, the black membership of the Methodist Episcopal Church, South—the Confederate-sympathizing branch of the Methodist Church—was down to 78,742 from a high of 207,776 black members in 1860.[43] Blacks involved in the founding of the CME emphasized their desire for autonomy not only from the white Methodist Episcopal Church, South, but also from the two independent black Methodist denominations of the North, the AME (African Methodist Episcopal) and the AMEZ (African Methodist Episcopal Zion).[44] White members of the Methodist Episcopal Church, South, sponsored and helped finance the CME while encouraging its remaining African American members to leave the Methodist Episcopal Church, South, and join the CME. It must have been clear to the blacks who were once members of the Methodist Episcopal Church, South, that they were no longer welcome in what was swiftly becoming an all-white denomination. "While presiding over his denomination's General Conference of 1890, [Bishop] John Christian Keener exulted that 'we have done our work grandly, conscientiously, and we now have a solidly white church, for which we thank God.'"[45]

By the early twentieth century, efforts to reunite northern Methodists (the Methodist Episcopal Church) and southern Methodists (the Methodist Episcopal Church, South) who had split in the years leading up to the Civil War succeeded at the cost of marginalizing the denomination's black members. Having decided that, "while black Methodists were men in the eyes of God, they were not fully men in the church," white Methodists created a segregated jurisdiction and placed their black members in it. By dismissing slavery and the Negro Question as points of regional contention and by dislocating their black members, the northern and southern Methodists were able to begin to put the Civil War's bitterness behind them and also to begin to construct a national unity myth centered on whiteness.[46] The segregated jurisdiction for blacks had the added consequence of spreading and normalizing southern racial segregation to northern Methodist churches.

Race played an even clearer role in the divisions inherent in modern Pentecostalism. The Azusa Street Revival began as a free-spirited, integrated experience guided by William J. Seymour, an African American and the son of former slaves. The services, which were held in a ram-shackle onetime AME church building on Azusa Street in Los Angeles, California, beginning in April 1906, were characterized by cross-racial interactions and female leadership (both of which were unusual for the time). Perhaps one of the most stunning statements about the Azusa services was uttered by a white eyewitness who commented that "the color line has been washed away in the Blood [of Jesus]."[47]

Pentecostal churches around the world claim origins in the Azusa Street Revival through the offices of those believers of all races who left Azusa and took the revival's message with them. Unfortunately, Seymour's leadership was undermined by whites who were offended by the integrated nature of the revival[48] or who disagreed with his decision to marry a black woman.[49] After a few years, the once-integrated revival had devolved into racially separate congregations that eventually gave rise to racially separate (although theologically similar) denominations: the Assemblies of God, which remains predominantly white, and the Church of God in Christ, which remains overwhelmingly black. Seymour felt personally betrayed by the whites he had trusted who nonetheless stole resources or members from him. Worse, white Pentecostals denied Seymour's role in leading the revival for most of the twentieth century, preferring instead to highlight the actions or teachings of marginal whites who had also been accused of sexual sins or financial mismanagement rather than to acknowledge the leadership of a man whose only failing was that he was a black man in a segregated nation.[50]

The Civil Rights movement to end de jure racial segregation only highlighted the huge, and continuing, racial divide between black and white churches in the United States. In 2016, the Presbyterian Church in America (PCA) responded to questions about the roles of race and racism in the denomination's founding during the Civil Rights era[51] with the following statement at its Forty-fourth General Assembly in Mobile, Alabama, June 20–23, 2016:

> Be it resolved, that the 44th General Assembly of the Presbyterian Church in America does recognize, confess, condemn and repent of corporate and historical sins, including those committed during the Civil Rights era, and continuing racial sins of ourselves and our fathers such as the segregation of worshipers by race; the exclusion of persons from Church

membership on the basis of race; the exclusion of churches, or elders, from membership in the Presbyteries on the basis of race; the teaching that the Bible sanctions racial segregation and discourages inter-racial marriage; the participation in and defense of white supremacist organizations; and the failure to live out the gospel imperative that "love does no wrong to a neighbor" (Romans 13:10).[52]

The statement is noteworthy for its specific mention of racism in relatively recent history ("during the Civil Rights era"), for the acknowledgment of pro-segregation teaching, and for recognition of members' "participation in and defense of white supremacist organizations." Further, the statement admits that the PCA did, as official policy and practice, segregate "worshipers by race" and exclude "persons from Church membership on the basis of race."[53] Perhaps most important of all, the PCA "voted to establish a PCA Unity Fund" to support ministries to "African-American and other minority Teaching Elders and Ruling Elders."[54] The fund represents not only repentance but also a quantifiable attempt at reparations for the consequences of past PCA racism.[55]

Although the resolution passed easily when presented to the 2016 General Assembly of the PCA, it had been preceded by years of scholarship and debate.[56] Discussions about racism often focus on slavery, but the PCA did not exist as a denomination during the antebellum era. Few members knew the actual history of the denomination with regard to race; discussions about race were often cloaked in theology, doctrine, and polity. As racism became less and less acceptable socially, denominational leaders denied or hid the more unsightly details of their history, including their complicity with Jim Crow segregation in society and in church. Anthony Bradley, describing how he came upon this history as a black seminarian who had to do his own digging to discover it, notes that "there are many PCA churches that have [racist] activities as a factual part of their histories but have swept them under the rug for decades. People need to know about them."[57]

For Bradley, the battle was nothing less than a fight for the soul and the future of the denomination:

Some in the PCA made every attempt to explain away these accusations as minor, dismiss the severity of the history, deflect the importance of the discussion by highlighting a few figures who were not pro-segregationists, and note that racism is everywhere. When nobody told me about the history, I suppose I could have dug into records and found out myself, but I didn't even know that history existed—and to suggest it's important only to blacks contributes to a dismissive disposition toward blacks in the PCA. Thankfully, the tendency to condescension and cover-up diminished over time, and the denomination was free to make an historic confession of past sin that could propel it forward into new growth opportunities.[58]

Eventually, the weight of the evidence of racism in the PCA became too heavy to ignore.

Racially segregated churches feel so normal—so regular a part of the landscape—that few people ask themselves why they are segregated. One finds theologically similar, racially divided congregations all across the country, but particularly in the South, where many towns boast two "First Baptist" churches—one black and one white. In cities all over the country it is not unusual to find a white United Methodist congregation on one side of town and a black Methodist congregation (AME, AMEZ, or CME) on the other side, or a white Assemblies of God congregation in the suburbs and a black Church of God in Christ congregation in the inner city.

A Theological Problem

Recently, theologians have begun to ask why Christian theology has failed so spectacularly to tackle issues of race and the racial divisions present in American congregations. Some theologians have concluded that theology itself must be redeemed from its role in supporting and undergirding (or even hiding) white supremacy, white hegemony, and white cultural normativity. J. Kameron Carter, for example, has examined "how the discourse of theology aided and abetted the processes by which 'man' came to be viewed as a modern, racial being." More specifically, Carter notes that "modern racial discourse and practice have their genesis inside Christian theological discourse and missiological practice, which themselves were tied to the practice of empire in the advance of Western civilization."[59] In his award-winning text,

The Christian Imagination: Theology and the Origins of Race, Willie James Jennings gives heartbreaking example after example of the ways that theology served empire from the colonial period onward and, in so doing, created racial hierarchies whose legacies linger today.[60] Rather than function as an anti-racism tool, Christian theology has too often operated in support of racism, colonization, land confiscation, slavery, segregation, anti-miscegenation policies, and the like. Carter and Jennings argue that, before theology can truly be redeemed as an anti-racism tool, its complicity in racism and its concomitant sins must be analyzed and denounced as the heresies they are.

Despite his condemnation of racial segregation in the church, H. Richard Niebuhr is also part of the broader problems of theology as some of the most famous white theologians of the twentieth century practiced it. Black Theology's James Cone indicts Niebuhr for his failure to speak out against the de jure segregation and lynching of the nineteenth and twentieth centuries. In this charge, Cone includes most of the "white theologians and ministers during that time." For Cone, "White Christianity was not genuine because it either openly *supported* slavery, segregation, and lynching as the will of God or it was silent about these evils." Cone then quotes anti-lynching activist Ida B. Wells: "Our American Christians are too busy saving the souls of white Christians from burning in hellfire to save the lives of black ones from present burning in fires kindled by white Christians."[61]

To be sure, there were some white Christians speaking out against slavery, segregation, and lynching, but far too few. Too often, theological debates about race have relied less on scripture about love and reconciliation and leaned more heavily upon now-discredited pseudo-scientific theories that declared race to be immutable and inviolable human categories and whites to be superior to blacks in every way: physically, mentally, and especially morally.[62] Moreover, theological debates (like those found in antebellum sermons and treatises arguing whether or not the Bible supported slavery) tended to obscure and to ignore the battles for political and economic power taking place at the same time under theological cover.[63] Too often regarding issues of racial inequality, theology seemed unable either to resolve the issues authoritatively or to reunite the feuding parties permanently.

The existence of theologically similar but racially segregated churches is the real theological problem here. "Here the races confess the same creeds, engage in the same forms of worship, nurture the same hopes, but do so in divided churches, where white and black find it easier to confess than to practice their common [kinship] to God."[64] Similar theology alone is apparently not enough to unite congregations, denominations, or individual members across lines of racial or ethnic division. Cultural norms, racialized viewpoints, and differing worldviews create a divide more enduring than shared theology can span, at least at present. In this damning indictment, H. Richard Niebuhr got it right: "Christendom has often achieved apparent success by ignoring the precepts of its founder.[65] Racially segregated congregations and denominations appear successful, even as they belie the power of a shared faith to unite them.

One must ask: Are these theologies really that similar? Are they serving the same function in black and white churches, even if they use similar words?

A Sociological Problem

Abolition and Civil Rights were two movements that were religiously motivated and made powerful use of religious organizations and symbols in their successful efforts to end slavery and de jure Jim Crow segregation. Nevertheless, it is important to remember that the Ku Klux Klans and many white supremacist groups also claim religious motivations and use religious organizations and symbols in defense of segregation and racial conflict. (There are still members of the PCA old enough to remember how theology was used as an excuse to expel blacks.) It must be remembered that in his struggles against Jim Crow, Martin Luther King, Jr., faced opposition from his own predominantly black denomination, the National Baptist Convention, as well as from white Christians. King penned his "Letter from Birmingham City Jail" to answer criticisms from those co-religionists, black and white, who questioned his methods and even his motives.[66] A shared religious language or even shared theology alone has not historically been enough to bridge the yawning racial divide.

Like theologians, sociologists have documented the impact of a wide variety of religious beliefs on racial interactions. They acknowledge race as a social construction and a cultural production even as they recognize that "some of the most important constructions sites can be found in religious institutions and organisations [sic]."[67] As a site of racial definition and performance, religious organizations developed theological justifications for their own group's social dominance or theological opposition to their own group's oppression:

> "Race" in America fostered the development of highly bounded [that is, racially segregated] human communities and like members of human communities everywhere, these racialized peoples engaged in the activities that constituted and constructed religious life. Those who defined and established themselves as white and dominant developed and shared religious ideas that justified their dominance, denigrated blackness and non-European cultures, and magnified the importance of whiteness and white supremacy. People in communities defined as inferior and targets of exploitation and discrimination developed religious ideas that questioned their suffering and fostered their survival.[68]

While the theologies of racially segregated congregations may be similar, they cannot be identical, given that they serve radically different purposes for the congregations involved, either questioning the social status quo or valorizing it.

Multiracial congregations alone cannot be the answer to theologies that protect white privilege. Investigators studying minorities in multiracial congregations have found that racial diversity was not enough to "promote progressive racial views among attendees of any race or ethnicity":[69]

> "Whose interests are multiracial congregations serving?" asked researcher Kevin Dougherty, Ph.D., associate professor of sociology in Baylor's College of Arts & Sciences. "We want to believe that [multiracial congregations] promote a shared, integrated identity for all. But the truth may be that many are advancing a form of Anglo-conformity instead."[70]

Multiracial congregations (1) leave dominant White racial frames unchallenged, potentially influencing minority attendees to embrace such frames and/or (2) attract racial minorities who are more likely to embrace those frames in the first place.[71]

If blacks initially fled white churches and denominations to escape the crippling impact of white supremacy, then reuniting them with multiracial congregations where the white supremacy has remained unchallenged will not resolve the deeper divisions between races in American society. Indeed, perhaps the only blacks attracted to multiracial congregations are those blacks willing to accept or to ignore hierarchical theologies of white supremacy and black insufficiency. For multiracial congregations to be able to address racial inequality, it would seem that they must first address their underlying theological presuppositions of white supremacy and black inferiority, even if those presuppositions are invisible to the whites in the congregation.

A Biblical Problem

If churches are as racially divided as this essay suggests, why even bother trying to unite them? Advocates for racial reconciliation point to several biblical ideas in defense of a world where people of different races worship together. Perhaps most compelling is this picture of heaven found in the Book of Revelation:

> After this I looked, and there was a great multitude that no one could count, from every nation, from all tribes and peoples and languages, standing before the throne and before the Lamb, robed in white, with palm branches in their hands. They cried out in a loud voice, saying "Salvation belongs to our God who is seated on the throne, and to the Lamb!" (Revelation 7:9–10, New Revised Standard Version)

In this vision of unity and diversity, people from every nation and tribe and language group are gathered in worship of Jesus, the Lamb of God. Although united geographically and theologically (in that they are all in the same place singing the same song), their differences in race, culture, and even language are still apparent.[72] Given that *fellowship, communion,* and even *love* are such central themes of the Bible, the continued racial division of American churches belies the message that most churches say they wish to communicate to the world.

A Problem of Survival

Perhaps the most compelling reason why white churches are now seeking to reach out to people of color is . . . institutional survival. Mainline denominational churches have seen steep declines in membership since the 1940s.[73] Although some commentators had suggested that Evangelical churches would continue to grow even as Mainline Denominations declined, the most recent portents do not support that conclusion. For example, the predominantly white and Evangelical Southern Baptist Convention, which had previously reported growth while Mainline Denominations declined, has recently acknowledged that baptisms, membership, and church attendance are all down.[74] Demographic changes expected to produce a United States where whites no longer consist of the numerical majority by mid-century[75] have combined with predictions of diminished influence for white Christians[76] to inspire predominantly white congregations and denominations across the country to try to improve the racial diversity of their congregations.

Anthony Bradley nailed it when he predicted that "the [PCA] was free to make an historic confession of past sin that could propel it forward into new growth opportunities."[77] White churches and denominations will be unable to expand their membership significantly into minority populations unless they address the theological teachings, cultural practices, and racial attitudes minorities find objectionable. (The few minority members that the predominantly white churches and denominations do already have probably represent that minority of minority folk willing to overlook or excuse the theological teachings, cultural practices, and racial attitudes of predominantly white churches and denominations that the majority of minority folk find objectionable. That minority of the minority will not be able to expand minority membership appreciably in white churches.) Given the slow growth of the white population in the United States, predominantly white congregations and denominations cannot continue to rely on white-only membership rolls.

Moving Past Integration; Moving toward Justice

Can we even call it "racial reconciliation" if all that is happening is blacks and whites are sitting together in the same church buildings on Sunday morning? In her book *Dear White Christians: For Those Still Longing for Racial Reconciliation* Jennifer Harvey blasts attempts at racial reconciliation that fail to confront white supremacy or to demand justice, noting that most white Christians still have not attended to Black Theology's challenges to racial inequality and white hegemony.[78] For Harvey, racial reconciliation cannot occur unless issues of justice and racial inequality are first addressed.[79]

Are blacks even interested in responding to whites' invitations to join congregations where whites predominate? Some are, but judging from the continuing strength of predominantly black churches, most are not. Nikole Hannah-Jones, an African American living in New York City, wrestled with the challenges of selecting an elementary school for her daughter in "Choosing a School for My Daughter in a Segregated City."[80] Her essay addresses the complications of residential and school segregation and the ways that the disproportionate economic and political power of whites in New York City has constantly and effectively counterbalanced that of poor and middle-class people of color such that the segregation produced appears natural and even unavoidable, although it is neither.

In many ways, Hannah-Jones's struggle to secure a high-quality education for her daughter, balanced with her desire for her child to be educated in an environment that regards African Americans positively, mirrors the concerns of African Americans who choose predominantly black churches for worship. Hannah-Jones had to do as many blacks must do, by balancing a desire for integration against a frank evaluation of the disadvantages and even dangers such integrated venues pose for minorities.

Blacks pay a high social and emotional cost for integrating predominantly white spaces. They must endure micro-aggression and outright racism as whites question their right to access predominantly white social spaces.[81] Stereotype threat can cause them (and others) to question their own competence.[82] Other blacks may question their commitment to the black community as a consequence of the integrated spaces they have chosen to inhabit. Forced to choose between allegiances, blacks in integrated spaces can become people without a community: They are suspect in the white communities they've joined, and they are suspect in the black communities they've left.

One way to avoid anti-black racism is to avoid non-blacks; for this reason, Hannah-Jones ultimately chose a predominantly minority school for her daughter. For similar reasons, many blacks choose predominantly minority churches. They represent safe spaces where black culture and life are celebrated; they also represent sanctuaries from the racism of broader society.[83]

Do Black Lives Matter? Do Black Deaths Matter, Too?

When Dylann Roof walked into Emanuel AME Church, he did not plan to study the Bible. He wanted to ensure that there would be no sanctuary for black people at Mother Emanuel AME on June 17, 2015. He went to a black church on a Wednesday night because he knew he would find black people there at that time and place. In a manifesto Roof posted online before the massacre, he admitted his cowardice about taking his fight to "the ghetto" presumably because his violence there might be met with equal and opposite force. Instead, he took his crusade to a city rich with the history of black-white conflict, but also to a place where no one would be likely to fight back. Roof explained his actions in an online statement posted before the shootings:

> "I have no choice," it reads. "I am not in the position to, alone, go into the ghetto and fight. I chose Charleston because it is most historic city in my state, and at one time had the highest ratio of blacks to Whites in the country. We have no skinheads, no real KKK, no one doing anything but talking on the internet. Well someone has to have the bravery to take it to the real world, and I guess that has to be me."[84]

Roof's website included references to Hitler and photos with Confederate flags at Confederate sites. In his manifesto, he lamented black inferiority and advocated white supremacy.[85] Then, he walked into a church and committed an act of racial genocide. But before he opened fire, Roof made one last statement justifying the murders as a necessary act: "You rape our women, and you're taking over our country. And you have to go."[86] Roof looked at a room filled mainly with middle-aged and elderly women holding Bibles, but saw only rapists taking over America. His racism had blinded him, as racism always does.

In the face of Roof's obvious racial animus and white supremacist ideology, the murders of the nine black congregants at Emanuel appeared all the more heinous. They were in church. They were reading the Bible. They had welcomed him to join them. Nothing about the peaceful setting or the Bible study he attended had deterred Roof. He never saw any of the church members as human beings, but only as enemies to be destroyed.

The Black Lives Matter Movement began as a protest against police-officer-involved shootings of unarmed African Americans, but it has since expanded to address multiple issues of concern to black people and communities. Initially, however, the movement focused not on black lives but black deaths, like the death of unarmed teenager Mike Brown.[87] Certainly, the deaths of the nine black congregants at Emanuel also provoked an outpouring of concern. White supremacy, which is so often invisible to whites, was visible to the entire world in that moment, and the contrast between Roof and those he martyred not only for their faith but also for their race, moved many—black and white—to action. In the aftermath of the shooting and in the scramble to replace the negative publicity the shooting generated with positive images of racial harmony, legislators removed the Confederate battle flag Roof had so eagerly embraced from the South Carolina Statehouse.[88] Later, the Southern Baptist Convention—the historical remnant of the Confederate Baptists—also renounced its use.[89]

If 11 A.M. Sunday morning is the most segregated hour in America, it is with good reason. For whites, Sunday morning segregation masks the history of using theology as a tool of empire, at worst justifying, and at best ignoring, slavery, Jim Crow, and countless other atrocities. For blacks, Sunday morning segregation protects one of the last social spaces where blackness is celebrated and black leadership is developed. In multiracial congregations, Sunday morning integration is a smokescreen and racial reconciliation a mirage in which white supremacy remains mostly unaddressed as a theological and a sociological issue. The massacres at Emanuel AME highlighted this single essential point: There is no true Christian brother- and sisterhood until white supremacy is addressed with appropriate repentance and reparation.

No justice; no peace.

What, then, might racial reconciliation look like in the aftermath of the murders at Emanuel? Korie L. Edwards describes hope in the context of Martin Luther King's dream:

> As churches seek to become interracial, they must not be satisfied with simply having people of different racial groups worship together. . . . If churches want to realize Dr. [Martin Luther] King's dream, they must first embrace a dream of racial justice and equality. Interracial churches must be places that all racial groups can call their own, where all racial groups have the power to influence the minor and major decisions of the church, where the culture and experience of all racial groups are not just tolerated but appreciated. This demands a radical approach and is certainly a high calling. Whites and racial minorities will have to resist white normativity and structural dominance and fully embrace the cultures, ideas, and perspectives of all racial groups. . . . So I encourage communities, religious or otherwise, that hold the dream of Dr. King as their own, not to accept the convenient counterfeit of mere racial integration but to strive toward becoming communities that celebrate racial justice and equality.[90]

But how do we become "communities that celebrate racial justice and equality" after the massacres at Emanuel AME? It seems to me that real reconciliation requires a frank acknowledgment of the ugly racial history, flawed theology, and sociological pathology that have brought us to this point. Real racial reconciliation requires repentance and redress of the very real injuries white Christians have done to black Christians *in the name of Jesus* throughout our history and into our present. Real racial reconciliation requires grappling with the differential social costs, and different levels of commitment and social capital for blacks and whites wishing to bridge the racial divide. Finally, it seems to me that real reconciliation will require the kind of laying down of power and privilege commended in the Gospel, where Jesus taught his disciples, "If any want to become my followers, let them deny themselves and take up their cross and follow me" (Matthew 16:24; see also Mark 8:34 and Luke 9:23). Real racial reconciliation in American churches will require whites to disavow their traditional privilege, power, and economic advantages and to honor blacks. It may also require blacks to give up their privileged places in black churches—their sanctuaries for blackness—in order to prepare the way for a heavenly vision in which all races are can feel at home.

In the years leading up to the massacre at Emanuel, rather than recommending that white churches should try to attract blacks—which would only reinscribe the existing power dynamics of the broader society by building white institutions at the expense of black ones—I had recommended that whites go to black churches. The point would be not to go as a spectator, an efficiency expert, a person in search of exotic entertainment, or a consultant ready to correct the institution's perceived flaws; rather, the point would be to go as a servant, ready to divest oneself, in an act of Christian integrity, of the nearly invisible white privilege that goes almost everywhere whites go in the United States and most of the world. By becoming part of institutions in which black culture and blackness are normative, whites would come to understand how it feels, on a very personal level, to be one of a minority among a majority that neither celebrates your culture nor regards it as normative.

Because white privilege remains invisible to many whites, those same whites often have difficulty seeing racial discrimination against blacks as an ongoing problem. Whites' immersion into the life of a black church (and by extension, in the lives of black people) would mean that those whites would gain a new sensitivity to what it means to be a minority in their majority culture. They would hear the testimonies of black life; they would see the struggles of black people. Having experienced the loss of some of their white privilege while interacting with blacks whose lives have been shaped by the poor state of race relations in the United States, these whites would be able to articulate their own experiences and understand those of the racial other.

Once there were a cadre of whites who had actual experience on the other side of the current church/color line, I reasoned—in the years before the massacre—that those whites would be able to begin a dialogue of racial reconciliation in earnest, armed with cultural empathy born of having been a minority in another's culture. Those whites would have an experience of what is at stake for blacks who see integration as an invitation to cultural and communal destruction and, as a result, a greater appreciation of the actual costs of integration for both sides.

At least that was what I used to recommend before Dylann Roof went to Emanuel AME with a gun. What Dylann Roof did at Emanuel AME was diabolical in that it undermined whites' ability to go to black churches confidently and blacks' likelihood of welcoming whites warmly when they do. He might not have started a race war, but did Dylann Roof make racial reconciliation much more difficult?

I fear that doing racial reconciliation has become more difficult since Dylann Roof went to Emanuel AME.

I believe that doing racial reconciliation has become more necessary since Dylann Roof went to Emanuel AME.

To start a race war, white supremacist Dylann Roof went to a black church. Nevertheless, I believe that the best way to heal the rift that whites have created historically and that Roof exacerbated recently is for white Christians to go to black churches and learn how to be *Christians* first and *whites* second.

Christianity is a faith centered upon the story of Jesus's crucifixion. According to the New Testament, Jesus went to the cross and willingly laid down his own life for others in an act Christians believe reconciled humanity to God and also reconciled humans to one another (2 Corinthians 5:18–21).[91] Further, for Jesus, going to the cross was the ultimate act of humbling himself (Philippians 2:5–8).[92] What Dylann Roof made clear during his visit to Emanuel AME was how very much might be required of those willing to practice real, justice-based racial reconciliation in the church. For the nine Emanuel martyrs, their commitment to welcoming the racial other into worship cost them their lives. Going forward, will whites, in an effort to follow Jesus, be willing to lay down their privilege and go serve black people in a black church even if it literally costs them their lives? Will blacks, in an effort to follow Jesus, lay down their hurts, their fears, their resentments and welcome whites into their midst as brothers and sisters?[93] Will we as a nation choose to move past our ugly racial history, our flawed theology, and our sociological pathology to make our churches less a war zone and more a beloved community?

Only time will tell.

NOTES

1 King, "Remaining Awake," 209.

2 King, "I Have a Dream (1963)," 104.

3 Dart, "Hues in the Pews," 6.

4 Roof probably did not appear dangerous at the time that members of Emanuel welcomed him into their Bible study. Emanuel's members would have had no idea of the danger they were in.

5 I will say more about this study later in this essay. See Christerson, Edwards, and Emerson, *Against All Odds*, 168.

6 For the purposes of this essay, "Mainline Denominations" are defined as those older, establishment denominations like the American Baptist Churches in the United States, the Episcopal Church, the Evangelical Lutheran Church in America (ELCA), the Presbyterian Church USA (PC USA), the United Church of Christ (UCC), and the United Methodist Church (UMC). "Historically Black Denominations" like the African Methodist Episcopal Church (AME), the African Methodist Episcopal Church Zion (AMEZ), the Christian Methodist Episcopal Church (CME), and the Church of God in Christ (COGIC) form a second category. The definition of a third category, "Evangelicals," is one upon which there is much scholarly and popular disagreement. In general, these Christians are predominantly white and tend to be more theologically conservative than those in mainline denominations. But by restricting the category to white denominations (as many other than myself tend to do), scholars and political pundits are able to overlook the theological similarities between the Evangelicals and the members of historically black denominations, who would qualify as Evangelicals by virtue of their theology if they were white. (I would argue that most black Christians are Evangelical in their theology and praxis.) However, for the purposes of this essay, Evangelicals include denominations like the Southern Baptist Convention (SBC) and the Assemblies of God (AOG) but not the AME, AMEZ, CME, or COGIC.

7 The index of dissimilarity "asks how diverse the congregations within the faith tradition are compared to the racial diversity of the entire faith tradition. . . . Its value *is the percentage of one racial group or the other that would have to switch congregations to end segregation.* Thus, if Hinduism had a dissimilarity score of .35, it would mean that 35 percent of racial group A (or 35 percent of racial group B) would have to strategically switch temples to end segregation" (emphasis in original). See Emerson and Woo, *People of the Dream*, 40.

8 Ibid., 40–41; emphasis in original. Here, Emerson and Woo's designation of "Conservative Protestantism" is roughly equivalent to my designation of "Evangelical."

9 Ibid., 41.

10 Ibid., 46.

11 Recent scholarship has highlighted the consistent and coercive methods used to keep people of color at an economic and political disadvantage while enforcing

residential racial segregation. See, for example, Loewen, *Sundown Towns*; Connolly, *A World More Concrete*; Desmond, *Evicted*; Duneier, *Ghetto*; and Sokol, *All Eyes Are upon Us*.

12 Today, American K–12 public schools are incredibly segregated by race and economic class, at least in part because government and community efforts to desegregate them have stalled. Poverty further complicates efforts to desegregate schools by race. Nevertheless, historic government and community efforts demonstrated that school segregation could be significantly ameliorated over time. See Strauss, "Report"; Layton, "Majority"; Boschma and Brownstein, "Concentration of Poverty"; and Childress, "Return to School Segregation?"

13 Haynes, *The Last Segregated Hour*.

14 Ibid., 4–5.

15 Ibid.

16 Ibid., 4–5, 244–245. Ironically, Independent Presbyterian Church (IPC) in Memphis, TN, eventually became part of the Presbyterian Church in America (PCA), a denomination that would repent in 2016 of its racism during the Civil Rights era.

17 Niebuhr, *The Social Sources of Denominationalism*, 3.

18 Ibid., 6.

19 Ibid., 9.

20 Michael Emerson, quoted in Dart, "Hues in the Pews," 6.

21 Ibid. Emerson's description of "historic Protestant churches" is roughly equivalent to my definition of Mainline Denominations.

22 Niebuhr, *The Social Sources of Denominationalism*, 236.

23 Dart, "Hues in the Pews," 6.

24 Ibid.

25 Smietana, "Sunday Morning Segregation."

26 Blake, "Why Many Americans Prefer Their Sundays Segregated."

27 Ibid.

28 Meckler, "How Churches Are Slowly Becoming Less Segregated."

29 Ibid.

30 Dougherty, Martí, and Martinez, "Congregational Diversity."

31 Christerson, Edwards, and Emerson, *Against All Odds*, 168.

32 Ibid., 152.

33 Ibid., 172.

34 Ibid., 175.

35 The popular press sometimes takes note of such demographic changes in predominantly black churches. See, for example, Freedman, "A Shift in Demographics." Nevertheless, in-depth scholarship examining the reactions of black congregants to an influx of whites is desperately needed. Anecdotal evidence from my years of sending white undergraduate and graduate students from Wake Forest University, the University of Virginia, and Duke University to visit predominantly black congregations suggests that whites are always greeted warmly and graciously.

36 In contrast, and speaking from my own experience as a black woman, I have often been the recipient of a cold shoulder at predominantly white congregations I have visited.

37 Irons, *Origins*; Slade, *Open Friendship*; Haynes, *The Last Segregated Hour*; Dupont, *Mississippi Praying*.

38 Schama, *Rough Crossings*, 97.

39 Ibid., 97.

40 Emanuel AME is an historic member of the African Methodist Episcopal denomination. See, for example, the church's own description of its history at its website. Just as Bethel AME in Philadelphia is referred to as "Mother Bethel," Emanuel is also often referred to affectionately as "Mother Emanuel" in recognition of its historic significance as a founding congregation of the AME denomination.

It is also noteworthy that, although Bethel left the Methodist Episcopal denomination, it kept that name—African Methodist Episcopal—as part of the name of the new denomination as an acknowledgment of the two denominations' shared origins and polity. It was not the way that Methodist Episcopal churches worshiped that was being critiqued here but the way that the denomination treated its black members.

41 Nash, *Forging Freedom*.

42 "In 1860, shortly after Emancipation, the total black population of the United States was 4.4 million. Of these, 4.2 million were in the South, while a mere 200,000 were in the North." See Ira Berlin, *Slaves without Masters* (New York: Oxford University Press, 1974), 46–47, as cited in Sawyer, "Sources," 61–62.

43 Murray, *Methodists*, 19.

44 Phillips, *History*.

45 Bailey, "The Post–Civil War Racial Separations," 453.

46 Davis, *The Methodist Unification*.

47 Bartleman, *Azusa Street*.

48 Charles Fox Parham was a segregationist who ascribed to a racist and heretical theology, "Anglo-Israelite Theory," which taught that white Anglo-Saxon Protestants were the descendants of the ten missing tribes of Israel and therefore destined to rule the world. Parham denounced the Azusa Revival's integrated nature, and in November 1906, he "attempted to take over the mission." Later, he established "a small, competing congregation just blocks from the mission." See Robeck, *Azusa Street Mission*, 40–41, 127. See also MacRobert, *Black Roots and White Racism*.

49 Clara Lum, a white woman, absconded with the *Apostolic Faith*, the newspaper of the Azusa Revival, removing it from William J. Seymour's control and giving it to another white woman, Florence Crawford, in Portland, OR. Robeck and others spectulate that Lum left Azusa and took the *Apostolic Faith* with her because she had fallen in love with William J. Seymour and was angry about his decision to marry a black woman, Jenny Evans Moore, rather than to marry her. See Robeck, *Azusa Street Mission*, 301–310.

50 "[Charles Fox] Parham may have been accused of homosexuality and [Ambrose Jessup] Tomlinson of financial mismanagement and megalomania, but [William J.] Seymour was less acceptable to most North American Pentecostal historians than either of them. They were white, he was black." See MacRobert, "Black Roots of Pentecostalism," 189.

51 Anthony Bradley, "Context"; Scherr, "Church Denomination Roots out Racism"; Grant, "What Catalyst Started the Presbyterian Church?"

52 Taylor, "Actions," 5.

53 Ibid. Also see Banks, "Presbyterian Church in America Repents."

54 Taylor, "Actions," 2.

55 Tisby, "Reflections." I should note that the use of the term "reparations" is my reading of the potential benefits of the fund, if developed and deployed successfully. Tisby does not use the word "reparations" to describe the Unity Fund.

56 Among those books that highlighted the racism present at the PCA's founding are Slade, *Open Friendship*; Alvis, *Religion and Race*; Haynes, *The Last Segregated Hour*; Dupont, *Mississippi Praying*; and Lucas, *For a Continuing Church*.

57 Bradley, "Context."

58 Ibid.

59 Carter, *Race*, 3.

60 Jennings, *The Christian Imagination*.

61 Cone, *The Cross and the Lynching Tree*, 131–132.

62 See Obasogie, "Race and Science," for a fuller discussion of such theories.

63 Noll, *The Civil War*.

64 Niebuhr, *The Social Sources of Denominationalism*, 11.

65 Ibid., 3.

66 King, "Letter from Birmingham City Jail (1963)."

67 Gilkes, "Still the 'Most Segregated Hour,'" 419.

68 Ibid., 420.

69 Cobb, Perry, and Dougherty, "United by Faith?"

70 *Phys.Org*, "Racial Attitudes of Blacks." Many hope that multiracial churches might be the answer to church racial segregation, but this study argues that such churches are not sites of the free exchange of ideas and norms between blacks and whites. Racial integration cannot be simply getting people of different races into the same sanctuary or denomination; it must also require actual, regular, positive, multidirectional interactions between people of different races. That the exchanges in multiracial congregations result in blacks who share whites' perspectives suggests strongly that the exchanges there only go in one direction: toward the perspectives of whites and away from the perspectives of blacks.

71 Cobb, Perry, and Dougherty, "United by Faith?"

72 When I think about the ideas this text invokes, I imagine all sorts of polyphonic harmonies and complex rhythms floating over the crowd. Although the congregants are singing the same song, each racial/ethnic/national group is presumably singing it in its own way. I imagine dancing, laughing, and joy as people mix

and mingle with others, learning each other's culture, rhythms, and ways. It is a picture I find endlessly hopeful: a heavenly jam session.

73 Finke and Stark, *The Churching of America*, 246.

74 Rankin, "Southern Baptists Decline."

75 Passel and Cohn, "U.S. Population Projections"; Kasperkevic, "What the US Population Will Look Like."

76 "In the United States, Christians will decline from more than three-quarters of the population in 2010 to two-thirds in 2050, and Judaism will no longer be the largest non-Christian religion. Muslims will be more numerous in the U.S. than people who identify as Jewish on the basis of religion." See Hackett et al., "The Future of World Religions." See also Jones, *The End*.

77 Bradley, "Context."

78 Harvey, *Dear White Christians*.

79 As I write this essay, the nation is reeling from the officer-involved shootings of two black men, Alton Sterling, who was killed in Louisiana, and Philando Castile, who was killed in Minnesota. Graphic cell-phone videos of the men's deaths provoked peaceful protests but also may have incited some blacks to fire on police in separate incidents in Texas and Louisiana. They have also inspired all sorts of comments on the legacy of Barack Obama, the first African American president; the state of U.S. jurisprudence (where none of the officers involved in a string of shootings of black and brown men and women has been convicted of anything); and the fairly toxic political campaign of Donald Trump, who many consider a racist and misogynist.

The summer of 2016 is not a time to be hopeful about race relations in America. But then, I have been unable to be consistently hopeful about race relations in America since the shootings at Emanuel AME during the summer of 2015.

Some have blamed the Black Lives Matter movement for producing a climate in which police officers might be shot at, but I do not confuse the peaceful protests of Black Lives Matter activists with the violent actions of a few angry, lone-wolf snipers unrelated to the movement. I believe that, in order to make policing safer for black and brown suspects and for the police as well, we need to make the legal system work for those who are victims of officer-involved shootings, to provide consistent national guidelines for the police use of deadly force, and to make sure that the legal consequences for those whose actions fall outside of those guidelines are quickly and consistently applied. Perhaps most important to the future of policing in the United States, however, is this: we need to stop racially profiling black and brown suspects. Not all people of color are criminals. Police who fear black and brown suspects disproportionately (because of racist preconceptions about black and brown people) are more likely to make fatal errors when dealing with them.

Finally, we must disentangle policies aimed at controlling people of color from modern policing methods. See Childress, "Michelle Alexander"; and, on race and policing, Naomi Murakawa, "Weaponized Empathy: Emotion and the Limits of Racial Reconciliation in Policing," in this volume.

Commentators like Stacey Patton see white supremacy at the core of the social unrest. She has critiqued American politics with a methodology similar to Jennifer Harvey's critique of American churches. See Patton, "We Don't Need Lincoln-Inspired Racial 'Unity.'"

80 Hannah-Jones, "Choosing a School."

81 Not surprisingly, medical researchers have begun to link such experiences of racism to health deficits among African Americans. See Zeltner, "Racism and High Blood Pressure Research"; and Silverstein, "How Racism Is Bad for Our Bodies."

82 Steele, *Whistling Vivaldi*.

83 Here I am playing with two different meanings of the word "sanctuary": It is the physical space of a church where worship takes place (and is derived from the Latin word meaning "holy"), but it can also designate a space where one is physically and legally protected from persecution or harm (like political asylum). At their best, churches ought to represent "sanctuary" in both senses of the word: holy spaces and safe spaces.

84 Notice that Roof capitalizes "White" but leaves "black" in lower-case letters. His view of blacks as inferior to whites is made evident by that choice. See Robles, "Dylann Roof Photos."

85 Robles, "Dylann Roof Photos."

86 Ortiz and Bruton, "Charleston Church Shooting."

87 Black Lives Matter, "Ferguson, 1 Year Later."

88 Hanna and Ellis, "Confederate Flag's Half Century at South Carolina Capitol Ends."

89 Banks, "Southern Baptists."

90 Edwards, *The Elusive Dream*, 140.

91 2 Corinthians, chapter 5: "18 All this is from God, who reconciled us to himself through Christ, and has given us the ministry of reconciliation; 19 that is, in Christ God was reconciling the world to himself, not counting their trespasses against them, and entrusting the message of reconciliation to us. 20 So we are ambassadors for Christ, since God is making his appeal through us; we entreat you on behalf of Christ, be reconciled to God. 21 For our sake he made him to be sin who knew no sin, so that in him we might become the righteousness of God" (New Revised Standard Version).

92 Philippians, chapter 2: "5 Let the same mind be in you that was in Christ Jesus, 6 who, though he was in the form of God, did not regard equality with God as something to be exploited, 7 but emptied himself, taking the form of a slave, being born in human likeness. And being found in human form, 8 he humbled himself and became obedient to the point of death—even death on a cross" (New Revised Standard Version).

93 I have already expressed my deep concern that interracial interactions in churches often cost blacks more than they cost whites. I remain deeply concerned about

that differential cost and the potential loss of black churches as sanctuaries for black people if whites join them. I fear that whites will go to black churches in search of salvation from their racial sins—and seek that salvation from blacks—rather than from Jesus. Too much black blood has been shed in pursuit of racial justice already. I do not believe that black churches can save white America. But I do believe that if whites go to black churches, learn to repent and put off their whiteness, learn to take up their crosses, and learn to earnestly follow Jesus, they will find him in black churches as black people have been doing for generations.

BIBLIOGRAPHY

Alvis, Joel L., Jr. *Religion and Race: Southern Presbyterians, 1946–1983*. Tuscaloosa: University of Alabama Press, 1994.

Bailey, Kenneth K. "The Post–Civil War Racial Separations in Southern Protestantism: Another Look." *Church History* 46 (December 1977): 453–473.

Banks, Adelle M. "Presbyterian Church in America Repents of 'Racial Sins.'" *Religion News Service*, June 27, 2016. http://religionnews.com.

———. "Southern Baptists: 'Discontinue the Display of the Confederate Battle Flag.'" *Religion News Service*, June 14, 2016. http://religionnews.com.

Bartleman, Frank. *Azusa Street*. Plainfield, NJ: Logos International, 1980.

Black Lives Matter. "Ferguson, 1 Year Later: Why Protesters Were Right to Fight for Mike Brown Jr." [2015]. http://blacklivesmatter.com.

Blake, John. "Why Many Americans Prefer Their Sundays Segregated." *CNN*, August 4, 2008. www.cnn.com.

Boschma, Janie, and Ronald Brownstein. "The Concentration of Poverty in American Schools." *Atlantic*, February 29, 2016. www.theatlantic.com.

Bradley, Anthony. "Context for the PCA's Repenting of Racism." *World*, June 29 2016. https://world.wng.org.

Carter, J. Kameron. *Race: A Theological Account*. Oxford: Oxford University Press, 2008.

Childress, Sarah. "Michelle Alexander: 'A System of Racial and Social Control.'" *Frontline*, April 29, 2014. www.pbs.org.

———. "A Return to School Segregation in America?" *Frontline*, July 2, 2014. www.pbs.org.

Christerson, Brad, Korie L. Edwards, and Michael O. Emerson. *Against All Odds: The Struggle for Racial Integration in Religious Organizations*. New York and London: New York University Press, 2005.

Cobb, Ryon J., Samuel L. Perry, and Kevin D. Dougherty. "United by Faith? Race/Ethnicity, Congregational Diversity, and Explanations of Racial Inequality." *Sociology of Religion* 76, no. 2 (2015): 177–198.

Cone, James H. *The Cross and the Lynching Tree*. Maryknoll, NY: Orbis Books, 2011.

Connolly, N. D. B. *A World More Concrete: Real Estate and the Remaking of Jim Crow South Florida*. Chicago: University of Chicago Press, 2016.

Dart, John. "Hues in the Pews: Racially Mixed Churches an Elusive Goal." *Christian Century*, February 28, 2001, 6–8.

Davis, Morris L. *The Methodist Unification: Christianity and the Politics of Race in the Jim Crow Era*. New York and London: New York University Press, 2008.

Desmond, Matthew. *Evicted: Poverty and Profit in the American City*. New York: Crown Publishers, 2016.

Dougherty, Kevin D., Geraldo Martí, and Brandon C. Martinez. "Congregational Diversity and Attendance in a Mainline Protestant Denomination." *Journal for the Scientific Study of Religion* 54, no. 4 (2015): 668–683.

Duneier, Mitchell. *Ghetto: The Invention of a Place, the History of an Idea*. New York: Farrar, Straus & Giroux, 2016.

Dupont, Carolyn Renée. *Mississippi Praying: Southern White Evangelicals and the Civil Rights Movement, 1945–1975*. New York: New York University Press, 2015.

Edwards, Korie L. *The Elusive Dream: The Power of Race in Interracial Churches*. Oxford: Oxford University Press, 2008.

Emanuel African Methodist Episcopal Church. www.emanuelamechurch.org.

Emerson, Michael O., and Rodney M. Woo. *People of the Dream: Multiracial Congregations in the United States*. Princeton, NJ, and Oxford: Princeton University Press, 2006.

Finke, Roger, and Rodney Stark. *The Churching of America, 1776–2005: Winners and Losers in Our Religious Economy*. New Brunswick, NJ: Rutgers University Press, 2005.

Freedman, Samuel G. "A Shift in Demographics at a Church in Harlem." *New York Times*, December 12, 2014.

Gilkes, Cheryl Townsend. "Still the 'Most Segregated Hour': Religion, Race and the American Experience." In *The Sage Handbook of Race and Ethnic Studies*, edited by Patricia Hill Collins and John Solomos, 415–440. Los Angeles: Sage, 2010.

Grant, Tobin. "What Catalyst Started the Presbyterian Church in America? Racism." *Religion News Service*, June 30 2016. http://religionnews.com.

Hackett, Conrad, Phillip Connor, Marcin Stonawski, and Vegard Skirbekk, primary researchers. "The Future of World Religions: Populations Growth Projections, 2010–2050: Why Muslims Are Rising Fastest and the Unaffiliated Are Shrinking as a Share of the World's Population." Pew Research Center, April 2, 2015. www.pewforum.org.

Hanna, Jason, and Ralph Ellis. "Confederate Flag's Half Century at South Carolina Capitol Ends." *CNN*, July 10, 2015. www.cnn.com.

Hannah-Jones, Nikole. "Choosing a School for My Daughter in a Segregated City." *New York Times Magazine*, June 9, 2016.

Harvey, Jennifer. *Dear White Christians: For Those Still Longing for Racial Reconciliation*. Grand Rapids, MI: Eerdmans, 2014.

Haynes, Stephen R. *The Last Segregated Hour: The Memphis Kneel-ins and the Campaign for Southern Church Desegregation*. Oxford: Oxford University Press, 2012.

Irons, Charles F. *The Origins of Proslavery Christianity: White and Black Evangelicals in Colonial and Antebellum Virginia*. Chapel Hill: University of North Carolina Press, 2008.

Jennings, Willie James. *The Christian Imagination: Theology and the Origins of Race*. New Haven, CT, and London: Yale University Press, 2010.

Jones, Robert P. *The End of White Christian America*. New York: Simon & Schuster, 2016.

Kasperkevic, Jana. "What the US Population Will Look Like in 2040." *Business Insider*, March 22, 2012. www.businessinsider.com.

King, Martin Luther, Jr. "I Have a Dream (1963)." In *I Have A Dream: Writings and Speeches That Changed the World*, edited by James A. Washington, 101–106. New York: Harper San Francisco, 1992.

———. "Letter from Birmingham City Jail (1963)." In *A Testament of Hope: The Essential Writings and Speeches of Martin Luther King, Jr.*, edited by James M. Washington, 289–302 (San Francisco: HarperSanFrancisco, 1986).

———. "Remaining Awake through a Great Revolution." In *A Knock at Midnight: Inspiration from the Great Sermons of Reverend Martin Luther King, Jr.*, edited by Clayborne Carson and Peter Holloran, 201–224. New York: Warner Books, 1998.

Layton, Lyndsey. "Majority of U.S. Public School Students Are in Poverty." *Washington Post*, January 16, 2015. www.washingtonpost.com.

Loewen, James W. *Sundown Towns: A Hidden Dimension of American Racism*. New York: Touchstone, 2006.

Lucas, Sean Michael. *For a Continuing Church: The Roots of the Presbyterian Church in America*. Phillipsburg, NJ: P & R Publishing, 2015.

MacRobert, Iain. *The Black Roots and White Racism of Early Pentecostalism in the USA*. New York: St. Martin's Press, 1988.

———. "The Black Roots of Pentecostalism." In *Down by the Riverside: Readings in African American Religion*, edited by Larry G. Murphy, 189–199. New York and London: New York University Press, 2000.

Meckler, Laura. "How Churches Are Slowly Becoming Less Segregated." *Wall Street Journal*, October 13, 2014. www.wsj.com.

Murray, Peter C. *Methodists and the Crucible of Race: 1930–1975*. Columbia and London: University of Missouri Press, 2004.

Nash, Gary B. *Forging Freedom: The Formation of Philadelphia's Black Community, 1720–1840*. Cambridge, MA, and London: Harvard University Press, 1988.

Niebuhr, H. Richard. *The Social Sources of Denominationalism*. Gloucester, MA: Peter Smith, 1987.

Noll, Mark A. *The Civil War as a Theological Crisis*. Chapel Hill: University of North Carolina Press, 2006.

Obasogie, Osagie K. "Race and Science: Preconciliation as Reconciliation." In this volume.

Ortiz, Erik, and F. Brinley Bruton. "Charleston Church Shooting: Suspect Dylann Roof Captured in North Carolina." *NBC News*, June 18, 2015. www.nbcnews.com.

Passel, Jeffrey S., and D'Vera Cohn. "U.S. Population Projections: 2005–2050." Pew Research Center, February 11, 2008. www.pewhispanic.org.

Patton, Stacey. "We Don't Need Lincoln-Inspired Racial 'Unity.' We Need Whites to Stop Being Racist." *Washington Post*, July 15 2015. www.washingtonpost.com.

Phillips, C. H. *The History of the Colored Methodist Episcopal Church in America: Comprising Its Organization, Subsequent Development and Present Status.* Jackson, TN: Publishing House C.M.E. Church, 1925.

Phys.Org. "Racial Attitudes of Blacks in Multiracial Congregations Resemble Those of Whites." August 17, 2015. https://phys.org.

Rankin, Russ. "Southern Baptists Decline in Baptisms, Membership, Attendance." LifeWay, June 09, 2011. *LifeWay.* www.lifeway.com.

Robeck, Cecil M., Jr. *Azusa Street Mission and Revival: The Birth of the Global Pentecostal Movement.* Nashville, TN: Thomas Nelson, 2006.

Robles, Frances. "Dylann Roof Photos and a Manifesto Are Posted on Website." *New York Times*, June 20, 2015. www.nytimes.com.

Sawyer, Mary R. "Sources of Black Denominationalism." In *Down by the Riverside: Readings in African American Religion*, edited by Larry G. Murphy, 59–67. New York and London: New York University Press, 2000.

Schama, Simon. *Rough Crossings: The Slaves, the British, and the American Revolution.* New York: Harper, 2005.

Scherr, Sonia. "Church Denomination Roots out Racism." *Intelligence Report*, Southern Poverty Law Center, May 30, 2010. www.splcenter.org.

Silverstein, Jason. "How Racism Is Bad for Our Bodies." *Atlantic*, March 12, 2013. www.theatlantic.com.

Slade, Peter. *Open Friendship in a Closed Society: Mission Mississippi and a Theology of Friendship.* Oxford: Oxford University Press, 2009.

Smietana, Bob. "Sunday Morning Segregation: Worshipers Feel Their Church Has Enough Diversity." *Christianity Today*, January 15, 2015. www.christianitytoday.com.

Sokol, Jason. *All Eyes Are upon Us: Race and Politics from Boston to Brooklyn.* New York: Basic Books, 2014.

Steele, Claude M. *Whistling Vivaldi: How Stereotypes Affect Us and What We Can Do.* New York: Norton, 2011.

Strauss, Valerie. "Report: Public Schools More Segregated Now than 40 Years Ago." *Washington Post*, August 28, 2013. www.washingtonpost.com.

Taylor, L. Roy, stated clerk. "Actions of the Forty-Fourth General Assembly of the Presbyterian Church in America." General Assembly, Mobile, AL, June 20–23, 2016. Lawrenceville, GA: Presbyterian Church in America Administrative Committee, 2016. www.pcaac.org.

Tisby, Jemar. "Reflections from a Black Presbyterian on the PCA's Overture on Racial Reconciliation." *Reformed African American Network*, June 27, 2016. www.raanetwork.org.

Zeltner, Brie. "Racism and High Blood Pressure Research in Black Patients." *Plain Dealer*, August 13, 2013. www.cleveland.com.

6

The "Post-national" Racial State, Domestication, and Multiscalar Organizing in the New Millennium

KIRSTIE A. DORR

To date, projects of racial reconciliation that have gained popular currency within the United States have often been articulated via demands for national redress, whether it be through legislative action, economic compensation, or civic inclusion. From the civil rights movement of the 1950s and 1960s, to the implementation of affirmative action policies in the 1970s, to the immigrant rights movements of the 1990s, U.S. communities of color have made strides in gaining greater access to economic opportunity, institutions of higher education, and representation in state and federal agencies. At the same time, the legacies of these critical social movements—specifically, how they have most often been institutionalized and memorialized—present some unique political challenges for the future of anti-racist organizing. With an eye toward the unique conditions that define our political moment—dramatic shifts in the heteropatriarchal organization and function of the U.S. racial state, the expansion of transnational accords and mechanisms of governance, and the unprecedented dominance of neoliberal capitalism—this essay explores how the logics and strategies of past anti-racist knowledge production and struggle must be retooled in order to effectively address extant globalized geographic arrangements of raced and gendered violence, vulnerability, and exploitation. It tackles two of the salient questions animating the dialogue of this forum—Is racial reconciliation a realistic possibility in early twenty-first-century America? and, How would social conditions have to be reorganized to foster a society in which racial justice could be achieved?—by pointing to some of the potential pitfalls of positioning the nation-state as the ideal or exclusive scale at which social justice agendas can or should be imagined and actualized. Anchoring my discussion in a series of thematic case studies that link moments of antagonism or crisis within institutionalized sites of racial knowledge production to those within popular campaigns of anti-racist organizing, I point to the oft-uninterrogated ideological baggage of "nation" as an organizational rubric for social justice work—most particularly, what I refer to as its *domesticating* logics and architecture.

This essay situates its analysis of the imperial U.S. racial state, then, within a global context, prioritizing attention to how "fatal couplings of power and difference"[1] are *relationally* constituted and organized across geographic scales. In doing so, it advances the argument that while structural racism is always mediated by its emplacement in, and expression through, geo-historically distinct contexts and modalities, it is likewise an enduring global phenomenon that is shaped by the exigencies of transnational regimes of governance, militarism, empire, and transregional flows of culture and capital. With the advent of global economic restructuring and the emergence of new informational and transport technologies, the territorial organization of racial capitalism has shifted dramatically over the last several decades. Significantly, these shifts have included the establishment of new, internationally dispersed, yet densely interconnected landscapes of (re)production and consumption.[2] For example, the outsourcing of labor-intensive manufacturing jobs in the United States has been accompanied by the creation of free trade zones in Mexico, Bangladesh, and the Philippines;[3] the dramatic restructuring of the U.S. welfare system by the 1996 Personal Responsibility and Work Opportunity Reconciliation Act occurred alongside the implementation of International Monetary Fund or World Bank–mandated structural adjustment programs throughout the Americas; and the intensification of U.S.-led warfare in the Middle East has been accompanied by an expansion of domestic carceral geographies and increased collaboration between domestic state and federal policing and military forces. In short, post–Cold War strategies of global capitalist expansion have generated diffuse yet articulated geographies of raced and gendered economic exploitation, social abandonment, and civil immobility and containment. In turn, as globalization has naturalized an internationalist "labor strategy that stresses minimizing cost and maximizing flexibility,"[4] the role and function of nation-states in mediating relations of race, gender, and capital have likewise decidedly shifted. Paradoxically, in the face of these global racial capitalist imperatives, post-national state making frequently entails the summoning of an increasingly transnational, increasingly mobile labor force to entertain nation-based solutions to global contradictions, even as domestic citizenries around the world are experiencing the denationalization of resources, opportunities, and political franchise.[5]

Given this, my essay argues for the importance of fostering anti-racist thought and action attentive to ever-shifting relations of race, gender, economy and place. Rather than framing social justice agendas within fixed or given geographic milieus such as the city, region, or nation, it avers that the organization of social space must itself be the subject of political scrutiny lest struggles for inclusion or redress recapitulate or fortify the geo-political structures of dominance that they seek to reform or destablize. Attention to geographic arrangements of difference, I suggest, enables activists to tackle an enduring, divisive obstacle within social justice pursuits: the domestication of political agendas. Here and elsewhere, I deploy the term "domestication" to index an interconnected ensemble of discourses and practices that commonly undergird processes of U.S. imperial, racial, national, and capitalist formation.

Defined by the *Oxford English Dictionary* as "the action of domesticating" or "the condition of being domesticated," the term stems from the verb "to domesticate," which alternatively denotes "to settle," "to naturalize," or "to attach to home and its duties." As such, domestication proffers a conceptual tool for both foregrounding and interrogating the geo-political entanglements of imperial expansion and colonial settlement; sites and structures of privatization, property, and the domestic; and finally, contested relations of race, gender, sexuality, and labor. Thus, building on women of color and other feminist critiques of "domesticity" and "the domestic" and their embeddedness in projects of racial capitalist nation- and empire-building, my use of the term connotes three interconnected critiques.

First, domestication signals the commonsense geo-political worldview that collective interests and capacities are most efficiently and effectively aggregated and managed under the rubric of the nation-state. While critiques of and contests over state power and violence are both urgent and imperative, anti-racist campaigns for inclusion or recompense are all too often leveraged via nationalist rhetorics and demands that unwittingly naturalize raced and gendered modes of social differentiation, such as distinctions between the foreign and the domestic, the citizen-subject and the undocumented migrant, or the dutiful patriot and the irrational terrorist. Second, domestication references a mode of organizing knowledge production in which political rhetorics of national reform, progress, and inclusion rely upon heteropatriarchal notions of domesticity and the domestic sphere. If the U.S. imperial nation was built on the imagination of a domestic territory to be protected and maintained, then that idealization of the homeland found its necessary analogue in the heteronormative home, where naturalized divisions between public and private and national projects of racial belonging conjoined.[6] At the same time, the U.S. racial capitalist state has long relied upon the home and the heteropatriarchal family as the base unit of racial capitalism.[7] Within racial capitalist logics, domesticity both naturalizes and conceals capital's raced and gendered divisions of labor, modes of exploitation, and systems of expropriation. Third, domestication references the tendency within U.S. popular and academic circles to discuss race relations in a manner that collapses race and ethnicity, that presumes the universality of U.S. racial categories, and that impose U.S.-based racial matrices to external contexts. As I demonstrate below, this domestication of global race relations recapitulates the Eurocentric racial-regional designs of area studies while internationalizing the racial-national architecture of the United States as both universal and exceptional. In doing so, domestication disavows the complexities, contradictions, and dynamism of racial formation and the transgeographic axes of power and difference that subtend relational contexts of racial capitalist expansion.

In sum, I argue that each of these entangled modes of domestication work to reinforce rather than interrogate the raced and gendered logics and spatial organization of capitalist expansion. In doing so, the domestication of anti-racist knowledge production and social movements often impedes our ability to effectively forge cross-community coalitions and transnational alliances rooted in intersectional social justice agendas. In what follows, I contend that in order to understand and confront racial antagonisms in this ostensibly post-racial, post-national era, (1) the internationalist impulses of 1960s–1970s activisms must be reinvigorated, (2) interracial and interethnic conflicts must be addressed, and

(3) anti-racist agendas must attend to the ways in which racial violence is always gendered, sexualized, and classed. To do so, I conclude, anti-racist thought and action must meaningfully address how, in today's world, relations of difference are geographically situated but are nonetheless relatively and relationally organized across urban, regional, and national boundaries.

Theoretical Frames

I enter into this critical conversation as a scholar whose intellectual training and professional appointments have straddled the fields of ethnic and gender studies. My essay thus approaches this volume's questions concerning the persistence of racial antagonism and pathways toward racial justice via the political genealogies and academic canons that have constituted these fields, as well as the debates that continue to animate them. I want to begin, then, with a brief overview of the key premises that formulate the analytical scaffolding of this essay, which draw upon and integrate the traditions of critical race studies, women and queer of color feminisms, post-colonial studies, and political geography. I understand these premises as a crucial point of departure for exploring questions of racial justice in the new millennium.

The first of these premises builds upon Michael Omi and Howard Winant's invaluable theory of racial formation.[8] Defined as the "the sociohistorical process by which racial categories are created, inhabited, transformed, and destroyed,"[9] racial formation proffers a useful framework for theorizing how racial hegemony is produced through the dynamic synthesis of commonsense racial discourse and white-supremacist social structures. At the same time, relations of empire and global capital inflect processes of racial formation such that racial categories are often constructed and solidified through social interrelations that by design exceed or transgress the boundaries of modern nation-states. As such, *analyses of contemporary racial politics in the United States must contend with how processes of racial formation in a particular site or landscape are structured relationally across geographic scales such as the city, region, or nation.*

The second premise involves theorizing race as one of multiple, co-constitutive modalities through which difference is lived. As feminist and queer of color scholars have exhaustively demonstrated, racial difference is most often articulated through vocabularies of gender aberrance and sexual pathology, while racial differentiation occurs in and through gendered, sexualized, and classed institutions and structures.[10] Thus, *the theorization of racial discourse and practice is enriched by intersectional approaches that highlight how gender, sexuality, nation, and economy inflect discourses and practices of racial differentiation.*

Third, given that social discourse and structures are mutually animating, *analysis of racial inequality must examine how institutional forms of racism are shaped by relations of representation in popular culture, the media, and academic inquiry, and vice versa.* Here, an expanded application of Omi and Winant's notion of "racial projects"—which are always simultaneously gender and sexual projects[11]—is useful for tracking how constructed perceptions of difference are explained and naturalized. At the same time, given how relations of culture, capital, and technology have shifted over the past several decades, racial projects must be examined as at once *geo-historically specific*—that is, emplaced in particular local, regional, and/or (inter)national contexts—as well as *geo-historically relational*—that is, as situated within and articulated with other geographies of racial capitalist formation and cultural circulation.

Taken together, these premises aim to grapple with the ways in which contemporary relations of difference are produced in and through the dynamic interaction of social and spatial formation. As I argue throughout, in our current moment, relations of space and place figure as both expressions of, and at times, as resolutions to, global racial capitalist contradictions. As the case studies that follow demonstrate, structural antagonisms are often intentionally organized across geo-political boundaries so as to foment inter-group competition and to deter inter-group solidarity and coalition. Given this, the next section pairs an examination of moments of tension or crisis within institutionalized sites of anti-racist knowledge production with corollary popular campaigns of anti-racist organizing. My aim is to tease out the ways in which the uncritical adoption of the nation-state as an ideal, default, or exclusive scale of social action risks undermining social justice agendas by subjecting them to the domesticating logics of statist nationalisms and the domestic architecture of nation.

Ethnic Studies Now! The Birth of a Field

Though rarely remembered as such, the creation of ethnic studies as an academic field of instruction and inquiry, inaugurated in the fall of 1969, was the product of coalitional struggle and cross-constituency solidarities that localized in a university setting one front of what was imagined to be a global struggle against racism and colonialism. Drawing momentum from the U.S. civil rights and anti-war mobilizations and decolonization movements around the world,[12] university students, staff, and faculty at San Francisco State College joined forces with activists, artists, and other community members[13] in the fall of 1968 to demand what they defined as the meaningful inclusion of "Third World peoples"[14] in California's state system of higher education. At that time the college's administration and student body was, like at most other colleges and universities nationwide, almost exclusively white and predominantly male.[15] The ensuing San Francisco State College Strike—the longest university student strike in U.S. history—was fomented by a coalition between the college's Black Student Union (BSU) and the Third World Liberation Front (TWLF)—an umbrella alliance among members of the Latin American Students Organization, Asian American Political Alliance, Pilipino American Collegiate Endeavor, and Native American Students Union. With the backing of a broad base of college and community members—many of whom were active in the Black Panther Party, the United Farm Workers Association, and the anti-war movement, the BSU and TWLF issued a list of fifteen demands for institutional changes that even today, on many academic campuses, remain unrealized, if not unimaginable. These included the establishment of a divisional "School of Ethnic Studies," the allocation of fifty full-time faculty lines, and that "all applications of non-white students be accepted" in the college's incoming spring and fall of 1969 classes.[16] In January of that same year, inspired by the militant action of San Francisco State activists, a separate Third World Liberation Front was formed on the University of California, Berkeley (UC Berkeley), campus, which allied members of its Mexican American Student Confederation, Asian American Political Alliance, African American Student Union, and the Native American group. There, the TWLF-led strike was met with militarized state resistance, as then-governor Ronald Reagan ordered five police departments, the California Highway Patrol, Alameda County Deputies, and finally, the California National Guard to occupy the campus. As the late Berkeley professor Ron Takaki recalled, "People thought the curtains were coming down. There were helicopters buzzing overhead, spreading tear gas; the campus was an armed camp. The student strike made it possible to extract from the university a commitment in the form of an Academic Senate resolution to build toward a College of Third World Studies, to include our three programs and Afro-American Studies."[17] In both cases, these strikes were successful at irrevocably reshaping the landscape of U.S. universities; in March 1969, the first College of Ethnic Studies was founded at San Francisco State, and the first Department of Ethnic Studies was established at UC Berkeley.

I open with this brief history because I believe that, as U.S. scholars committed to feminist, anti-racist, and anti-colonial struggle, we are at a political crossroads that occasions its retelling. Recalling the formation and subsequent formalization of the field of ethnic studies, which has arguably served as an institutional nexus for knowledge production by and about communities of color on many college and university campuses over the last half-century, is germane to contemporary conversations on racial justice and racial reconciliation for several reasons. On the one hand, we can turn to recent contexts in which ethnic studies curricula have come under siege as a barometer for measuring mounting racial antagonisms as they are localized in particular regional geographies across the nation. Arizona governor Jan Brewer's 2010 endorsement of the widely popular HB 2281, for example, evidences how current neoconservative attacks on the field have appropriated the rhetoric of post-racialism to reinvigorate what literary and cultural critics such as Lisa Lowe, Mary Louise Pratt, and Jodi Melamed have referred to as "the Culture Wars" of the 1990s.[18] Significantly, such campaigns for "[national] cultural unification" and the "recanonization of Western classics"[19] patently illustrate the extent to which, for a significant economic and geographic cross-section of white America, the histories and intellectual contributions of racialized communities within the United States continue to be viewed as external and/or antithetical to the cultural ethos of the national popular. Moreover, as Chris Newfield has astutely observed, these culture wars provided an ideological foundation for subsequent efforts to defund public universities.[20]

On the other hand, tracing the institutional history of ethnic studies as an interdisciplinary site of inquiry is equally productive: it occasions reflection on how a field produced in the crucible of grassroots struggle has been (re)shaped by subsequent political debates and administrative challenges as well as shifting political conditions and contexts. This story is relevant to all of us engaged in academic anti-racist knowledge production, as ethnic studies departments and programs shoulder a disproportionate load of the "diversity" work on our college and university campuses: demographic work, in terms of faculty and student of color representation, recruitment, and retention; instructional work, in terms of curricular offerings that meet "diversity course" requirements; and intellectual work, in terms of providing a center of gravity for anti-racist thought. Of course, ethnic studies formations are in no way monolithic, stable, or consonant. At present, there are more than seven hundred ethnic-specific programs and departments in U.S. colleges and universities, each with its own organizational history, curricular contours, intellectual mission, and so forth.[21] And it is arguably the elasticity of the ethnic studies project—that is, its ability to float amid the tides of intervention and adapt to the winds of reorientation—that conditions its institutional precarity yet bulwarks its radical potential. Nonetheless, I believe it is both possible and useful to focus on some of the "growing pains" that ethnic studies collectivities and practitioners have commonly confronted over the last four-and-a-half decades because these confrontations are often reflective of larger trends within social justice organizing outside academe—particularly, in battles waged against structural racism within public organizations and other social institutions. It is to this history that I now turn.

* * *

In his seminal 1969 essay "Internal Colonialism and Ghetto Revolt," sociologist Robert Blauner wrote, "It is becoming almost fashionable to analyze American racial conflict today in terms of the colonial analogy."[22] Blauner goes on to historicize the ways in which the concepts of "internal" or "domestic" colonialism had first become popular among U.S.-based Black militants,[23] later expanding in usage among other U.S. communities of color. Inspired by the writings of anti-colonial activists such as Patrice Lumumba, Mahatma Gandhi, and Frantz Fanon, identification with the struggles of African, Asian, Caribbean, and other colonized peoples became increasingly important for U.S. activists who viewed their political work as part of an inherently—and thus necessarily—internationalist struggle against racial oppression. Indeed, this conceptualization of white supremacy as a global problem inexorably tied to inter-relational, inter-continental histories of (settler) colonialism, chattel slavery, xenophobia, and capitalist expansion informed the internationalist and coalitional impulses of various social movements that took root in throughout the United States during the mid-century.[24] This was certainly a common political ethos of the aggrieved community struggles throughout 1960s California, where Blauner had completed his doctoral work and initiated his academic career. For example, the Delano grape strike of 1965 led to the merging of the predominantly Filipino Agricultural Workers Organizing Committee and the Mexican-American National Farmworkers Association, forming the United Farm Workers of America in August 1966.[25] A protest organized at the San Francisco Bay island of Alcatraz by Sioux demonstrators in March 1964 set the stage for the nineteen-month pan-Native occupation initiated in 1969, which brought international attention to the ongoing U.S. state violation of international treaties and centuries of struggle for Native sovereignty.[26] The Black Panther Party was formed in Oakland, California, in 1966, deploying armed citizen patrols to monitor and contest racial profiling and police brutality. By the late 1960s, the group expanded its mission to political education and community-based social programs and sent delegates around the world to connect with other socialist and anti-imperialist leaders. These "radical anti-racisms"[27] indelibly shaped the coalitional imaginary that united campus populations at San Francisco State and UC Berkeley, who framed their demands for the creation of ethnic studies around the need to establish an interdisciplinary field of inquiry that foregrounded the histories of "Third World" peoples. This vision of ethnic studies was both analytically and geographically capacious, as it emerged from grassroots labors that emphasized cross-community coalition, internationalist solidarity, and the university campus as one of numerous fronts within a necessarily protean anti-racist, anti-colonial struggle.

The institutionalization of ethnic studies as an academic field, indexed by the creation of programs at Berkeley and San Francisco and the formation of its first professional association in 1972,[28] dovetailed with the advent of what we now call "globalization" and the global victory of U.S.-led neoliberal racial capitalism. Yet, paradoxically, in the decades that followed the formalization of the field, the transnational impulses that informed its creation gave way to an increasingly domestic scholarly and curricular focus. The reasons for this domestic turn are many. On several campuses, fledgling ethnic studies programs were pressured by administrators to distinguish themselves from the well-established area studies programs that were former hubs of academic knowledge production about racialized migrant and non-western communities. As Evelyn Hu-DeHart has noted, "area studies programs arose out of American imperialism in the Third World" and were designed to "train specialists to uphold U.S. hegemony in regions in which the U.S. had heavy economic and political investments."[29] Defined by an ethos of Cold War militarism and anti-communist conservatism, mid-century area studies programs benefited from access to state department funding and grants from external agencies vested to protect U.S. corporate interests. Although these interdisciplinary programs became more critical in the wake of the anti-war movement of the 1960s, their center of gravity remained entrenched in traditional disciplines, and their leadership, predominantly white and/or male.[30] Thus, in order to differentiate themselves from these well-established, well-funded programs that largely strengthened rather than contested existing university structures, ethnic studies programs such as those at San Francisco State and UC Berkeley delimited their intellectual focus to the U.S.-based histories of communities of color and indigenous nations in North America. While addressing a significant gap within extant liberal arts curricula, this geo-political bifurcation of area and ethnic studies following the latter's institutionalization significantly eroded the internationalist impulses that defined the field's inception while undermining the sovereignty of the indigenous nations that punctuate hegemonic, settler colonial mappings of U.S. territoriality. Moreover, this reorientation of the field's geo-political purview reconfigured the racial/ethnic subject of knowledge production, fracturing its historical, cultural, and kinship ties with those peoples and places that exceeded the bounds of the U.S. nation-state.

Ethnic Studies in Crisis: Domestication and Minoritization

Nearing the thirty-year anniversary of the creation of the Department of Ethnic Studies at UC Berkeley, Chair Ling-chi Wang expressed his support for a controversial proposal: the subsuming of Ethnic Studies within the university's American Studies Program. The plan recommended the creation of an American Studies Department with five concentrations— African American, Chicano, Asian American, and Native American and Comparative Ethnic Studies—along with the existing group major in American Studies. Conceding that this move was in part designed to stabilize the ailing department, which had suffered a significant decline in majors since its peak in the early 1990s, Wang was hopeful that the merger offered an opportunity "to redefine not just American Studies, but what it means to be American."[31] Indeed, throughout the 1990s, competing conceptions of citizenship and national belonging dominated both state and federal debates. Following the introduction and passage of a series of conservative initiatives between 1994 and 1996, California in particular established itself as an electoral testing ground for the adoption of anti-immigrant and anti–affirmative action legislation. Following the passage of Proposition 209, which prohibited state governmental institutions from considering race, gender, or ethnicity in decisions related to public employment, contracting, or education, ethnic studies programming came under statewide public scrutiny. African American University of California regent Ward Connerly, a vocal proponent of the deceptively titled "California Civil Rights Initiative," called for the review of ethnic studies programs systemwide, dubbing them bastions of "self-imposed isolation for students of color."[32]

This legislative backlash was no doubt a significant contributing factor to the mid-1990s crisis in ethnic studies; as then ethnic studies Ph.D. candidate Caroline Streeter observed, "We've suffered a lot of political losses, with the passage of Prop. 209 and the declining number of black and Latino students [at UC Berkeley]."[33] Nonetheless, the domesticating logics of what Melamed has dubbed "official anti-racisms" likewise undermined the role and function of the department within the larger university.[34] In 1989, following widespread protests among students and faculty of color across the campus, Berkeley adopted the "American cultures" requirement for all undergraduates, which were courses that compared the "American experience" of at least two ethnic groups in the United States. However, unlike other campuses with similar requisites, which were introduced to expose students to the histories of communities of color in the United States, Berkeley allowed all departments on campus to offer "American cultures" courses and for these to focus exclusively on European immigrant groups. For those who had imagined that the requirement would serve to educate students across campus about histories of racial formation in the United States, the unanticipated material and symbolic effects of its incorporation were particularly devastating. While American Studies was only a program sustained by faculty affiliates, enrollment increased dramatically, as the program served as a hub of cross-listed courses in conventional disciplines that met the newly instituted requirement. Meanwhile, the campus's historic ethnic studies major suffered a significant decline. Wang explained that this was in large part owing to financial pressures to offer a greater number of lower-division courses that fulfilled the American cultures requirement, which led to fewer upper-division offerings, and thus, fewer ethnic studies majors. Moreover, the introduction of the American cultures requirement had the symbolic effect of equating course offerings focused on the study of race and ethnicity with "service learning" or "diversity training," rather than as being representative of themes of academic inquiry.

Given these challenges, the proposal to consolidate ethnic studies under the institutional banner of American studies may seem pragmatically sound, if not ideal. Indeed, American studies programs and departments across the East Coast have served as the long-standing institutional home for ethnic studies research and teaching. And Wang's rhetorical insistence that subsuming ethnic studies under the umbrella of American studies could potentially serve to rearticulate Americanness in a way that questions its long-standing equation with a transparent white masculine citizenry is certainly compelling. Yet, when considered within the longer history of the struggle for ethnic studies—that within three short decades, the grassroots organizing, creative coalitions, and astute analysis of the 1969 Third World Liberation Front could be reduced to a set of discrete subfields to be incorporated into an American studies department—this begs for deeper interrogation. A reading of this crisis and its proposed resolution is instructive for examining the logics and implications of domestication at work.

The notion that a freestanding department with eighteen full-time faculty and a twenty-nine-year institutional history should be absorbed into a much younger program dependent upon affiliate faculty and cross-listed courses, rather than vice versa, is, structurally speaking, somewhat perplexing. Yet read through the commonsense logic of domestication, this maneuver appears both rational and desirable. First, the notion that ethnic studies is a subfield of American studies, available for incorporation when expedient, privileges assimilation into extant structures of national belonging over their reconfiguration and, in doing so, both echoes and extends the long-standing idealization of "American" citizenship as normatively white and masculine. Next, it recasts racial-ethnic communities in the United States as domestic "minorities" rather than global majorities, thus distinguishing them from the purported default national population constituted by a normative white "majority." It bears mention that this move occurred at a moment when the bulk of UC Berkeley's student population was of color and conservative ideologues deemed California's eminent classification as the nation's first "majority minority" state a moral and political crisis. Third, in distinguishing between domestic "minorities" and external racialized populations, this move compels and naturalizes allegiance to the U.S. nation-state over solidarity with inter- and transnational anti-racist and anti-neocolonial struggles. And finally, this national domestication and nativist minoritization of racial-ethnic groups undermines Native sovereignty struggles by recasting Native nations as domestic(ated) populations within the United States rather than independent states that punctuate its geo-political boundaries.[35]

The institutional domestication of ethnic studies—and, by extension, of racial-ethnic knowledge production—has both shaped and been shaped by the geo-political contours of contemporary popular organizing platforms. Take, for example, the "Change the Mascot" campaign initiated by Oneida Indian Nation. This robust, multi-media movement is described on its website as demanding an "end the use of the racial slur 'r*dskins' as the mascot and name of the NFL team in Washington, D.C."[36] Spearheaded by Oneida Indian Nation leader and multimillionaire CEO Ray Halbritter, "Change the Mascot" has released radio ads, polls, academic studies, media interviews, YouTube videos, and social media drives to foment a multi-pronged attack on the use of the disparaging name and images associated with the District of Colombia–based NFL team. "No group deserves to be treated as a target of racial epithets," urged Halbritter in a recent radio ad. "We deserve to be treated as what we are: Americans." While a continuation of the anti-mascot struggles that have been active throughout North America since the 1960s, "Change the Mascot," as noted by Professor Bruce E. Johansen of the Native American Studies Program at the University of Nebraska at Omaha, differs from its predecessors in one significant way: "Money. When you have Halbritter's wealth, it buys media access. It buys attention."[37]

Indeed, "Change the Mascot" has been incredibly successful. Renowned sports journalists such as Bob Costas have agreed to discontinue the use of the established name of the NFL team, as have numerous television and print media outlets; civil rights groups and professional athletes across the nation have professed their solidarity with the campaign; fifty U.S. senators signed a letter to the NFL commissioner calling for his attention to the issue; and six of the team's registered trademarks were revoked by the Patent and Trademark Office, which conceded that these were indeed "disparaging."[38] Most recently, the Oneida Nation has initiated dialogue with U.S. government officials regarding a proposed ban on the sale of NFL R*dskin merchandise on military bases and other public land. And Halbritter and his cohort have approached Target, Walmart, and Amazon with a similar proposal following the corporations' collective agreement to discontinue the sale of the Confederate flag in the wake of the mass shooting at Emanuel African Methodist Episcopal Church in Charleston, South Carolina, in June 2015.

The anti-mascot movement has accomplished a critical step in reshaping how relations of racial representation are understood and organized in popular cultural spheres. "Change the Mascot" has brought wide-scale attention to connections between the material and the symbolic by educating the national public about the lived effects of racist stereotypes for Native peoples in general and Native youth in particular. As decades of research has shown, Indian mascots reinforce the myth of "the disappeared noble savage," promote historical inaccuracies, invite non-Native people to participate in settler colonial rituals of "playing Indian," sanction the use of disparaging language and images, undermine the ability of American Indian Nations to portray accurate images of themselves and their culture, create a general climate of racial hostility, and foment conflict among aggrieved communities.[39] Indeed, the wholesale retirement of Indian mascots is long overdue, and "Change the Mascot" has made significant contributions to this important struggle. At the same time, however, Halbritter's strategies and methods of change raise some vexing questions for the future of anti-racist, anti-colonial organizing: Can racism be defeated by the power and allure of cold, hard cash? Should U.S. social justice agendas prioritize the brokering of business deals over grassroots organizing and action? If transnational corporations such as Walmart and Target retire enduring symbols of white supremacy such as the Confederate flag or Indian mascots, will broader structural changes automatically follow? If so, where, for whom, and to what end?

I want to frame these questions within the broader context of globalized racial capitalism, shifting our focus from the consumption of Indian mascot merchandise in the United States to international landscapes of free trade manufacture where such items are typically produced. 47 Brand, a prominent U.S. sportswear franchise, has a significant manufacturing base in the outskirts of Lima, Peru. There, indigenous migrants are paid less than a dollar per twelve-hour workday to assemble, sew, and finish hats, T-shirts, and tracksuits depicting Indian "mascots" for teams such as the Florida State Seminoles, the Washington R*dskins, and the Cleveland Indians. Indigenous peoples make up nearly 50 percent of Peru's national population and are among the very poorest peoples in the hemisphere. Over the last three-and-a-half decades, the U.S.-led "War on Drugs," the introduction of structural adjustment programs, Cold War interventionism, market liberalization and foreign investment, and forced sterilization campaigns funded by the Reagan and Bush administrations have all contributed to the mass displacement and dispossession of indigenous Andeans. Most have migrated to the capital city of Lima, where they live in expansive *pueblos jovenes* (shantytowns) without access to basic necessities such as electricity, running water, roads, schools, and health care. A hyper-exploitable surplus labor pool, these indigenous migrants—particularly young women and girls—constitute the bulk of Peru's garment industry workforce. Returning to the "Change the Mascot" movement, what does it mean that indigenous women in the global south have, by social necessity, been conscripted to reproduce racist symbols that arguably disparage indigenous peoples throughout the Americas? In a recent address at Carlisle College, Halbritter applauded the "critical mass of Americans will no longer tolerate, patronize and cheer on *commodified bigotry*."[40] Yet his campaign has failed to interrogate the relationship *between* commodification and bigotry. If 47 brand were to discontinue the production of R*dskin and other mascot paraphernalia, would this significantly alter the conditions of precarity and vulnerability that both impel and maintain the raced and gendered international division of labor?

Returning to my critique of the domestication of anti-racist knowledge production and social justice agendas, I want to emphasize the ways in which struggles for racial equality that appeal to U.S. state mediation and popular support may unwittingly forestall the possibility of drawing deeper connections regarding how relations of power and difference are geographically organized, as well as opportunities to forge transnational solidarities that confront racial capitalist contradictions on a global scale. My aim is neither to critique nor condemn the Oneida Nation's "Change the Mascot" campaign, which is one that I wholly support. That to date the movement has focused its organizational efforts and energies on the English-speaking audiences of the northern portion of the continent makes absolute strategic sense, given the logistical challenges to organizing across regional, cultural, and linguistic divides. At the same time, I am interested in thinking through how geographically circumscribed struggles such as these can eventually be extended beyond the boundaries of the imperial U.S. racial state. Economic success among Oneida Nation members such as Halbritter has enabled the unprecedented popularization of a crucial anti-racist, anti-colonial struggle. However, as numerous scholars and activists have argued, shifts in relations of representation do not guarantee a material redistribution of power, privilege, and resources—in fact, as the sociologist Rod Ferguson, among others, has astutely observed, the former is often deployed as a strategy for impeding the latter.[41] Thus, bearing in mind both the obstacles to and the possibilities of "imagining alliances" in today's globalized world, anti-racist thought and action must vigilantly confront the seductions of U.S. state recognition and national inclusion for, as Wahneema Lubiano reminds us, "state interests are often unexamined and critically internalized among us—whether or not the 'us' is made up of people marginalized by the overlapping social realities of racism, classism, and sexism, or those who think of themselves as existing within the comforting parameter of the mainstream."[42]

Race, Gender, and the Domestic[43]

If the late twentieth-century Americanization—and concomitant minoritization—of ethnic studies has been one form of its domestication, then the field's historic separation from women's and gender studies reflects another aspect of its reliance on normative conceptions of domesticity, with attendant intellectual and political pitfalls. Like the racial and ethnic studies programs whose history I outlined above, women's studies—and its latter-day iteration of gender studies—first emerged out of student and community struggle in the late 1960s and reflected larger political currents in the global women's liberation movement. Just as ethnic studies programs became intellectual formations for theorizing race as a material and discursive structure of power rather than a fixed category of biological or cultural difference, women's and gender studies programs became vital institutional sites for the production of knowledge that challenged long-held presumptions regarding the naturalness and fixity of gender, sex, and sexuality as social categories and relations.

Despite—or perhaps because of—their parallel histories and similar political and intellectual projects, however, scholarship on race emerging in the field of ethnic studies has historically attended to the construction, negotiation, and transformation of racial categories, structures, and meaning without a comparable attentiveness to the complexities and contingencies of gender, and vice versa. Indeed, all too often, even nuanced social constructionist analyses of race have failed to apply a similar critique to the biological determinism that undergirded their own characterizations of sex, if not gender, as unchanging, natural binaries. Conversely, for decades, while feminist scholars explored gender's multi-faceted function as a terrain of discursive signification and structuring logic of power relations, they failed to adequately attend to or theorize race's discursive power or political materiality beyond phenotype. Of course, in recent years, much has been written critiquing both fields' failures to adequately grapple with the mutual constitution of race and gender, and my goal is not to reiterate it all here.[44] Suffice it to say that, from the radical anti-racist movements of the 1960s and 1970s, which found liberation in the imagined successful reinstantiation of heteropatriarchal gender roles, to Omi and Winant's easy dismissal of sex as an unquestionably biological category, and from early liberal feminism's near-exclusive emphasis on the liberation of white, middle-class women via their thorough incorporation into the capitalist labor force, to the esteemed feminist philosopher Judith Butler's repeated con-flation of race and skin color, the concurrent and mutual theorization of race, gender, and sexuality has persisted as an epistemological problem.

This historical tendency to posit men of color as the transparent proper subjects of racial and ethnic studies, while white women stand as the presumed natural subjects of women's and gender studies, has several pitfalls. First, as feminists of color have frequently observed, uni-versalizing the political interests, privileges, and burdens experienced by men of color as representative of all people of color, and those experi-enced by white women as representative of all women, fails to address the experiences and political interests of women of color. Traditional claims to "universal sisterhood" or demands for "racial solidarity" all too often rely upon the prioritizing of a single category of identity or axis of power over attending to the complex, multi-faceted, and interacting re-lations of race, class, gender, sexuality, and other forms of difference that make up the structural and quotidian aspects of women of color's lives. Indeed, as the members of the Combahee River Collective observed in their 1977 Black Feminist Statement, for women of color, race, gender, and class oppression are "interlocking." "It remains difficult," they ar-gued, "to separate race from class from sex oppression because in our lives they are most often experienced simultaneously."[45] Some fifteen years after women of color began to actively publish and share their di-verse modes of naming that "form of racial-sexual oppression which is neither solely racial nor solely sexual,"[46] the concept of race, class, gen-der, and sexuality—as not just simultaneously experienced but mutually constitutive—cohered under the rubric of "intersectionality"—a term developed by legal theorist Kimberlé Crenshaw in the late 1980s and early 1990s.

Yet as Crenshaw points out, it is not only the experiences of women of color that are left shortchanged or under-analyzed by the codifica-tion of race and gender as distinct and universal categories.[47] For if the production of a universal political subject requires rendering abstract and normative that which is particular and specific, then the creation of the universal raced subject *or* gendered subject necessarily effaces the complex intersections of race and gender at work in the lives of men of color and white women, just as surely as it does in the case of women of color. Or, to put it differently, a failure to attend to how race is *always already* gendered, and gender is *always already* raced, makes it impossible to account fully for any of our experiences, desires, political stakes, and future possibilities.

To be certain, the above critiques, so urgently and cogently argued by a number of feminist of color theorists and activists over the last half-century, continue to be relevant in the current political moment. For the interests of this essay, however, I would like to briefly focus on how the continued difficulty of working against and across the institutional and intellectual divides between ethnic studies and gender studies is, in part, a consequence of each field's reliance on narrow constructions of domesticity. Within ethnic studies, all too many contemporary considerations of racial politics delineate the realm of the political through heteronormative distinctions between public and private that rely on gendered notions of the domestic for their coherence. Within this version of racial politics, the political is what happens in the public sphere—the terrain of street protests, electoral rights, legal battles, and labor conflicts. Within this implicit gendered dyad, the private sphere is by definition *not* political but instead social, cultural, or personal. Such a definition of the political obscures the racial politics at work in those ostensibly private places of raced and gendered struggle: the home, the body, the family. Why, for example, does it remain so difficult, more than two decades after Crenshaw originally published "Mapping the Margins," to discuss the rape of women of color as a form of gendered and sexualized racial violence? Why is it only in the last few years that the vastly disproportionate brutal and often fatal violence experienced by transwomen of color has received national attention, and why has such attention remained almost exclusively circumscribed within queer and trans political and academic communities?

Nor have scholars of gender studies fully escaped the thrall of the domestic, despite the rich body of work by feminist theorists critiquing the so-called Cult of Domesticity and the perceived impermeability of separate gendered spheres.[48] From Betty Friedan's famed denouncement of the "problem that ha[d] no name" but that permeated the stifling suburban homes of white middle-class women through the 1960s, to subsequent radical feminist condemnation of the devaluation of "women's work" and demands for wages for housework, to contemporary scholarly and popular obsessions with the so-called Mommy Wars, white feminist scholars and public intellectuals have—rightfully—explored at length how naturalizing the domestic as women's place means that the gendered notions of domesticity serve to domesticate women—that is, to contain, discipline, and disempower them. Yet all too often, these ongoing debates, analyses, and studies of domesticity's gendered construction fail to explore how the domestic has never been simply a site of gendered meaning making but a crucible for producing and negotiating racial categories in ways that far exceed normative conceptions of white gendered domesticity. (And here, of course, I am excepting the work of feminist and queer of color scholars, who frequently find themselves caught between these two fields of ethnic studies and women's and gender studies—a status reflected in the series of slashes that conjoin subject fields on the backs of their books or the service-heavy joint appointments they find themselves occupying at universities and colleges large and small.) Indeed, despite these numerous interventions by feminist and queer of color scholars, mainstream gender studies scholarship still struggles to address domesticity as a raced and gendered construct that operates in vexed and complex ways in the lives of women of color, who historically have been denied access to their own homes as a legitimate, let alone protected, private sphere, even as the ideals of heteronormative domesticity have been continuously used to police, surveil, and punish them for their presumed racialized and gendered non-normativity.

Consider the case of Daniel Holtzclaw, the Oklahoma City, Oklahoma, officer who was arrested and charged in the summer of 2014 for using his power as a policeman to harass, detain, assault, and rape at least thirteen Black women and girls over a six-month period. Occurring as it did during the apex of public protest over the killing of eighteen-year-old African American teen Michael Brown and the subsequent police occupation of Ferguson, Missouri, the thirty-six acts of first-degree rape, second-degree rape by instrumentation, forcible oral sodomy, sexual battery, assault, coercive oral sodomy, and stalking that

Holtzclaw was charged with committing against these predominantly poor, socially vulnerable Black women were largely overlooked by both mainstream and alternative media. Indeed, the Holtzclaw case only received significant attention after his trial commenced in November 2015, initially from Black women scholars and activists calling into question the seeming political apathy regarding the police violence these women had experienced at the height of the Black Lives Matter movement. National media interest soon followed, particularly with Holtzclaw's conviction on 18 counts and sentencing to 236 years in prison.

Some might read this narrative, from virtual obscurity to national attention, from police impunity to carceral "justice," as a legal and social progress narrative. Putting aside, for a moment, the utter dubiousness of "justice" as a goal or result of the current U.S. carceral system, I instead want to take a moment to ask how notions of the domestic and domesticity shaped the political responses of both anti-racist and feminist activists. At the start of the trial, the predominantly Black women activists who attended the opening week expressed shock that not only were there very few representatives from anti–police violence or Black civil rights organizations present, but also there were very few from the national feminist organizations that regularly attend rape trials.[49] Certainly, one might attribute the lack of popular outrage regarding Holtzclaw's violent predation, the subsequent stacking of the all-white jury with eight men, or the defense's aggressive attempts to characterize the testifying victims as social rejects and criminal deviants to what Black Youth Project 100 member Samantha Master described as "the blind eye turned to the particular types of violence faced by Black women and girls."[50] Not only have long-standing tropes of hyper-sexualized Black women undermined popular and legal recognition of their right to sexual autonomy and safety, but as the African American Policy Forum's Say Her Name public education and advocacy campaign avers, when it comes to gender, some Black lives may, indeed, seem to matter more than others. Yet it is not just the race and gender of Holtzclaw's victims that led to their lack of support: It is the set of domesticating logics against which they, and their demands for justice, were measured and found wanting.

For the Oklahoma City organizers who reached out to national organizations about the Holtzclaw case and received minimal response, the very factors that made these women vulnerable to police violence was what led to them being ignored and dismissed, first by the police and then by mainstream feminist organizations. Working and non-working poor women and girls, many of those whom Holtzclaw targeted had prior or concurrent violations for drug use or possession or for sex work. Not only did their criminal records render them more vulnerable to surveillance and police search, but as women whose labor and leisure took place on streets, cars, and alleys, rather than offices, homes, or other legitimated places of work and play, their claims to the gendered protections of domesticity were undermined from the outset. Even those women and girls whose first entanglements with the police was Holtzclaw's intimidation and brutality were represented as outside the proper domestic sphere. When reading the description of each complainant's testimony, they are all described by their shared spatial vulnerability of being outside. Parked in cars by the side of the road, or walking to their friends', cousins', or own houses, or conducting business on the street—each of the women and girls in the Holtzclaw case is literally caught by him outside the boundaries of recognized domesticity, a status that was naturalized as permanent by both their race and their poverty.

While these women and girls were perceived as operating beyond the limits of the domestic, the acts of raced and gendered violence committed against their flesh were not. To return to Samantha Master's observation, the lack of a robust response to the Holtzclaw case by anti-racist activists was not simply because this violence was enacted on the bodies of Black women but due to the *particular kinds* of violence inflicted on Black women and girls. Within the binaries of public and private, political and personal that shape mainstream racial justice campaign, the murder of a Black person by the police is perceived as a political act of racial violence. The near ubiquitous sexual assault of Black women and other women of color by police officers (a recent study placed the number over the last six years in the hundreds), in contrast, is at worst, individualized, or at best, treated as a problem of gender politics, rather than an issue of racial justice. Within this calculus, the gendered domestic dyad of public and private—killing and sexual assault—operates as all such Manichean logics do: to valorize one term over the other. In the case of police shootings versus police sexual assaults, (masculinized) Black death is foregrounded, while (feminized) Black rape is depoliticized, obscuring the two act's shared function as forms of sexualized racial terrorism and control exercised in the service of white supremacy.

Internationalizing the Racial Domestic: Beyond the "Black/ Brown" Divide

A third tension that ethnic studies formations have negotiated since their inception concerns the representation of various racial/ethnic groups within institutional sites and structures of inquiry. The inaugural departments adopted at UC Berkeley and San Francisco State introduced programmatic subfields that reflected the ethnic nationalist movements that fought for their establishment: African American/Black Studies, Asian American Studies, Native American/American Indian Studies, and Chicano/La Raza Studies. These concentrations, with some regional and institutional variations, have continued to dominate academic landscapes of anti-racist thought and knowledge production, from university departments and programs, to professional associations and thematic tracts within them, to "minority" scholarship foundations. At best, the preservation of these has served to unpack the white/non-white binary in a manner that recognizes the distinctive histories, experiences, and struggles of racial/ethnic/national communities. However, this tetrad model of anti-racist thought and scholarship has rightly been the subject of ongoing critique for over two decades, for reasons both logistical and ideological. For the purposes of this essay, I want to focus on some of the many limitations of this model as they relate to the terrains of anti-racist thought and action.

The above-mentioned organizational rubrics encourage a comparative rather than relational approach to the study of race, ethnicity, and nation. Racialization is understood as an independent rather than interdependent process, thus obscuring the ways in which racial meanings have been configured, both historically and contemporarily, through and against shifting and unstable definitions of blackness, indigeneity, whiteness, and so on. This nationalizes the experience of racialization in a manner that naturalizes whiteness as normative and transparent while collapsing relations of race, ethnicity, and nation into seemingly discrete, stable, and universal deviations from that norm. Moreover, this domesticating move, common within both popular and academic circles, presumes the universality of U.S. racial categories and encourages the uncritical imposition of U.S.-based racial/ethnic matrices to external contexts.

An example of this domestication of racial/ethnic categories at work can be found in the bi-national Memín Pinguín controversy that emerged in 2005. On July 29 of that year, the Servicio Postal Méxicano (Sepomex) announced its release of a five-stamp postage series commemorating the internationally known comic book character, Memín Pinguín. A racialized caricature of a boy of African descent frequently described as "apelike" and "Sambo-like," Memín Pinguín is the protagonist of an eponymous comic series that has been sold throughout the Americas, Asia, and Europe for over six decades. The comic icon only recently gained media notoriety in the United States, however, following its controversial acclamation by Sepomex. Issued only weeks after President Vicente Fox's contentious public assertion that Mexican immigrants in the United States "are doing jobs that not even blacks want to do,"[51] the postage series sparked public outcry among of U.S.-based civil rights organizations, including the National Association for the Advancement of Colored People, the Rainbow PUSH Coalition, and the Urban League. An equally ardent public defense of the comic character was articulated by pundits ranging from Mexican governmental officials, to prominent Mexican journalists, to a chorus of fans throughout the hemisphere. This pro-Memín camp countered charges of racism with a vehement condemnation of U.S. cultural imperialism and what they described as the uninformed imposition of a U.S. racial imaginary upon an iconic figure historically and culturally Mexican in origin.[52] Within days of their release, the Memín postage stamps catalyzed an enduring international controversy that far outlasted their relatively brief production life.

Of particular interest here are the ways in which U.S. and Mexican public opinion makers alike commonly depicted the dispute as the by-product of "culture wars" between Mexico and the United States and, analogously, between African Americans and Latinos.[53] The purportedly essential and oppositional racial-national character of the pro- and anti-Memín camps was popularized through both Mexican and U.S. press coverage. The *New York Times* and *Washington Post* headlined the controversy: "Fight Grows over a Stamp US Sees as Racist and Mexico

Adores" and "White House Denounces Art on Mexican Stamps; Aide to Fox Says Cartoon Is Cultural Icon."[54] Mexican news conglomerates *El Universal* and *La Jornada* respectively reported that "Memín stamps offend African Americans" and "Memín's Mischief Jeopardizes Bilateral Relations between Mexico and the US."[55] In short, public discourse on both sides of the border spotlighted the aggrieved position of the African American public, largely neglecting or minimizing the scale and import of Afro-Mexican responses to the controversial stamps. Moreover, English- and Spanish-language news media alike repeatedly emphasized the demands of U.S.-based civil rights activists and organizations, which included a demand that the Mexican government issue a formal apology for what Rev. Jesse Jackson dubbed an "insult to African Americans."[56] The bi-national terms in which the dispute was framed set a conceptual stage for the unabashedly statist nationalist platforms put forth by Memín protestors. In a startling performance of U.S. patriotism, Rev. Al Sharpton issued President Fox a July 4 deadline for the stamps' withdrawal.[57] Marc H. Morial, executive director of the National Urban League, joined Sharpton and Jackson in calling upon President George W. Bush and Secretary of State Condoleezza Rice to denounce the stamps.

The Bush administration declined to officially censure the Mexican postal service. Nonetheless, drawing upon the ethical authority ceded to the U.S. state by civil rights leaders, White House press secretary Scott McClellan issued a statement urging the Mexican government to recognize that "racial stereotypes are offensive, no matter what their origin." Such images, McClellan concluded, "have no place in today's world."[58] This proposed cooperation among strange bedfellows set the stage for Washington politicians to position themselves, and by extension the U.S. state, as the hemispheric arbiters of racial political rectitude. In the process, Washington's seemingly benign condemnation of anachronistic racial stereotypes became an opportunity for the White House leadership to assign itself a privileged moral (and, by extension, political) authority in the international sphere.

In keeping with the internationalization of U.S.-based racial matrices, media discourses on both sides of the border conjointly mapped seemingly stable geopolitical boundaries between African Americans in the global north and (non-Black) Latinos in the global south. Both proponents and critics of Memín anchored their defense of, or opposition to, the comic in national terms that elaborated corollary racial, cultural, and spatial imaginaries. In doing so, media pundits and cultural workers enabled state actors to opportunistically frame the controversy in terms of competing "national interests" and irreconcilable cultural differences. In the end, these abstractions of race and place empowered both states to exploit the fracas as an opportunity to call forth their respective citizens in defense of the cultural territory of the nation, even as these very subjects experienced increased alienation from that nation's resources, opportunities, and political franchise. How do we make sense of this tendency of contemporary state makers and other conservative ideologues to garner support and authority by linking themselves to "national" cultural imaginaries at a moment when economic and cultural interactions have become increasingly denationalized?[59] How do these "post-national" nationalisms align themselves with contemporary processes of racial formation, and what do such processes reveal about how racialized bodies, communities, and fields of knowledge are spatially imagined?

Reading the Memín controversy as a bi-national articulation of Mexican and U.S. post-national nationalisms reveals the extent to which neoliberal state-making strategies in both countries have entailed the popularization of an amended geo-cultural imaginary of nation. In both cases, these post-national nationalisms retooled notions of state belonging to inhere not in stable or bounded geo-political territoriality but rather in abstract and diffuse modes of "modern" and "nostalgic" racial-cultural belonging. These tactics for rationalizing the contradictions of racialized economic restructuring were arguably distinct in content and form. However, they were rooted in similar logics (the strategic management of difference) and deployed through similar strategies (the de-localization of nation). They also pursued similar goals: the garnering of state support and the entrenchment of state authority at a moment when the private interests of transnational corporatism are prioritized over—and often at the expense of—the common interests of impoverished national publics. In the end, these distinctive yet compatible racial-national projects served to obscure the procedures (global economic restructuring) and effects (racialized exploitation) of neoliberal racial capitalism through the concomitant governmental disciplining of difference and reconsolidation of fixed racial-national divides.

This reterritorialization of the Memín polemic and of blackness itself both depended upon and fed existing narratives of "race relations" within the United States that depicted an intra-class conflict between two seemingly stable racial groups: on the one hand, a U.S.-born "Black" community, and on the other, immigrant and U.S.-born Latinos, euphemistically described as "Brown." In recent years, the notion of a Black/ Brown divide has been so naturalized as to become both a popular and academic truism. The alacrity with which the U.S. state has embraced this commonsense rhetoric underscores its significant strategic functions. By imposing a stable and predictable racial order upon complex sites and forms of difference, it sutures contested relations of gender, race, and class within racialized communities in the United States through what is at best a disavowal and at worst a cynical leveraging of material conflicts and contradictions that exist within both so-called Black and Brown communities: inter-class or inter-cultural tensions, urban-rural divides, and strained relations between migrants and citizens. A state-making tactic that the anthropologist Allen Feldman has referred to in another context as "individualizing disorder,"[60] public discourses that reinvent socioeconomic crises as conflicts between "Black and Brown" communities conceal the complicity of the U.S. imperial racial state in producing and managing structural inequalities by reterritorializing the origin of and responsibility for such contradictions from the scale of the nation-state to the scale of individualized raced and gendered bodies.

Conclusion

Following Ruth Wilson Gilmore's astute assertion that moments of social crisis are likewise moments of political opportunity, I have organized this essay around a series of thematic case studies that link moments of antagonism and constraint within the development of ethnic studies as a field to similar frictions within popular anti-racist organizing campaigns. In doing so, my aim has been to explore how past lessons and current shifts in relations of racial formation might inform future anti-racist knowledge production and political action. Toward this end, I have introduced domestication as an analytic for critiquing the oft-uninterrogated imperial, racial capitalist, and heteropatriarchal designs that undergird the ideologies and architecture of U.S. nationalism and nation. Drawing upon the insights of women and queer of color feminisms, I have argued that domestication as a political force in the United States strategically conjoins imperial and settler colonial agendas with ideologies and structures of racial/sexual regulation and capitalist expansion. To support this claim, I have highlighted examples of the ways in which the domestication of political agendas have figured as an enduring, divisive obstacle within social justice pursuits. Whether it be the domestication of anti-imperialist struggles demonstrated in my discussion of the "Change the Mascot" campaign, the domestication of categories and terrains of struggle as revealed in my evaluation of the Memín Pinguín postage stamp controversy, or the domestication of feminist struggles against racial violence illustrated in the media and activist silence around the Daniel Holtzclaw case, its is clear that domestication must be understood as a naturalized if flexible ideological force that engenders and exploits emplaced frictions and fractions that inhibit critical solidarities across the boundaries of race, gender, and place.

In today's globalized world, the role and function of nation-states in mediating relations of race, gender, capital have shifted in accordance with the expansion of transnational accords and mechanisms of governance and the unprecedented dominance of neoliberal capitalism. Yet, paradoxically, post-national state formation frequently entails the hailing of an increasingly transnational, increasingly mobile labor force to entertain nation-based solutions to global contradictions, even as domestic citizenries around the world are experiencing the denationalization of resources, opportunities, and political franchise. Accordingly, I have argued that the pursuit of racial justice within the United States will require thinking through the discursive logics and material conditions that organize "group-differentiated vulnerability to premature death"[61] both within and beyond U.S. borders and across axes of difference. For anti-racist scholars and activists, this will require active analytical engagement with the ways in which processes of racial formation are at once *geo-historically specific*—that is, as temporally emplaced in particular, local, regional, and national contexts—and *geo-historically relational*—that is, as situated within and articulated with other geographies of racial capitalist formation and networks of cultural circulation. To do so, we must think and work across and beyond the domesticating logics of the nation-state to imagine new, relational, and intersectional models of racial, social, and economic justice. This will no doubt necessitate moving beyond nation-based demands for redress and toward broader systemic challenges to the contemporary U.S. racial state's inextricability from global systems of racialized violence and exploitation.

NOTES

1 Ruth Wilson Gilmore, "Fatal Couplings of Power and Difference: Notes on Racism and Geography," *Professional Geographer* 54.1 (2002): 15–24.

2 David Harvey, "Space as a Keyword," paper, Marx and Philosophy Conference, Institute of Education, London, 29 May 2004; Sallie A. Marston, "The Social Construction of Scale," *Progress in Human Geography* 24.2 (2000): 219–242; and Katharyne Mitchell, "Transnational Discourse: Bringing Geography Back In," *Antipode* 29.2 (1997): 101–126.

3 Evelyn Hu-DeHart, "Globalization and Its Discontents: Exposing the Underside," *Frontiers: A Journal of Women Studies* 24.2 (2004): 244–260; and Grace Chang, *Disposable Domestics: Immigrant Women Workers in the Global Economy* (Cambridge, MA: South End Press, 2000).

4 Hu-DeHart, "Globalization and Its Discontents," 248.

5 For example, Alicia Schmidt Camacho brilliantly argues that the free trade zones such as the maquiladora sector along the U.S./Mexico border are dependent upon the unprotected labor of "denationalized citizens." See Alicia R. Schmidt Camacho, "Ciudadana X: Gender Violence and the Denationalization of Women's Rights in Ciudad Juarez, Mexico," *CR: The New Centennial Review* 5.1 (2005): 255–292.

6 Amy Kaplan, "Manifest Domesticity," *American Literature* 70.3 (1998): 581–606.

7 Friedrich Engels, *The Origin of the Family, Private Property and the State*, introduction by Tristram Hunt (London: Penguin UK, 2010).

8 Michael Omi and Howard Winant, *Racial Formation in the United States* (London: Routledge, 2014).

9 Ibid., 55.

10 See, for example, Mary Pat Brady, *Extinct Lands, Temporal Geographies: Chicana Literature and the Urgency of Space* (Durham, NC: Duke University Press, 2002); Gilmore, "Fatal Couplings"; Katherine McKittrick, *Demonic Grounds: Black Women and the Cartographies of Struggle* (Minneapolis: University of Minnesota Press, 2006); Katherine McKittrick and Linda Peake, "What Difference Does Difference Make to Geography?" In *Questioning Geography: Fundamental Debates*, ed. Noel Castree, Alisdair Rogers, and Douglas Sherman (Malden, MA: Blackwell, 2005), 39–54; and Natalie Oswin, "Critical Geographies and the Uses of Sexuality: Deconstructing Queer Space," *Progress in Human Geography* 32.1 (2008): 89–103.

11 Priya Kandaswamy, "Gendering Racial Formation," in *Racial Formation in the Twenty-First Century*, ed. Daniel Martinez HoSang, Oneka LaBennett, and Laura Pulido (Berkeley: University of California Press, 2012), 23–43.

12 Evelyn Hu-DeHart, "The History, Development, and Future of Ethnic Studies," *Phi Delta Kappan* 75.1 (1993): 50–54.

13 Helene Whitson, "Introductory Essay," n.d., *The SF State College Strike Collection*, San Francisco State University, J. Paul Leonard Library, http://jpllweb.sfsu.edu; and Helene Whitson and Anne Reynes, "'On Strike! Shut It Down!' An Interview with Helene Whitson on the San Francisco College Strike and Strike Collection," *E-rea: Revue électronique d'études sur le monde anglophone* 10.2 (2013), hosted at OpenEdition, www.openedition.org.

14 This term is used throughout the strike literatures at both San Francisco State University and the University of California, Berkeley.

15 Hu-DeHart, "The History, Development," 50. Notable exceptions to this trend are, of course, Historically Black Colleges and Universities and Tribal Colleges.

16 "Third World Liberation Front: Notice of Demands," n.d., *The SF State College Strike Collection*, San Francisco State University, https://diva.sfsu.edu.

17 Gloria Bowles, Clara Sue Kidwell, and Ron Takaki, "Ethnic Studies and Women's Studies at UC/Berkeley: A Collective Interview," *Radical Teacher* 14 (December, 1979): 12.

18 Lisa Lowe, *Immigrant Acts: On Asian American Cultural Politics* (Durham, NC: Duke University Press, 1996); Jodi Melamed, *Represent and Destroy: Rationalizing Violence in the New Racial Capitalism* (Minneapolis: University of Minnesota Press, 2011); and Mary Louise Pratt, "I, Rigoberta Menchú and the 'Culture Wars,'" in *The Rigoberta Menchú Controversy*, ed. Arturo Arias (Minneapolis: University of Minnesota Press, 2001), 29–48.

19 Lowe, *Immigrant Acts*, 39.

20 Christopher Newfield, *Unmaking the Public University: The Forty-Year Assault on the Middle Class* (Cambridge, MA: Harvard University Press, 2008).

21 Hu-DeHart, "The History, Development."

22 Robert Blauner, "Internal Colonialism and Ghetto Revolt," *Social Problems* 16.4 (1969): 393. Blauner's essay is not without its shortcomings; as Native feminist scholar Jodi Byrd astutely argues, "internal colonialism" as an analytic is often deployed in a manner that erases the ongoing violation of Native sovereignties. She writes, "One might argue that the idea of "internal colonialism" services the construction of the United States as a multicultural nation that is struggling with the legacies of racism rather than as a colonialist power engaged in territorial expansion since its beginning." See Jodi A. Byrd, *The Transit of Empire: Indigenous Critiques of Colonialism* (Minneapolis: University of Minnesota Press, 2011), 125.

23 Stokely Carmichael and Charles V. Hamilton, *Black Power: The Politics of Liberation in America* (New York: Random House, [1967]).

24 Melamed, *Represent and Destroy*, x.

25 Susan Feriss, Ricardo Sandoval, and Diana Hembree, *The Fight in the Fields: Cesar Chavez and the Farmworkers Movement* (New York: Houghton Mifflin Harcourt, 1998).

26 Adam Fortunate Eagle, *Alcatraz! Alcatraz! The Indian Occupation of 1969–1971* (Berkeley, CA: Heyday Books, 1992).

27 Melamed, *Represent and Destroy*.

28 The National Association of Ethnic Studies (NAES) was formed by a small cadre of scholars in the Midwest in 1972. See National Association of Ethnic Studies, "About: NAES Herstory," *NAES*, ethnicstudies.org.

29 Hu-DeHart, "The History, Development."

30 Ibid., 51.

31 Joan Walsh, "What If American Studies and Ethnic Studies Were One in the Same?" *Pacific News Service*, 2 Sept. 1998.

32 Ibid.

33 Ibid.

34 Melamed, *Represent and Destroy*.

35 See, for example, David E. Wilkins, "Indian Peoples Are Nations, Not Minorities," in his *American Indian Politics and the American Political System* (Lanham, MD: Rowman & Littlefield, 2002), 41–62.

36 *ChangeTheMascot.org*, www.changethemascot.org.

37 Ariel Sabar, "The Anti-Redskin," *Atlantic*, Oct. 2015, www.theatlantic.com.

38 Ibid.

39 Philip Joseph Deloria, *Playing Indian* (Princeton, NJ: Yale University Press, 1998). Examples of quantitative and qualitative research regarding the violent material, ideological, and psychic effects of Native mascots and other colonial stereotypes include Stephanie A. Fryberg et al., "Of Warrior Chiefs and Indian Princesses: The Psychological Consequences of American Indian Mascots," *Basic and Applied Social Psychology* 30.3 (2008): 208–218; Ellen J. Staurowsky, "American Indian Imagery and the Miseducation of America," *Quest* 51.4 (1999): 382–392; and Lawrence R. Baca, "Native Images in Schools and the Racially Hostile Environment," *Journal of Sport and Social Issues* 28.1 (2004): 71–78.

40 Emphasis mine. See Indian Country Today Media Network Staff, "Ray Halbritter Discusses Native Imagery in Sports at Carlisle Journeys," *Indian Country Today*, 11 Oct. 2016, indiancountrytodaymedianetwork.com.

41 Roderick A. Ferguson, *The Reorder of Things: The University and Its Pedagogies of Minority Difference* (Minneapolis: University of Minnesota Press, 2012).

42 Wahneema Lubiano, "Talking about the State and Imagining Alliances," in *Talking Visions: Multicultural Feminism in a Transnational Age*, ed. Ella Shohat (Cambridge, MA: MIT Press, 1998), 441.

43 The following section draws upon work from a book in progress I am co-authoring with Sara Clarke Kaplan, *Ethnic Studies and the Problem of the Domestic*. See also Sara Clarke Kaplan, *The Black Reproductive: Feminism and the Politics of Freedom* (Minneapolis: University of Minnesota Press, forthcoming 2018), for

an extended discussion of raced domesticity and gendered reproduction in the context of Black Lives Matter.

44 See, for example, Kandaswamy, "Gendering Racial Formation"; Evelyn Nakano Glenn, *Unequal Freedom: How Race and Gender Shaped American Citizenship and Labor* (Cambridge, MA: Harvard University Press, 2009); and Sumi Cho, Kimberlé Williams Crenshaw, and Leslie McCall, "Toward a Field of Intersectionality Studies: Theory, Applications, and Praxis," *Signs: Journal of Women in Culture and Society* 38.4 (2013): 785–810.

45 Combahee River Collective, "A Black Feminist Statement (1977)," in *The Black Feminist Reader*, ed. Joy James and T. Denean Sharpley-Whiting (Oxford: Blackwell, 2000), 261–270, quote at 266.

46 Ibid.

47 Kimberlé Crenshaw, "Mapping the Margins: Intersectionality, Identity Politics, and Violence against Women of Color," *Stanford Law Review* 43 (1991): 1241–1299.

48 Cathy N. Davidson and Jessamyn Hatcher, eds., *No More Separate Spheres! A Next Wave American Studies Reader* (Durham, NC: Duke University Press, 2002); Barbara Welter, "The Cult of True Womanhood: 1820–1860," *American Quarterly* 18.2 (1996): pt. 1:151–174.

49 Molly Redden, "Daniel Holtzclaw: Former Oklahoma City Police Officer Guilty of Rape," *Guardian*, 10 Dec. 2015, www.theguardian.com.

50 Kanya D'Almeida, "Trial Resumes for Ex-Cop Charged with Sexually Assaulting 13 Black Women," *Rewire*, 11 Nov. 2015, https://rewire.news.

51 "Fox 'Regrets' Remark about Blacks," *CNN. com*, 17 May 2005, www.cnn.com.

52 Darryl Fears, "White House Denounces Art on Mexican Stamps; Aide to Fox Says Cartoon Is Cultural Icon," *Washington Post*, 1 July 2005, A18.

53 Elisabeth Malkin, "Fight Grows over a Stamp U.S. Sees as Racist and Mexico Adores," *New York Times*, 2 July 2005.

54 See Fears, "White House Denounces Art"; and Malkin, "Fight Grows over a Stamp."

55 EFE, "Ofenden estampillas de Memín a afroamericanos," *El Universal*, 30 June 2005; and David Brooks, "Travesura de Memín Pinguín pone en jaque la relación bilateral entre México y EEUU," *La Jornada*, 1 July 2005.

56 Dave Goldiner, "Mexico Prez: Cartoon Not Racist," *New York Daily News*, 1 July 2005, 18.

57 Ibid.

58 Malkin, "Fight Grows over a Stamp."

59 Schmidt Camacho, "Ciudadana X."

60 Allen Feldman, *Formations of Violence: The Narrative of the Body and Political Terror in Northern Ireland* (Chicago: University of Chicago Press, 1991).

61 This is an excerpt from Ruth Wilson Gilmore's compelling definition of racism as "the state-sanctioned or extralegal production and exploitation of group-differentiated vulnerability to premature death." See Ruth Wilson Gilmore, *Golden Gulag: Prisons, Surplus, Crisis, and Opposition in Globalizing California* (Berkeley: University of California Press, 2006), 28.

ABOUT THE EDITORS

Charles J. Ogletree, Jr., is Jesse Climenko Professor of Law and Executive Director of the Charles Hamilton Houston Institute for Race and Justice at Harvard Law School. He is the author of *All Deliberate Speed: Reflections on the First Half-Century of* Brown v. Board of Education (2004) and co-editor of *From Lynch Mobs to the Killing State: Race and the Death Penalty in America* (NYU Press, 2006).

Austin Sarat is Associate Dean of the Faculty and William Nelson Cromwell Professor of Jurisprudence and Political Science at Amherst College. He is author or editor of more than ninety books, including *When the State Kills: Capital Punishment and the American Condition; Mercy on Trial: What It Means to Stop an Execution;* and *Gruesome Spectacles: Botched Executions and America's Death Penalty.*

ABOUT THE CONTRIBUTORS

Valerie C. Cooper is Associate Professor of Black Church Studies at Duke Divinity School.

Kirstie A. Dorr is Assistant Professor of Ethnic Studies at University of California, San Diego.

Matthew Pratt Guterl is Professor of Africana Studies and American Studies at Brown University.

Naomi Murakawa is Associate Professor of African American Studies at Princeton University.

Osagie K. Obasogie is Professor of Law at University of California, Hastings.

Carla Shedd is Assistant Professor of Sociology and African American Studies at Columbia University.

INDEX

abolition, 130

adolescence: distinction of, 81; inequality in, 81–83; as protected role, 82; social and criminal injustice and, 82

Affirmative Action, 27

Afghanistan, 97

African Americans: arrests of, 103–4; micro aggressions of, 2; reparations for, 8; safety in Christian churches, 120; white people passing as, 26; as youth, 68–69, 83–84. *See also* Black churches; *specific topics*

African Methodist Episcopal (AME) Church denomination, 123–24

Agricultural Workers Organizing Committee, 159

Alba, Richard, 6

Alexie, Sherman, 42

Allen, Richard, 123

Allport, Gordon, 5

ambivalence, 3

AME. *See* African Methodist Episcopal Church denomination; Emanuel African Methodist Episcopal

American Indian Nations, 163–65

American studies programs: as ethnic studies programs assimilation, 18–19, 161–63; increased enrollment in, 162; minorities in, 163; Wang proposal for, 161

anti-mascot movement, 163–64

anti-racism: agendas of, 153–54; of American Indian Nations, 163–65; and ethnic studies programs, 177–78; lack

of response to Holtzclaw, 171–72; racial formation and, 178–79; radical initiatives of, 159

appropriation: Dolezal material difference from, 41; as faddish, 31

Assemblies of God, 126

assimilation, 6; of ethnic studies programs, 18–19, 161–62; of Rockefeller, 36

Azusa Street Revival, 125–26, 142n49

Baltimore Police Department, 93

Bartusch, Dawn, 69

Belhaven University, 9

BiDil drug, 58

bigotry, 166

biological race: emergence, of, 50–51; FDA on, 58–59; in Holocaust, 11, 49; hypocrisy of, 54–55; as ideology, 54–55; racial antagonism based on, 49; racial reconciliation moments in, 52–54; racism from, 49–50

The Black Child Savers (Ward), 68

Black churches: alongside slavery and Civil War, 124–25; history of, 122–28

blackface, 26

Black Feminist Statement (1977), 168

Black like Me (Griffin), 26

Black Lives Matter movement, 15, 90, 149n79; beginning of, 136

blackness, 44–45

Black on the Block (Pattillo), 85

Black Panther Party, 159

Black Reconstruction in America (Du Bois), 41

Black Student Union (BSU), 156

Black Youth Project 100, 171

Blauner, Robert, 158

Blink, 6

Book of Revelation, 132

Bradley, Anthony, 127–28, 133

Bratton, William, 93

Brewer, Jan, 157

Brewer, Marilynn, 6

Broadly, 43–44

Brown, Michael, 136, 170

Brown v. Board of Education, 1; as point of change, 3–4; racial reconciliation from, 5; in Section 5 of Fourteenth Amendment, 56

BSU. *See* Black Student Union

Bubandt, Nils, 91

Bush, George W., 175

Butler, Judith, 168

Cabrini-Green Public Housing Projects, 13

"California Civil Rights Initiative," 161

Capote, Truman, 38

Carby, Hazel, 3

carceral humanism, 102

Carlisle College, 166

Carter, J. Kameron, 128

"Change the Mascot" campaign, 163–64; domestication in, 178; indigenous Peruvian women and, 165–66

Charleston, South Carolina: Dolezal and, 34; murders in, 32–34

Chicago schools: gangs in, 72, 74; interviews in, 70–81; place and injustice perception in, 75–81; predominately white schools in, 76; race and space intersection in, 13; racial composition in, 70–75; school choice in, 70–75; youth perception of, 67

child-saving movements, 65–66

Christerson, Brad, 121

Christian churches: African American safety in, 120; Biblical problem of, 132–33; conflict in, 121–23; cultural assault perception in, 119; integration in, 17, 119–20, 143n70; justice in, 134–35; kneel-ins in, 116–17; minorities in, 121; problem of survival for, 133; racial divide of, 115; racism in, 127; segregation history of, 122–28; segregation of, 16, 113–17, 128–33, 139; segregation proponents in, 120–22; sociological problem in, 130–32; theological problem of, 128–30; white supremacy in, 132. *See also* Black churches

The Christian Imagination: Theology and the Origins of Race (Jennings), 129

Church of God in Christ, 126

civil rights movement, 3; kneel-in of, 116–17; on segregation, 126–27; successes of, 4

Civil War, 124–25

class: crossing lines of, 10; in white-to-black racial passing, 36–37

Clinton, Bill, 53

Cobb, Jelani, 31, 32

Cold War interventionism, 165

Collins, Francis, 53

colonialism, 156; anti-colonial activists, 158–59; as domestic, 158

Combahee River Collective, 168

commodification, 166

Confederate flag, 164

Confederates, 124–25

Congregations Project, 118–19

Connerly, Ward, 161

Constitution, U.S., 4; Section 5 of Fourteenth Amendment to, 50, 55–57, 60n17

Contact Theory, 5

Corlett, J. Angelo, 7

Costas, Bob, 164

counterinsurgency tactics, 96–97

Crenshaw, Kimberlé, 168

cross-racial progressive movements, 46
crucifixion, 139
Cult of Domesticity, 169–70
culture wars: of Mexico and United States, 174–76; of 1990s, 157

Dawkins, Marcia, 42
de Blasio, Bill, 92–93
The Debt: What America Owes to Blacks (Robinson), 8
decriminalization, 16
Delano grape strike, 159
discrimination: justifications for, 7; progress on, 2; reverse discrimination, 9; without subterfuge, 117–20; of youth, 65–66
Dolezal, Rachel, 9–10; biography of, 39–41; blackness of, 44–45; Charleston murders and, 34; fictionalized past of, 30–31; at Howard University, 31; Humphrey, J., interview with, 28–30; Jenner similarity to, 45; material difference from appropriation, 41; on matrilineal descent, 28; with NAACP, 28–29; post-racialism of, 26; press and media on, 29–32; profit of, 34; psychological wage of, 41–43; racial reconciliation of, 27; as remaking white matriarchy, 44; small-town escape of, 35; triviality of, 45–46; visions of, 25–26
domestication: in "Change the Mascot" campaign, 178; definition of, 152; of ethnic studies programs, 163–64, 167; Holtzclaw and, 171; internationalizing of, 173–77; Memín Pinguín controversy example of, 174; in nation-state system, 152–53; of politics, 152
domesticity: in gender studies, 169–70; race, gender and, 167–73; women of color and, 172
Dresinger, Baz, 26
Du Bois, W. E. B., 41

Eastern Washington University, 9, 25
Edwards, Korie L., 121, 137
ELCA. *See* Evangelical Lutheran Church of America
Ellis, William, 37
Emanuel African Methodist Episcopal (AME) Church massacre, 10; in AME denomination, 124; historicism of, 142n40; racial reconciliation after, 137–38; racism in, 114–15; Roof murders at, 16, 113, 135–36
Emerson, Michael O., 115, 118, 121
empathy, 109n14; observations or feelings of, 96; police violence and, 103. *See also* tactical empathy
equality: in Verbal Judo, 98–99. *See also* inequality
ethnic nationalist movements, 173
ethnic studies programs: anti-racism and, 177–78; assimilation to American studies programs, 18–19, 161–63; backlash to, 18; birth of, 156–60; in crisis, 161–67; diversity and, 158; domestication of, 163–64, 167; gender studies divide with, 169; institutional history of, 157–58; institutionalization of, 159–60; subjects of, 168
eugenics movement, 51–52
Evangelical Lutheran Church of America (ELCA), 121

FAS. *See* Free African Society
FBI. *See* Federal Bureau of Investigation
FDA. *See* Food and Drug Administration
Federal Bureau of Investigation (FBI), 59
Federal Trade Commission, 59
Feldman, Allen, 177
feminism, 167; of feminists of color, 168; intersectionality in, 168
Ferguson, Missouri, 26, 170
Food and Drug Administration (FDA), 58–59
forced sterilization, 51

Fordham Law Review, 54
47 Brand, 165–66
Fox, Vicente, 174–75
Frank, Waldo, 26
Free African Society (FAS), 123
Friedan, Betty, 170
Fullwiley, Duana, 54–55

gangs: in schools, 72, 74; stigmas of, 80–81
gay marriage, 3
gender: aberrance of, 155; in police violence, 169–72; in power relations, 167; race, domesticity and, 167–73
gender studies: domesticity in, 169–70; ethnic studies programs divide with, 169; subjects of, 168
geographies of exclusion, 69
George, David, 123
Gilligan's Island, 36
Gilmore, Craig, 104
Gilmore, Ruth Wilson, 104, 177
Gladwell, Malcolm, 6
Graham, Billy, 97
Gray, Freddie, 93
Greenhouse, Carol, 3
Griffin, John Howard, 26
Guthrie, Savannah, 32

Halbritter, Ray, 163–66
Hammonds, Evelynn, 51
Harper High School, 13, 73–74, 81
Harris-Perry, Melissa, 32
Hartman, Saidiya, 107
Harvard Implicit Associations Test, 6
hate crimes, 28
hate mail, 28–29
Haynes, Stephen, 116–17
Herzig, Rebecca, 51
Hispanic youth, 83–84
Hoban, Jack, 98
Hobbs, Allyson, 31, 45
Hoberman, John, 55
Holly Golightly (fictional character), 38

Holocaust: biological race in, 11, 49; inhumane science experiments in, 52–53; racial reconciliation efforts from, 11
Holtzclaw, Daniel, 170–72, 178
hospitals, 12
Howard University, 9; Dolezal at, 31
Hu-DeHart, Evelyn, 160
Hudson, Michael Derrick, 42
humane policing, 108
Human Genome Project, 53–55
Human Rights Institute, 40
Humphrey, Jeff, 28–30
Humphrey, Robert, 98–99

IACP. *See* International Association of Chiefs of Police
Independent Presbyterian Church (IPC), 117
indigenous Peruvian women, 165–66
inequality: in adolescence, 81–83; representation and, 155; of youth, 64–65
injustice: place and perception of, 75–81; youth experiences of, 81. *See also* social and criminal injustice
"In Rachel Dolezal's Skin" (Sunderland), 43–44
integration: in Christian churches, 17, 119–20, 143n70; critics of, 6; for racial reconciliation, 5
"Internal Colonialism and Ghetto Revolt" (Blauner), 158
International Association of Chiefs of Police (IACP), 93, 105–6
internationalizing, 173–77
interracial relations, 145n93
intersectionality, 46; in feminism, 168
interventionism, 165
IPC. *See* Independent Presbyterian Church

Jackson, Jesse, 175
Jacobson, Matthew Frye, 42
Jenkins, Jerry, 97

Jenner, Caitlyn, 27; Dolezal similarity to, 45; on *Vanity Fair* cover, 30
Jennings, Willie James, 129
Jesus, 121; crucifixion of, 139
Jim Crow era, 4, 83, 124, 130
Johansen, Bruce E., 164
Johnson, David, 5
Johnson, Roger, 5
Joint Center for Politics and Economic Studies, 2
Jones, Absalom, 123
justice, 64; in Christian churches, 134–35. *See also* injustice

Kaling, Mindy, 42
Katzenbach v. Morgan, 56–57
Khalili, Laleh, 96–97
Kilgore, James, 102
King, Martin Luther, Jr., 16, 113, 130, 137
Klarman, Michael, 4
kneel-ins, 116–17
Krivo, Lauren J., 65

Lansdale, Edward, 97
The Last Segregated Hour: The Memphis Kneel-ins and the Campaign for Southern Church Desegregation (Haynes), 116
Lee, Bruce, 100
Left Behind (Jenkins), 97
"Letter from Birmingham City Jail" (King), 130
LGBTQ people of color, 90; as scholars, 154–55
Liele, George, 123
Lincoln Park High School, 13, 66–67
Lofton, Katie, 43
Los Angeles Times, 58
Loving v. Virginia, 56
Lowe, Lisa, 157
Lubiano, Wahneema, 166

Mainline Denominations, 133, 140n6
"Mapping the Margins" (Crenshaw), 169

Mark Watson (fictional character), 26
mass incarceration, 42
Master, Samantha, 171
matrilineal descent, 28
McClellan, Scott, 175
media. *See* press and media
medical schools, 12
medicine: preconciliation in, 57–59; as race-based, 58
Melamed, Jodi, 157
Melissa Harris-Perry Show, 32
Memín Pinguín (fictional character): controversy of, 174–78; reterritorialization of, 177
Methodists, 125
Mexican-American National Farmworkers Association, 159
Mexican immigrants, 174
Mexico: Memín Pinguín controversy of, 174–78; racial-national divide in, 176; United States culture wars with, 174–76
micro aggressions, 2
militarization, 104–5
minorities: in American studies programs, 163; in Christian churches, 121; criminalization of, 3
Mommy Wars, 170
Morial, Marc H., 175
multiracial congregations, 31
murders: of Brown, 136, 170; in Charleston, 32–34; by police, 104–5, 107. *See also* Emanuel African Methodist Episcopal Church massacre
Myrdal, Gunnar, 3

NAACP. *See* National Association for the Advancement of Colored People
Natapoff, Alexandra, 104
National Association for the Advancement of Colored People (NAACP), 9; Dolezal with, 28–29; on Memín Pinguín controversy, 174
National Football League (NFL), 164

National Human Genome Research Institute, 53

national poverty rate, 2

National Urban League, 174–75

nation-states: domestication in, 152–53; mediation of, 178; racial capitalism of, 153

Native sovereignty, 159

The Nature of Difference (Hammonds and Herzig), 51

The Nature of Prejudice (Allport), 5

neighborhoods, 12; racial/ethnic ambiguities in, 66; schools and comparative contexts for, 64–66; surveillance of, 62–63

Newfield, Chris, 157

Newsome, Bree, 10, 32–33

New York Times, 174–75

NFL. *See* National Football League

Niebuhr, H. Richard, 117–18, 129–30

Nuremberg Codes of 1947, 11, 52

Obama, Barack, 89–90; Task Force on 21st Century Policing of, 106

Omi, Michael, 154

Oneida Indian Nation, 163–66

Orientalism, "gentle," 101

Oxford English Dictionary, 152

parens patriae, 63

parents, 85–86

Parham, Charles Fox, 142n48

passing: historical act of, 36–37; Rockefeller as, 36–37; wealth in, 37–38. *See also* white-to-black racial passing

Patent and Trademark Office, 164

Pattillo, Mary, 85

PCA. *See* Presbyterian Church in America

PCUS. *See* Presbyterian Church in the US

Pentecostal churches, 126

People of the Dream: Multiracial Congregations in the United States (Emerson and Woo), 115

performative, 10

Personal Responsibility and Work Opportunity Reconciliation Act of 1996, 151

Peterson, Ruth D., 65

Petraeus, David, 97

Pinckney, Clementa C., 113

place: injustice perception and, 75–81; movement across boundaries in, 13–14; race intersection with, 13, 66–69; racial subordination and mobility of, 70; segregation by, 13–14; significance of, 70

police, 14; mistrust of, 108n3; murders by, 104–5, 107; power of, 16; sexual assault by, 170–72; youth on, 62, 86. *See also* tactical empathy; Verbal Judo training framework

Police Chief, 93

police violence, 144n79; empathy and, 103; gender in, 169–72; language of, 14; victims of, 107; towards women of color, 169–72

policing: dehumanizing subjects in, 99; emotion-centered perspective of, 107; humane policing, 108; scale and scope of, 14; Task Force on 21st Century Policing, 106; trust-centered framework of, 105

politics: domestication of, 152; racial polarization in, 2; of racial reconciliation, 150

Post, Emily, 38–39

post-racialism, 3; of Dolezal, 26

power: gender in, 167; of police, 16; racial reconciliation and, 15

Pratt, Mary Louise, 157

preconciliation, 11; preventative remedies as, 56–57; as reconciliation, 55–59; in science and medicine, 57–59

Presbyterian Church in America (PCA), 126

Presbyterian Church in the US (PCUS), 117

press and media, 141n35; on Dolezal, 29–32; on Memín Pinguín controversy, 174–75
privilege: of being white, 138; in white-to-black racial passing, 26
Proceedings of the National Academy of Sciences, 55
profiteering, 41–42
Progressive Era, 65–66
Proposition 209, 161
psychological wage, 41–43
public education, 11; formation and transformation of, 82–83

race: dignity in, 70; domesticity, gender and, 167–73; fluidity of, 27; impact assessments on, 12; medicine based on, 58; place intersection with, 13, 66–69; in politics, 2; stereotypes of, 174–75; of teachers, 87; UNESCO statements on, 53; war on, 113. *See also specific topics*
racial antagonism, 12; based on biological race, 49; face of, 83–84; roots of, 64. *See also* structural antagonisms
racial capitalism, 39, 151; as framing, 165; of nation-state, 153
racial differences: through gender aberrance and sexual pathology, 155; quantifying, 51
racial fakery, 10; as escape, 35; profit in, 34; of Rockefeller, 38. *See also* Dolezal, Rachel; white-to-black racial passing
racial formation: anti-racism and, 178–79; dynamic process of, 19; as theoretical framework, 154–55
racialization, 173
racial reconciliation: after AME Church massacre, 137–38; in biological race, 52–54; from *Brown v. Board of Education*, 5; of Dolezal, 27; as domesticated, 18; from Holocaust, 11; integration for, 5; politics of, 150; power and, 15; preconciliation as, 55–59; projects of,

150; as realistic, idealistic, or fatalistic, 84–87; respect and tolerance for, 3; restitution and, 7; Roof and, 139
racial-spatial divide, 65
racial state, imperial U.S., 151
racial violence, 179; of Holtzclaw, 170–71; rape of women of color as, 169–73; of sexual assault, 170–72. *See also* murders; police violence
racism, 4; from biological race, 49–50; in Christian churches, 127; global struggle against, 156; legacy of, 114–15; of Roof, 135–36; from science, 51–52. *See also* anti-racism
Rahr, Sue, 101
Rainbow PUSH Coalition, 174
rape, 169–72
Reagan, Ronald, 156–57
Real Housewives, 38
reparations, 7; for African Americans, 8
representation, 155
respect, 3, 8
reterritorialization, 177
reverse discrimination, 9
Rice, Condoleezza, 175
Rice University, 16, 113
Robinson, Randall, 8
Rockefeller, Clark, 36–38
Roof, Dylann, 10; AME shooting by, 16, 113, 135–36; blind racism of, 135–36; danger of, 140n4; racial reconciliation and, 139; white supremacy commitment of, 136
Rosenberg, Gerald, 4

safety: of African Americans in Christian churches, 120; Thompson on, 98
Samuels, Allison, 33
sanctuary, 145n83
San Francisco Peace Officers Association Journal, 106
San Francisco State: College of Ethnic Studies at, 157, 173; strike at, 156

Schept, Judah, 102
schools: as formative, 63, 65; of medicine, 12; neighborhoods and comparative contexts for, 64–66; racial composition of, 70–75; social and criminal injustice perceptions in, 83–84; socialization in, 63–64; surveillance of, 62–63; teachers in, 87. *See also* Chicago schools; public education
science: inhumane Holocaust experiments for, 52–53; preconciliation in, 57–59; racism from, 51–52
Second Presbyterian Church (SPC), 117
Section 5 of Fourteenth Amendment, U.S. Constitution, 50, 55, 60n17; application of, 56–57; in *Brown v. Board of Education*, 56
segregation, 1, 141n12; as Biblical problem, 132–33; of Christian churches, 16, 113–17, 120–33, 139; Christian church history of, 122–28; civil rights movement on, 126–27; as norm, 2; normalcy of, 128; by place, 13–14; as problem of survival, 133; proponents of, 120–22; sociological problem of, 130–32; as theological problem, 128–30; for white supremacy, 69
"self-mastered man" Orientalist notion, 100
Servicio Postal Méxicano (Sepomex), 174–76
sex, 168
sexual assault, 169–72
sexual pathology, 155
Seymour, William J., 125
Sharpton, Al, 175
Sibley, David, 12, 69
slavery, 124–25
Smith, Andrea, 42
social and criminal injustice, 12, 78; adolescence and, 82; school perceptions of, 83–84

social constructionism, 49
socialization, 63–64
social justice movements: agendas of, 155; operation of, 18
The Social Sources of Denominationalism (Niebuhr), 117–18
Soul Man, 26
SPC. *See* Second Presbyterian Church
state violence, 90–91; aesthetic solutions to, 15
structural antagonisms, 18
structural changes, 9
Suhr, Greg, 106–7
Sun, Tzu, 100
Sunderland, Mitchell, 43–44
Supreme Court, U. S., 19
surveillance, 62–63

tactical empathy, 15; authenticity question in, 102–3; carceral humanism and, 102; in other training modules, 101; "self-mastered man" Orientalist notion in, 100; Thompson on, 94; in Verbal Judo, 91–92, 94
Takaki, Ron, 157
Task Force on 21st Century Policing, 106
teachers, 87
terror, 15–16
theology, 128–31
theory of institutionalized self, 69–70
Third World Liberation Front (TWLF), 156–57, 162
Thompson, George: on safety, 98; on tactical empathy, 94; on Verbal Judo, 91–94, 96
three Cs, 5
Tilden High School, 13, 71; cross-racial affiliations at, 72–73
tolerance, 3, 8
Toomer, Jean, 26, 45
transracial: historical precedent for being, 45. *See also* Dolezal, Rachel
TWLF. *See* Third World Liberation Front

UC Berkeley Department of Ethnic Studies, 161, 173
UNESCO Statement on Race, 53
United Farm Workers of America, 159
United Nations, 7
United States: Mexico culture wars with, 174–76; racialized communities in, 177
Universal Declaration of Human Rights, 7
University of Chicago, 73
University of Connecticut, 91
University of Wisconsin, 36
urban institutions, 12

Values for a New Millennium (Humphrey, R.), 98–99
Vanity Fair, 30
Verbal Judo Institute, 102
Verbal Judo: The Gentle Art of Persuasion (Thompson), 92, 94
Verbal Judo training framework: core belief system of, 97–98; counterinsurgency tactics similarity to, 96–97; equality in, 98–99; goal of, 93–94, 109n15; of police, 92–93; tactical empathy in, 91–92, 94; techniques of, 95–96; Thompson on, 91–94, 96

Walter Payton College Prep, 13; selectivity of, 75
Wang, Ling-chi, 161
Ward, Geoff K., 68
war on drugs, 165
Washington Post, 174–75
white matriarchy, 44

whiteness: advantage of, 10–11; as normative, 173
Whiteness of a Different Color (Jacobson), 42
white privilege, 138
white supremacy, 42–43; in Christian churches, 132; segregation for, 69. *See also* Roof, Dylann
white-to-black racial passing: class in, 36–37; as historically temporary, 35; privilege in, 26; as profiteering, 41–42. *See also* Dolezal, Rachel
Wilkinson, J. Harvie, 4
Willerslev, Rane, 91
Williams, Armstrong, 7–8
Winant, Howard, 154
W. K. Kellogg Foundation, 8
women of color: domesticity and, 172; police violence towards, 169–72; rape as racial violence towards, 169–73; sexual assault of, 169–72
Woo, Rodney M., 115
World War II, 11

Young, Alford, 77
youth: African Americans as, 68–69, 83–84; Black Youth Project 100, 171; on Chicago Public School system, 67; discrimination of, 65–66; gang stigmas of, 80–81; Hispanic youth, 83–84; inequality experiences of, 64–65; injustice experiences of, 81; parents as teachers of, 85–86; on police, 62, 86. *See also* schools